T0304320

Shipping Strategy

With roughly three-quarters of the earth's surface covered with water, it is needless to say that shipping plays a major role in world trade. In fact, it is one of the most international industries, and has an impact on each and every one of us every day. Ships transport the food we eat, the clothes we wear, the cars we drive, the materials used to build our homes, and the fuel that heats them. Yet traditional shipping companies – ones that combine various aspects of shipping under one organizational roof – are on the decline. They are gradually being replaced by new, more specialized companies with more strategic clarity and managerial focus. In *Shipping Strategy*, Peter Lorange draws on his extensive experience in the shipping industry to show how companies can adapt to the fast-moving and volatile world of maritime business by devising strategies for future success, including specialization and innovation.

PETER LORANGE is the Kristian Gerhard Jebsen Professor of International Shipping at IMD in Lausanne, Switzerland. He retired in 2008 after fifteen years as President of IMD, is a former president of the Norwegian School of Management BI and, before this, was affiliated with the Wharton School, University of Pennsylvania, and The Sloan School of Management, Massachusetts Institute of Technology. Professor Lorange is the former owner of a Norwegian shipping company and is also a board member of several shipping firms. He has written or edited 15 books and some 110 articles on the topics of global strategic management, strategic planning, and entrepreneurship for growth. His most recent book is *Thought Leadership Meets Business* (Cambridge, 2008).

Shipping Strategy
Innovating for Success

DR. DR. H. C. MULT. PETER LORANGE

Kristian Gerhard Jebsen Professor of International Shipping
Former President, IMD

CAMBRIDGE
UNIVERSITY PRESS

CAMBRIDGE UNIVERSITY PRESS
Cambridge, New York, Melbourne, Madrid, Cape Town,
Singapore, São Paulo, Delhi, Tokyo, Mexico City

Cambridge University Press
The Edinburgh Building, Cambridge CB2 8RU, UK

Published in the United States of America by Cambridge University Press, New York

www.cambridge.org
Information on this title: www.cambridge.org/9780521761499

First published 2009
Third printing 2010

A catalogue record for this publication is available from the British Library

ISBN 978-0-521-76149-9 Hardback

In memory of Kristian Gerhard Jebsen, 1927–2004.

Contents

List of figures   *page* ix
Foreword   xiii
Acknowledgements   xix

Part I   World shipping: the context   1

1 Drivers of change in the shipping industry   3

2 Major shipping markets   15

3 Shipping freight rates   31

4 Shipping industry clusters   62

Part II   Strategic archetypes in shipping   77

5 Specialized strategies   79

6 Owning steel   112

7 Using steel   142

8 Operating steel   170

9 Innovating around steel   175

Part III   The firm's portfolio strategy   185

10 Portfolio management   187

11 Risk and revenue management   215

Part IV   In conclusion   233

12 Two unique issues in shipping – family and governance   235

13 In the end … a question of management capabilities   248

Epilogue   260
References   262
Index   266

Figures

2.1 Price of oil per barrel   *page* 17
2.2 Very large crude carrier (VLCC) earnings vs. oil price   17
3.1 Bulk freight rates   32
3.2 Panamax bulk carrier earnings   32
3.3 Suezmax tanker earnings   33
3.4 Chinese iron ore imports by source, 1997–2007   34
3.5 Port delays   38
3.6 Order book-to-fleet ratio (dry bulk, tanker, and fully
     cellular containership fleet)   39
3.7 Freight market behavior as a consequence of fleet
     employment rate   40
3.8 Capesize bulk carriers – expected freight market
     behavior   41
3.9 Major bull market every thirty years? Commodity cycles   45
3.10 Vessel earnings (Cape, VLCC, and 4,000 TEU – one-year
     time charter rate)   46
3.11 Rate of growth of trade (measured in tonne/mile or TEU/
     mile terms)   47
3.12 Gross freight earnings by vessel type, 1960–80   50
3.13 Typical shipping market freight rate development   51
3.14 Abnormal shipping market freight rate developments   52
4.1 Share of revenues invested in R&D compared with level
     of innovativeness in five national maritime industries   66
4.2 Personnel mobility within the Dutch maritime cluster   67
4.3 The relationship between preferences for keeping
     headquarters in the home country and satisfaction with
     public policy   68
4.4 Maritime clusters (European Union)   69

4.5   Global market capitalization   72
5.1   Conceptual model for shipping strategies   81
5.2   Four archetypes of specialist firms   85
5.3   The specialist movement within the shipping industry   87
5.4   Owning steel, using steel, operating steel, innovating
      around steel   90
6.1   Container supply/demand balance   119
6.2   Crude tanker supply/demand balance   119
6.3   Segmentation of ship types   121
6.4   Shipbuilding activities in Germany   122
6.5   Ships on order per country (of control)   122
6.6   Container ships in existence by country
      of ownership, 2006   123
6.7   Shipyard capacity by country   123
6.8   Major yards: capacity growth – ships delivered   125
6.9   Newbuilding prices   126
6.10 Matching demand and supply   128
6.11 Top twenty liner companies – new orders
      at March 10, 2008   130
6.12 Market share (%) of the five largest container ship lines   133
6.13 New ships on order as % of existing fleet (including ships
      chartered in)   134
7.1   In/out and long/short strategies (various market
      assumptions)   144
7.2   Buy/sell/place second-hand ships and newbuilding orders   144
7.3   DFDS overall strategy   166
7.4   DFDS ownership share per ship type (%)   167
8.1   Proportional distribution of operating costs for bulk
      carriers   171
8.2   Proportional distribution of operating costs for tankers   172
9.1   Slow steaming: vessel power vs. speed   179
9.2 CO_2 emissions per unit load for various types of
      transportation (comparison by transport mode)   180
10.1 Peter Georgiopoulos' sphere of shipping companies   189

10.2	Risk/return tradeoffs in shipping (based on time charter rates for the period 1980–2002)	192
10.3	Risk/return tradeoffs in shipping (based on time charter rates for the period 2003–2007)	193
10.4	Portfolio, owning ships/infrastructure firms – Seaspan example	196
10.5	Seaspan's stakeholder-based portfolio strategy	197
10.6	Portfolio – using ships – Clarkson Shipping Hedge Fund example	199
10.7	Growth vs. yield in the public market since 2002	200
10.8	Portfolio – innovating around steel – Marsoft example	201
10.9	Portfolio shipping firm – owning, using, operating, innovating	202
10.10	Container terminals business model	210
10.11	From customer relations niche specialist to infrastructure low-cost specialist	213
12.1	Public vs. private company ownership	236
12.2	Family business vs. publicly traded firms – two different systems	237

Foreword

With roughly three-quarters of the earth's surface covered in water, it is needless to say that shipping plays a major role in world trade. In fact, it is one of the most international industries, and it has an impact on each and every one of us every day. Ships transport the food we eat, the clothes we wear, the cars we drive, the materials used to build our homes, and the fuel that heats them. Nowadays, however, shipping is largely out of sight and out of mind. Shipping facilities are usually beyond city limits, fenced in and unapproachable. Outsiders are not meant to go there, so most of us have no idea what goes on. But in my view, managers in a broad variety of mature industries can learn a lot from understanding and tracking developments in the shipping industry.

The general image of shipping is one of permanence and predictability as ships ply traditional routes with their cargoes, linking industries and consumers. But in reality the industry has experienced extraordinary changes over the last few years. The global landscape is shifting, with emerging nations driving global demand, and, until recently, the industry had been enjoying an unprecedented period of sustained profitability and increased investor interest. Many new fortunes were made – and lost – during these exceptional times. With its heavy exposure to global market mechanisms, the shipping industry is both unique and fascinating, attracting some of the world's most risk-taking and charismatic entrepreneurs and fortune-builders.

These changes have been accompanied by a dramatic increase in the ship freight derivatives business, so-called forward freight agreements (FFA) trading. It is estimated that the volume of FFA trading for dry bulk shipping from mid-2007 to mid-2008 might be at virtually the same level as physical trading in ships. Derivatives trading has become critical in several of the business segments in shipping, almost notably in the dry bulk segment but also in tankers. The container shipping segment, on the other hand, has not so far become subject to derivatives trading.

Over the last few years, there has been a strong influx of capital, largely from sources that were previously not generally available to this industry, such as general investors, asset management funds, and bank financiers. Coupled with this, there has been an equally strong influx of new professional talent, many with very different backgrounds from those traditionally found in shipping. At the same time, experience and shipping judgment still count. Additionally, hedge funds and financial brokers showed increasing interest in shipping derivatives following the rise in freight rates caused by economic growth in China and elsewhere. To sum up, this is an exceptional time for the shipping industry.

As a result, the level of shipbuilding was at a record high with tonnage output rising fast. Many foresaw an oversupply of shipping capacity in the near future, or even another industry depression, perhaps similar in magnitude to that of the 1980s. However, the financial crisis in 2007–8 has created new shortages of capital and widespread uncertainty about the future of the economy. What can we learn today from the way shipping markets have behaved in the past? How deep will the dip be, and how long will it last? And, perhaps most importantly, how can shipping companies respond proactively to the vast array of challenges they are now facing?

For companies that aspire to be global winners, specialization may be the answer. This seems to be the case for most, if not all, mature industries. Perhaps the major insight of this book is the call for strategic clarity, by distinguishing between four primary archetypes – owning steel, using steel, operating steel, and innovating around steel – that is, between owning ships, chartering ships, trading in the markets, ship operations, and innovations related to the technical as well as commercial aspects of shipping. I shall discuss the critical success factors behind the strategies for each of these archetypes. My claim is that the hour of integrated shipping companies is largely past and that the future trend is toward firms that are decomposing the value chain and focusing on one aspect, or possibly two, through autonomous units. The result is less complexity, less coordination, less bureaucracy, and more strategic clarity and managerial focus. Still, there will be a need for an overall portfolio strategy, and the management of overall risk to the shipping corporation is becoming more important than ever – all of which I will discuss in this book.

I sold my own shipping company, S. Ugelstad A/S, in January 2007. While I benefited from the strong market by obtaining a satisfactory price for my company, the major rationale for selling was that I began to feel increasingly uncomfortable attempting to combine various aspects of shipping under one organizational roof. With varying degrees of success, I tried to combine owning, chartering, and innovating. As the sole owner – and the one ultimately responsible – it became an increasingly complex situation for me to handle, so I sold the firm. However, my interest in shipping – broadly speaking – remains the same. I am engaged in various investments, many involving holding ownership stakes in ships. By freeing myself from direct company ownership, I have been able to diversify my holdings rather than being caught up in the increasingly tangled reins of an integrated shipping company.

So, who is this book for? The target reader is clear – the sophisticated shipping industry practitioner. There is a lot of sophistication among most shipping industry executives today. Accordingly, this book attempts to develop the most relevant critical success factors for the shipping business in general, as well as for the various key shipping strategies that can be identified. For each strategy, I shall attempt to identify the most relevant drivers, including the most pressing implementation challenges, critical risk/return considerations, and performance measures. I shall also indicate ways of benchmarking a specific category vis-à-vis other industries, past history, etc. There are a number of unique challenges that will make this book valuable to savvy shipping executives:

- I see a specialization trend within the shipping industry into more clearly focused businesses, namely:
  - owning steel/ships
  - using steel/ships – chartering/trading ships
  - operating steel/ships
  - innovation around steel/ships.[1]

  This book deals with how to develop effective strategies around each of these focused businesses. It concentrates on the main shipping business segments – tankers, bulk carriers, and container ships – and less on specialty ships, including ro-ro/ropax ships, ferries, cruise/passenger ships, and others. This is an intentional choice, to maintain a reasonable focus.

- At the same time, the new reality is the development of effective overall portfolio strategies, with particular emphasis on managing overall exposure to risk. This book covers approaches to these challenges.
- Financial understanding is becoming more and more of a must. But what does competent financial management entail?
- Derivatives trading – FFA contracts – in shipping is increasingly prominent – certainly when it comes to the dry bulk markets, but also for tankers. This means that a new set of trading-related capabilities is needed.
- Underlying all of this is a keen understanding of the market mechanisms in shipping. Growth in demand, i.e., in world trade, is the key driver for this but the supply side is important too. How can we better understand the growth outlook? When shipowners put up too many new buildings, supply will outstrip demand and rates will fall. How can we learn from key developments in markets in the past?
- The shipping industry is becoming more and more professional. But what does this professionalism involve? What are the key agenda items for today's successful shipping executives?

---

[1] I do not use the term "steel" literally to indicate ships built solely from steel. I include ships, notably fast ferries, cruise liners, and so on, that are built from composite materials and aluminum.

When considering key success factors, we must make a distinction between commodity shipping and specialty shipping. For the former, low costs are critical and the financial aspect – to enjoy the lowest possible capital cost – is increasingly important. It is essential to understand the basic shipping markets well enough to be able to decide on appropriate "in/out" and "long/short" decisions. In contrast, the customer is the focal point in specialty shipping, which is a customer-based business. To succeed, you need to understand your client.

Another critical question is how fast a specialty shipping business niche will evolve into merely another commodity business. Imitation is inevitable and barriers to new entrants typically low. How effective is each particular shipping market then?

I should state at this point that I have possibly not been entirely objective when it comes to discussions drawing on Marsoft or Seaspan as examples: I am a board member and outside director of both of these companies. However, to my best ability, I have tried to be objective and balanced.

At the time of completion of this manuscript in mid-2008, the shipping markets had been experiencing an unprecedented period of growth – over an equally unprecedented period of time – almost five great years! There were, however, clouds on the horizon. Newbuilding orders, relative to existing fleets, were growing rapidly and financing was becoming more difficult to obtain. During the latter part of 2008, the shipping markets did indeed collapse. The fall was more dramatic – faster and deeper – than anything ever experienced in the past. The shipping industry was perhaps in a deeper crisis than ever before in its history.

So, what can a book on shipping strategy offer during these difficult times, particularly when the book was essentially written during the earlier period of extreme optimism? While I have made some adjustments to the text, the book's production schedule would not allow for an extensive rewrite. However, it is important to note that this should not diminish the book's value. The basic "messages" remain more valid today than ever.

- Pursue highly focused business strategies for shipping companies, with heavier emphasis on understanding the relevant underlying critical success factors within each specific shipping business segment.
- Be cognizant of the need to manage overall risk through a more robust, overall corporate portfolio strategy.
- The level of the professionalism of management practice within the shipping industry can certainly be further advanced. Paradoxically, times of crises tend to enhance such managerial breakthroughs. I hope that the book might have a positive impact on this as well.

All in all, my sense is that this book is timelier than ever. I have also added a brief epilogue, which further reflects on the unprecedented changes that have recently had an impact on the shipping industry. An open-minded, flexible view is now called for.

Peter Lorange
Kristian Gerhard Jebsen Professor of International Shipping
Lausanne, March 2009

Acknowledgements

A large number of individuals have discussed emerging issues in shipping with me – all of whom I thank sincerely here: M. Adland, P. Aury, C. Bardjis, S. Chu, P. Curtis, P.L. Eckbo, P. Engeset, O. Espeland, R. Francis, K. Hazel, C. Hennig, J. Howat, E.W. Jakobsen, T. Janholt, O. Jessel, B.T. Larsen, W. L'Orange, K. Low, K. Møgstad, P. Monsen, G. Porter, O. Rosendahl, J. Schoolkate, P. Shaerf, I. Skaug, A. Sterling, N. Su, Aa. Svendsen, G. Wang, E. van Weering, A. Vizilbash, several anonymous referees, and many others. E. Ferrari and A. Polzer typed the manuscript. B. Lennox did an outstanding job of editing the text, which was finalized for publication by S. Simmons of the Cambridge Editorial Partnership. I am highly indebted to all. Approximately 95 percent of this book is entirely new material. Approximately 5 percent is taken from my previous book *Shipping Company Strategies: Global Management under Turbulent Conditions*, Elsevier, Oxford, 2005. The overall responsibility for the content and messages of this book remains with me.

Peter Lorange

Part I   World shipping: the context

1   Drivers of change in the shipping industry   *page* 3
2   Major shipping markets   15
3   Shipping freight rates   31
4   Shipping industry clusters   62

I Drivers of change in the shipping industry

Like it or not, the shipping industry is currently experiencing a business environment characterized by radical change – and there seems to be an explosive acceleration in the speed of change. The traditional shipping company can no longer thrive in this environment. To succeed, the shipping company of the future may have to undergo a fundamental restructuring of the way it operates. This will call for new strategies and business models. So what's behind all this change? This chapter focuses briefly on the more striking drivers of change in the industry. These may have a high impact not only on the future role of the traditional, asset-based shipping company, but also on reshaping shipping companies for the future.

But before I go into this, what is the formal definition of a shipping company? A shipping company is a commercial firm that is active in one or more of the following:

- shipowning
- trading, including ship brokerage, forward freight agreement (FFA) trading and liner shipping
- operations
- commercial and technical innovations.

The shipping industry is institutionally more broadly defined than might be conventionally assumed. It is the overall industry's value chain that matters, not merely ship ownership, a relatively small part of the industry as a whole.

GLOBALIZATION
Globalization is shaping our modern world. It is perhaps also the single biggest force in the shipping industry – indeed, in most industries.

Markets are becoming larger and larger – and more global. And the pace of globalization has gathered speed because of a number of factors, including the almost complete opening up of world markets. With the advent of multinational, multilateral agreements, we have also begun to see large homogenous trading blocs, such as the European Union (EU), the North America Free Trade Agreement (NAFTA) and the Association of Southeast Asian Nations (ASEAN). As the barriers to cross-border trade and ownership continue to break down, goods will move even more freely around the world.

DISPERSED MANUFACTURING

In the not-too-distant past, many durable consumer goods were made in Japan and then shipped to countries such as the US and Europe. Over time, cost levels in Japan increased and countries like Taiwan and Korea took over. This led to changes in shipping patterns. Since China has become the "manufacturer of the world," one-third of the world's container shipping is now going to and from China. Even though the recent economic slowdown has impacted China negatively, it still remains the dominant manufacturer in the world. One could speculate that a future low-cost manufacturing country might be Vietnam. There is already an increase in ocean/sea freight route activity to and from this country. As these low-cost manufacturing centers continue to grow, meaning that goods are produced further and further away from major consumers, we are likely to see an unprecedented increase in the demand for container-based shipping.

INCREASED GLOBAL DEMAND FOR COMMODITIES AND CONSUMER GOODS

With these changes in world patterns of manufacturing, China and other so-called low-cost developing nations are becoming even more important in today's global economic scene. And, as these developing nations become wealthier, we are seeing an increase in global demand for commodities such as various types of ore, steel, and energy to support their booming infrastructure needs.

The newfound wealth of the low-cost manufacturing nations will also become more of a driving force in the global demand for consumer goods. Also, the interrelationships among consumers are becoming more immediate and transparent. Masses of new consumers will enter the world arena.

WORLD TRADE

With most of the world's economies slowing down in the latter part of 2008, the level of world trade has also dropped. The consumer sector is definitely having problems, mostly in the US, but also in Europe. An important consequence of the decline in consumer confidence is the fall in container-based demand for the shipping of finished goods in particular – mostly from China to both the US and Europe. Despite this decline, China remains the major exporter of manufactured goods. As a reflection of this, many of the container liners are, as of the end of 2008, implementing extensive reductions in employee levels, laying-up ships, sharing ship capacity, and streamlining route systems.

The flow of raw materials is also falling. Steel production is down, not least due to the slowdown in the purchase of consumer durables such as cars. As a consequence, iron ore imports are also down, as are the trading flows of most other commodities. Commodity prices, therefore, have also come down – perhaps a good sign for having a potentially stimulating effect on the world economy, but with significant negative consequences for many developing economies.

Hence, from an unprecedented period of growth in most economies, we find ourselves, as of the end of 2008, in the grip of a worldwide recession and weakened trade flows.

DEMOGRAPHIC SHIFTS

The growth in the world's population is heavily centered in Asia today. India is the planet's most heavily populated country, with slightly more than one-quarter of the world's total population within its borders. China is also huge, with slightly less than one quarter, and

Southeast Asia is growing fast. In contrast, European countries, North America, and Japan are not growing at the same rate. These demographic shifts will certainly have longer-term impacts on the world's ocean freight patterns and shipping rates. The countries with young populations, such as the countries in Asia, are mainly producers today, but they can be expected to be the major consumers of the future. Asia-focused shipping can be expected to become even more dominant.

UNEVEN ECONOMIC GROWTH AND TURBULENCE

Economic sustainability and robust growth are becoming critical. However, economic volatility may also become more extreme. There are strong economic ups and downs within each trading bloc. Higher capacity utilization within many industries represents a major reason for this.

Before mid-2008, China, in particular, proved to be *the* major source of sustainable and rapid growth in the world economy. China's economy was growing, on average, 10 percent per year and inflation was relatively low. As China became the world's manufacturing center, it was estimated that its gross national product (GNP) per capita would be 50 percent of that of the US by 2030. However, China has five times the population of the US, which means that its total GNP will be 2.5 times larger. In addition to China, India, Eastern Europe, Russia, and Latin America were all experiencing strong growth. Never before has three-quarters of the world's population seen such a strong cycle of growth.

While China's impressive growth over the last few years has indeed been a major factor in propelling a strong level of prosperity throughout the entire world, it was slowing down by the end of 2008 for two classes of reasons.

First, a series of endogenous factors had a negative impact on China's economy. The earthquake in Sichuan in the summer of 2008, while relatively limited in physical scope, affected China's entire economy. The Summer Olympics in August 2008 similarly brought the entire country to a virtual standstill for two weeks. A stricter focus on the environment has also taken its toll on the economy.

Second, the world slowdown, particularly in the consumer goods sector in the US and Europe, has led to fewer exports of finished goods from China, which, in turn, has led to less basic metal production – particularly steel – and thus fewer raw material imports, particularly iron ore.

Finally, China has been putting a lot of emphasis on shipbuilding. As of the end of 2008, there were estimated to be approximately 400 shipyards capable of building ocean-going ships in China. Experts think that this number will have to shrink to perhaps as few as 100 in the next three to four years.

All of this has led to a slowdown in China's economy – and we can, in all likelihood, expect to see more.

Western Europe, on the other hand, is experiencing relatively slower growth compared to the rest of the world. Germany and France, for instance, have had problems maintaining their economic dynamism. Germany is still a larger exporter than China, but the products being exported generally have more value-added content. The same can be said of Japan. In North America, the entire economy has gone through large swings, including extended periods of depression. Innovation remains high within many sectors of the US economy, of course.

While shipping companies must adapt in order to compete globally, they must also be aware of their exposure to ups and downs in various parts of the world, at various points in time. For instance, while the transpacific volume of containers shipped is now flat because of the economic slowdown in the US, growth in container shipping has shifted to the China–Europe routes. When things are good in one place, they are often not so good elsewhere, resulting in volatility in the global portfolio of corporate activities (Fischer, 2004). But it is not only macro-economic shifts that are driving change. There are also many forces at the micro-economic level that are causing turbulence. The credit crisis, which began at the end of 2007, and fluctuating interest and currency exchange rates, are just a few examples. As a result of this economic volatility and the shift in growth regions, we are bound to see further changes in ocean transportation patterns.

To sum up, rapidly growing world trade is driving many of the major changes in the world today – and world trade is more or less synonymous with world shipping (Bernstein, 2008).

GEOPOLITICAL SCENE

The geopolitical scene is also changing. Things are becoming more turbulent, not less, after the collapse of the former Soviet Union and the emergence of the United States as the sole superpower. Regional instability is a major reason for this. Consider, for instance, the tensions in the Indian subcontinent; China and its relationship with Taiwan; Korea – North and South; the Israeli–Palestinian conflict; Iran; Iraq; the many gruesome local and civil wars in Africa; conflicts in Central America; the Balkans – with several years of terrible wars behind them and continuing tensions ... one could go on and on.

Are these countries politically stable? China is run by an authoritarian regime. Although it is certainly more and more pragmatically liberal in its view of economic matters, it is still not a democracy. Will the present balance last? Are we talking about a feeble stability here? Similarly, India – the world's largest democracy – is still fraught with tensions. Can relative stability be sustained in this enormous country? Will the path toward more economic liberalism continue?

We could continue speculating about the political forces that are currently at play, or latent. Clearly, this has an impact on the business order. In general, political stability is a condition for economic stability and prosperity, as well as for investment attractiveness and meaningful economic value creation (Courtney, 2001). The relationship between stability and growth in ocean shipping remains strong. Still, it may be seen as a paradox that ship freight rates tend to shoot up during periods of political instability and war. While such events often create bursts of unexpected growth within the shipping sector, the long-term growth trajectory of shipping is a function of political stability.

TERRORISM

The threat of terrorism is another dimension that has been heightened, particularly since the attacks on the United States on September 11, 2001. Despite the efforts of many of the established world powers, it seems to be difficult to limit the threat of terrorism, anywhere in the world. An immediate sense of violence and political instability is the result. The risk of global terrorism and the cost of security measures to combat it will continue to be an ongoing concern. These issues are sure to have an impact on the shipping industry. How can safety be ensured in container shipping, for instance? Piracy, particularly from bases in Somalia, also represents a serious problem for world shipping – with respect to both safety and costs.

TECHNOLOGY

Technologies are changing fast and product life cycles are becoming shorter. More substantial research and development (R&D) invest-ments are needed to come up with new products and/or processes with global reach. Contemporary R&D seems to be a matter of going for larger gains and global scope, but it also comes with larger financial commitments and risks. The impacts for shipping are numerous – new navigational equipment, engines with more sophisticated fuel injec-tion, new hull designs, more efficient propulsion, low-friction, etc. However, the basic design and characteristics of a ship tend to be very stable – in an overall sense, the lifecycle for ships may be remark-ably long. Several fundamental innovations have been driven by legislators, for example, the requirement to have double-hull tankers from 2010. Will legislators increasingly require the implementation of more environment-friendly ships too? I expect so.

ENVIRONMENTAL AND SAFETY CONCERNS

In the developed world, environmental and safety concerns are high on the agenda for most industries, and shipping is no exception. After the Exxon Valdez oil spill disaster in Alaska in 1989, new legislation was introduced in the US in 1990, which required double hulls on all new tankers and established a phase-out schedule for existing single-hulled vessels. The EU followed suit, and double-hull construction in tankers became mandatory in 1994. Subsequent events – the Erica and the Prestige incidents – have led to an acceleration in the phase-out dates of single-hulled tankers to 2010 and, in some cases, 2015.

While the biggest environmental challenge is how to control carbon dioxide (CO_2) emissions, there is also a drive toward limiting nitrogen oxide (NOX) and sulphur oxide (SOX) emissions. The world's shipping fleet produces five percent of global CO_2 emissions in the world – twice as much as the world's fleet of aircrafts, and the same as that produced by Africa. The Kyoto Protocol does not yet cover ocean shipping; however, one cannot overlook the possibility of forced obsolescence of ships due to new legislation.

Additionally, certain ports – notably in Western Europe and the US – require ships to use relatively clean diesel as bunker fuel. They have disallowed the use of heavy oil, which is a greater source of pollution.

It must be stressed, however, that there is a major difference between an international agreement and national legislation. One would not necessarily be breaking the law by failing to adhere strictly to national legislation.

REBALANCING THE COMPETITIVE EDGE:
DEVELOPED VS. EMERGING SHIPPING NATIONS
The rising costs resulting from environmental, safety and crewing legislation are making it more and more difficult for shipping companies in the developed world to compete with those in the new economies. Environmental and safety-enhancing legislation in developed countries has resulted in increased investment costs. However, this legislation may not be strictly adhered to by certain countries. This means that less expensive tonnage (e.g., single-hull tankers), typically from the developing world, might still be allowed to operate. Because this tonnage is less expensive, it is highly competitive. Increased global transparency may ameliorate such differences to some extent, however.

A MORE CAPITAL-INTENSIVE INDUSTRY

For many industries the emphasis is on reducing costs, enhancing efficiency, providing higher quality products and services, and gaining market accessibility. Many companies do this by maximizing their buying power on a global basis, leveraging their economies of scale by maintaining larger and more sophisticated physical plants, and globally sourcing and reconfiguring the manufacturing-based part of the value chain. The worldwide shipping industry is no exception. The days when plants – or shipping companies – were focused on individual national economies seem to be largely gone. One consequence, of course, is that the investment requirements per installation – or per ship – have increased, which means that many industries have become much more capital intensive. We see this en masse within the shipping industry. Seaspan Corporation, for example, one of the world's largest container shipping companies, which charters its ships out to major shipping lines under long-term, fixed-rate contracts, recently ordered eight 13,100 TEU mega-container vessels, representing a staggering investment of US$1.5 billion.[2] And the capital intensity of modern container operations has become huge.

CAPITAL: ABUNDANT – AND NOT SO ABUNDANT

The credit crisis that emerged in 2007 has grown progressively serious, particularly for companies that have launched substantial newbuilding programs. Financing costs have gone up, and the availability of debt capital is an issue. Ship finance banks are increasingly having problems syndicating their ship loans, which as a result must often remain on the banks' books, leading in turn to less capacity to allocate funds to the shipping sector. The Basel II Accord, which sets limits on the number of certain types of loans that can be issued, including those made to the shipping industry, also contributes to the scarcity of capital.

---

[2] Container capacity is often expressed in 20-foot equivalent units (TEU).

However, up until mid-2008 despite occasional credit squeezes, cost-of-capital increases, higher interest rates, more restrictive debt repayment conditions, and so on, there nevertheless seemed to be an abundance of available capital, which was having an impact on many industries including shipping. Good projects were financed, which was not always the case. This resulted in new entrants joining the shipping industry. New projects and a new breed of investor – based on new money – were challenging the old order. At the same time, as we discussed earlier, from early 2008 the availability of capital was becoming tighter. While the credit squeeze emerges in shipping, the opportunities in the markets remain large. Thus, opportunity-based optimism is accompanied by uncertainty around whether or not the financial crisis might expand.

Needless to say, financial understanding is key today. The ability to raise capital efficiently is becoming more and more of a competitive issue – and can lead to significant competitive advantage.

FINANCIAL MARKETS

As the banking/financial markets crisis deepened during the fall of 2008, liquidity for the shipping sector has virtually dried up, particularly when it comes to debt financing for new ships. In general, credit is rarely available. One reason for this is that the inter-bank paper market for ship debt has more or less collapsed – banks now typically have to keep their total ship finance commitments on their own books.

The equity market for shipping companies has also become very tight. Typically, new equity can only be raised in limited amounts and with significant price discounts, implying large dilution for existing shareholders. The German Kommanditgesellschaft investment funds (KGs) market has also more or less disappeared.

The one potential benefit from all of this might be delays in the delivery of new tonnage – perhaps even cancellations. Needless to say, some shipowners may have to liquidate or even declare bankruptcy.

ACCELERATED PROFESSIONALISM

Many industries – shipping included – are experiencing an infusion of spirited young talent that is better trained and more professional. Often coming from other industries before entering shipping, they advance much more quickly than in the past. This has brought more dynamism to the shipping industry. Shipping is no longer the industry-specific silo it used to be. Innovation, driven by increased professionalism, is particularly noticeable when it comes to the need for strong financial competencies within the shipping sector. And this cache of "new" professionals is also much more international than before.

OVERALL IMPLICATIONS FOR SHIPPING

The effects of these drivers, along with others, and the interplay between them, means that this period of radical change in the shipping industry is likely to be a pattern for the future. New growth opportunities will always emerge. The increased global demand for commodities and consumer goods, which resulted in new growth opportunities for the shipping industry, particularly in Asia, is only one example of this.

It is thus important to bear in mind that turbulence creates opportunities. There seems to be a stronger and stronger first-mover advantage. For instance, Seaspan was one of the first companies to see the growth potential of the "lease-inspired" ship-owning niche and was able to establish itself firmly early on in the game. (The first firm to pursue this fully was probably Ship Finance Inc.) Others, such as the Greek firm Danaos, are now trying to follow a similar strategy to Seaspan. However, it can be difficult to catch up with a strong first mover. Interestingly, Danaos has also diversified its portfolio strategy to include ownership of conventional bulk-carriers (since sold), and even state-of-the-art information technology (IT) services that can provide totally integrated solutions to shipping companies and their vessels. Logistics may increasingly become a critical competence for the industry and perhaps even another first-mover advantage!

As shipping companies respond proactively to this array of exogenous forces in their quest to compete in the global economy, they must adapt themselves to heightened levels of flexibility and change, to meet the competition in the marketplace. They must find new ways to operate and organize themselves. It is increasingly difficult to find a sustainable traditional niche in this new global world. And this will have implications for the shipping industry, which will call for new winning strategies. As Darwin (1859) said, almost a century and a half ago, "It is not the strongest species that survive, nor the most intelligent, but the ones most responsive to change." Response to change is what this book is all about.

CONCLUSION

The shipping industry is driven by a number of recent and important changes – we have briefly discussed them – all of which are very different. One could justifiably claim that shipping is one of the most complex industries and that this is at the heart of what makes shipping so interesting. Its complexity opens up huge opportunities to see options early, before they become obvious to everyone else. Shipping is – and always has been – entrepreneurial. But the competence-base needed to succeed has changed, with much more focus on international professionalism, and with the emergence of executives who are comfortable with a raft of changes – technological, environmental, legislative, and logistical – as well as skilled in competent financial management.

2 Major shipping markets

While cyclicality and turbulence characterize much of the shipping industry, successful ship owners see these two forces as an opportunity, not a threat. Taking advantage of the opportunity, however, requires the ability to understand and execute an effective, commodity-based strategy. Successfully executing a commodity strategy rests on three principles:

1 Timing is everything – short term (spot) and long term (futures); getting in and/or out at the right time, and turning points in the markets are key.
2 Cutting your losses – a stop-loss attitude; run with the winners, but don't be greedy – good times do not last forever.
3 Margins – squeezing them out of the business; a low cost base is key.

There are also opportunities to pursue niche strategies in shipping. Identifying market segments where there is strong demand for your unique set of competencies, and where the competition may still be weak, can allow a shipping firm to serve a set of customers more or less alone. Identifying and executing non-commodity niche strategies seems to be an important part of the successful shipping company's overall strategic agenda. However, niche markets tend to provide short-lived bonanzas. Other shipping companies copy the niche pioneers, which typically triggers a general move toward commoditization of the niche market over time.

Seaspan's focus on increased containerization to and from China is a good example of a company pursuing a niche market with a first-mover advantage. Seaspan chartered a significant number of its ships to China-based container liner companies. Obviously, an understanding of the more general ship market developments will remain very important, as will understanding developments in the financial and stock markets. For example, in Seaspan's case a difficult equity market could drive up the effective cost of capital for the company, and hinder its ability to fund growth along the lines anticipated. The debt market could also become more restrictive, with less availability for liquidity, thus perhaps also hampering growth. Movements in the ship freight rates, newbuilding and second-hand markets will always continue to be important. For example, once Seaspan's ships come off their initial long-term charters, there will be a rechartering risk that will depend on the general freight market level at that point in time. These factors will dictate whether the firm can enjoy long-term satisfactory rates of return in the end.

There are different general markets for tankers, as opposed to bulk carriers and container ships, each of which are analyzed in more detail below (Zannetos, 1966, 1999). And, as we shall see, there are important sub-segments – indeed separate markets – within each of these broad categories. There are several other markets, too – reefers, gas carriers, offshore supply ships or passenger ships, for example. In practice all of these markets are relatively small – a comprehensive analysis of bulk, tanker and container shipping would have to cover a lot.

TANKER MARKETS

Tanker markets, and the prevailing freight rates for these "wet" markets, are largely driven by the demand for oil – again largely a function of oil prices. As we know, the price of oil reached an exceptionally high level in 2008. I have also argued that when oil prices are exceptionally high, we might expect a fall in the consumption of oil and thus less ocean transportation of oil products, resulting in falling tanker freight rates. In fact, this is what we are now seeing.

Figure 2.1 gives a long-term historical picture of the development of the oil price per barrel from 1860 until today, measured in US dollars using the 2006 exchange rate. We see that the oil price shot up during the period 1973–88, a time when the tanker daily freight rates were down too.

Oil prices peaked in mid-2008 at US$147 per barrel and then fell dramatically to US$50 per barrel by the end of November 2008. Worldwide consumption of oil, in fact, has gone down because of the

FIGURE 2.1 Price of oil per barrel
Source: *24 Heures*, 10–12 May 2008, p. 9, plus subsequent updating.

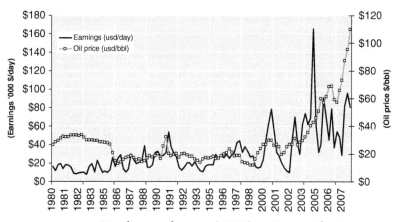

FIGURE 2.2 Very large crude carrier (VLCC) earnings vs. oil price
Source: Marsoft (2008b).

world recession. The consumption of oil in the US, for instance, fell from a peak of 20.8 million barrels per day in 2005 to 20.7 million barrels per day in 2007, falling further to a record low of 19.7 million barrels per day in 2008. One could normally expect tanker freight markets to rise or at least stabilize when oil prices fall because this typically results in an increase in oil shipment activity. This has not been the case this time.

Figure 2.2 provides a closer examination of the relationship between tanker rates for very large crude carriers (VLCCs) and oil prices from 1980 until today. We see that when oil prices were at relatively high levels in the early 1980s, tanker rates were down, which was then followed by a decade of relatively low oil prices and only slightly higher tanker rates than before. Again, we see a new era starting around 2003, with oil prices rising steadily – to the extraordinarily high levels they have reached today. Tanker rates have also gone up, but not as dramatically as oil prices. Again, it seems to be true that high oil prices have a dampening effect on the consumption of oil, with a consequent weakening of tanker rates.

It must generally be said, however, that tanker rates – in an absolute sense – have not fallen to the same low levels as bulk carrier rates. The demand for oil is of course still relatively strong – for aircraft fuel, automotive uses, heating of buildings, petrochemical applications, etc. – even though other sources of fuel, above all coal, are clearly being substituted for oil whenever possible.

Within the tanker category, there are at least four major sub-markets, all somewhat correlated:

1. VLCCs – ships with typically more than 200,000 dead-weight tonnage (dwt) capacity.
2. Suezmax market – ships typically of around 150,000 to 180,000 dwt.
3. Aframax/Panamax market – ships of 60,000 to 120,000 dwt.
4. Product tankers/Handysize market – ships typically around 25,000 to 50,000 dwt.

As a result of the International Maritime Organization (IMO) regulations regarding the requirement of double hulls, outlined in Chapter 1, there has been an unprecedented newbuilding program for tankers over the last few years, and the order books remain high. Still, the phasing out of single hull tankers may significantly affect the future crude tanker freight market – and most likely lead to higher project rates. The effects of this phasing out have not yet shown, as the old tonnage has been partly absorbed by countries ignoring the IMO regulations. These vessels are still plying the seas.

There are two additional factors that impact the tanker market – the existence of ore-bulk-oil carriers or OBO ships and the conversion of newer single-hull tankers to bulk carriers.[3]

---

[3] OBO ships are multipurpose ships that can carry ore, heavy dry bulk goods and oil.

1 OBO ships can command particularly strong freight rates at times. Although they are considerably more expensive to build, they can often make return journeys with cargo. This makes them ultimately more economical than single-purpose ships, which must often return empty. That said, most OBOs today carry exclusively dry cargo, because dry bulk rates are considerably higher than wet cargo rates. However, there are instances when trade routes can be worked out with both wet and dry cargo, which allows for excessive ballast legs, typical for most tankers and many bulk carriers, to be avoided.

2 Conversion of relatively new single-hull VLCC tankers to large bulk carriers is another growing trend. The Taiwan-based TMT shipping group and Hong Kong-based BW Group have had extensive conversion programs. But with tight yard capacity – including repair yards – conversion costs have gone up rapidly. Some owners, notably John Fredriksen, have converted some of their single-hull tankers to offshore storage capacity for oil.

BULK CARRIER MARKETS

The dry bulk carrier market can be broken down into three major segments:

1 Capesize bulk carriers – comprised of ships of more than 80,000 to 100,000 dwt and typically within the 150,000 to 180,000 dwt range.

2 Panamax market – typically comprised of ships of around 65,000 to 80,000 dwt.

3 Handymax/Handysize market – typically comprised of ships of 25,000 to 60,000 dwt.

Ship safety is also of concern for bulk carriers, and regulations are being tightened. Although the IMO has recommended that bulk carriers should be built with double hulls from 2007, this is not a regulation, and the phasing out of single-hull bulk carrier vessels has not been put into international law (Whittaker, 2003).

Demand for iron ore is higher than ever, and China is the major market. Supply comes particularly from Australia and Brazil, and the three major producers (Vale, Brazil; BHP Billiton, Australia; and Rio Tinto, UK) are rapidly increasing their production of iron ore. Indeed, these three firms have a higher concentration in the iron ore trade than the Organization of the Petroleum Exporting Countries (OPEC) countries have ever had in the oil trade (Eckbo, 1976). Hypothetically, they could push prices up, which would result in a reduction in global trade and lower shipping markets. To date, this does not seem to have happened. While expansion projects by the oil producers have speeded up significantly in response to the heavy growth in demand, port and infrastructure improvements have been lagging, and these, as discussed, result in higher freight rates because ship capacity is tied up by port congestion.

How much further can bulk-shipping markets rise or fall? What are the turning points? Historically, the market peaks have been short and the downturns brutal. But continued strong iron ore imports to supply the Chinese steel industry seem to be the key to understanding the overall market cycle this time and, as with electricity, the critical importance of shipping is easily forgotten until there is not enough of it. Today, the utilization rate for bulk carriers is at an all-time high. Many industrial users of ships, e.g., oil companies, mining companies, steel mills, and power utilities, have fostered a belief that low-cost shipping would always be readily available. Consequently, many companies decided not to take longer-term cover for their shipping needs.

While the tanker markets and bulk freight markets are largely independent of each other, there are of course also interdependencies, partly due to the existence of the fleet of OBO ships that can serve both markets, and above all due to the effects of newbuilding activities in the shipyards. The yards deliver capacity in whichever of the two ship types is the most advantageous, given the price they can ask for a newbuilding at any given time. This, again, is a function of the freight rate outlook as seen through an owner's eyes. This expectation regarding the likely development of freight rates for the ship type will impact the owner's appetite for placing orders, willingness to pay the yard a reasonable price for the ship, and the length of time he or she is willing to wait before delivery. Until now, this has led to too many newbuilding orders in a particularly popular category of ships. Over time, this brings down the freight rate in this category, making the other ship categories relatively more attractive for owners. Thus, in the end, this evens out the long-term differences between tanker rates and dry bulk rates – indeed, in general, between any types of ships.

What is exceptional about newbuilding orders today is that tanker orders remain relatively high, despite the slump in tanker rates. Bulk carrier orders booked also remain high, despite the collapse of the high dry bulk rates. Since the general collapse of the ship freight markets, there have been little to no newbuilding orders. However, we would have expected relatively more bulk carrier orders, and relatively fewer tanker orders. Hence, the evening out effects in rates between the two markets may not be as strong as usual. Maybe tanker owners want to be prepared for the 2010 double hull requirement. And maybe "irrational exuberance" is having an effect – no tanker owner would want to be left behind (Shiller, 2000).

CONTAINER MARKETS

The impact of containerization on the shipping business cannot be overstated. Large-scale shipping of finished consumer goods from China, for instance, would not have been feasible without container-ization. Strong exports of finished goods, coupled with strong technology developments in container ships, have led to spectacular growth in this shipping segment, which has, in general, been highly profitable. The size of ships has increased from around 1,000 TEU to more than 14,500 TEU for so-called mega ships. Ship speed has also increased. Today, a speed of 25 knots is not uncommon. Initially, the container shipping business could be seen as a specialized niche business; today, however, it has many of the characteristics of a commodity business. A growing fraction of today's container ship capacity is run on the open market, on either short-term contracts or time charter/bare boat charter contracts. The bulk of the container ships are part of the operations of a specific liner business. And this business segment is becoming fiercely competitive.

What would a downward, worst-case scenario be for the con-tainer shipping business segment? A major slowdown in the world's leading economies would have a negative effect on world trade and hence on container shipping. Also, of course, the risk of terrorism in a major consumer country, such as the US, might lead to a downward adjustment of consumers' activities, and with it, a corresponding slow-down in imports to the US, particularly from China. In the end, it will be the overriding developments in the final consumption patterns in industrialized countries that could represent the biggest source of vulnerability for the container business.

According to Gerry Wang, CEO of Seaspan, there are perhaps three major factors that are particularly important for China's further development and economic growth (Lorange, 2007):

1 The challenge of transforming the state-owned firms for a market economy: these have all now largely become privatized, with broader ownership structures. Consequently, this factor no longer seems to represent a major impediment to growth – perhaps rather the contrary.
2 Revitalizing and strengthening China's banking sector: this has recently been overhauled, and seems to be performing reasonably well. Again, there no longer seems to be a major problem here, and the banking sector can now potentially have a positive impact on the future growth of China.
3 China's huge farming population still represents a problem and a challenge: with 70 percent of China's population relatively poor farmers, the Chinese government faces a huge task to develop a plan that would allow this group to benefit from the overall wealth that is being created in the country. This still represents a major challenge for the Chinese government.

There are clearly additional potential challenges for the Chinese gov-ernment and for continued economic growth in the country, such as:

• Environmental issues relating to antipollution. Here, the challenge of upgrading the country's stock of automobiles, as well as how to clean its coal-fired plants, will be key.
• Energy efficiency issues. China's economy is primarily based on coal as its major energy source – not oil, as is the case for the other major world

economies. Although coal is relatively abundant, it may increasingly have to be imported – another boost for shipping.

- The legal system, especially as it relates to human rights, property rights, intellectual property protection, etc.
- The currency system. With its peg to the US dollar, the Yuan might now be thought undervalued, which would stimulate exports. Will the rest of the world continue to "allow" this?

While the future economic development of China will be key for predicting the future strengths for worldwide shipping markets, the rates of economic development in the rest of the world will clearly be important too. Japan, Europe and the US are all major consumer blocs. Continued growth of the world economy is thus vital for shipping, but in general there seems to be more uncertainty about it today than there has been for many years.

The growth in demand for container ship revenues has been around 10 percent per annum over the last few years. Now, however, it is being adjusted down, to around 5 or 6 percent per annum (*Berlingske Tidene*, September 23, 2008, pp. 16–17). The US-based import flow via the container market is expected to be more or less zero – in keeping with the slowdown in the US economy. In 2007, the Far East–Europe container trade grew by 20 percent, but this strong growth is unlikely to be sustained.

These considerations may have a particularly strong impact on container shipping. Wang describes the container ship system as "ocean highways," greatly important for the stimulation of world trade, connecting producers and consumers. Container lines must, however, attempt to be more cost efficient too, for instance, by operating larger container ships to achieve economies of scale. Many lines have also associated themselves with port operations, storage, and even door-to-door truck delivery. These associated activities tend to be run as separate businesses. An efficient route pattern will also be essential. Reducing speed – slow-steaming – from (say) 25 knots to 18 knots can also lead to savings of up to 50 percent in bunkers, for example:

result – decreased costs. But to maintain the same frequency of service would mean that more ships would be needed: result – increased costs. So there is a trade-off. The overall trend in container lines is nevertheless generally to go for larger and larger ships, often with higher and higher speeds, complemented by smaller feeder ships, warehousing, door-to-door activities, etc., – and building a strong brand to support everything. Competition among the various players is fierce. A. P. Moller-Maersk has approximately 16 percent of the world's capacity for container ships, followed by MSC of Switzerland.

The size of container ships has continually increased. Ten years ago, a 3,000 TEU ship was considered large. Today, the largest ships are in the region of 15,000 TEU. We also need to differentiate between major container ships and container feeder ships. Feeder ships typically have a capacity of 1,000 TEU or less. Their main purpose is to bring containers to or from smaller ports or larger ones, where the containers are unloaded from major container ships or reloaded onto them. Thus, a container line typically consists of several classes of ships, creating an effective network of hubs and spokes.

CONTAINER LINES VS. CLASSICAL LINER BUSINESSES – CAR CARRIERS AND RO-RO SERVICES

Considerable resources are needed to be a top player in the container liner industry. Interestingly, one of the shipping industry's largest groups of players, the Norwegian shipowners, has been largely absent when it comes to the container shipping segment. Why? From a historical point of view, Norwegian owners may have been more focused on tramp shipping, where the vessels do not have regular routes or service; instead there is heavy emphasis on adapting to market swings. The container liner business, on the other hand, can be seen as more industrial, even more marketing oriented (business-to-business – B2B), and with a need to build up an integrated infrastructure – on sea and on land – based on long-term thinking. Admittedly, several Norwegian shipowners need to operate conventional liners. But they seem to have largely stuck to pallets as a transportation solution.

Also, several Norwegian players focused heavily on ro-ro ships. (I discuss ro-ro ships and car carriers in depth later.)[4] Examples would be Wallenius Wilhelmsen Logistics, the world's largest company in the car transportation/ro-ro segment, with strong ties to the classical Wilh. Wilhelmsen Lines, as well as the former HUAL, now Höegh Autoliners – the car carrier company owned by Leif Höegh & Co.[5] Norwegian owners seem to have gotten themselves trapped in these transportation concepts, and have largely missed out on the boom in growth in the container market.

Where ro-ro car carriers are concerned, the Korea-based EUKOR is part-owned (40 percent) by Wallenius Lines, 40 percent by Wilh. Wilhelmsen, and 20 percent by Hyundai. Wallenius Wilhelmsen Logistics (WWL) is owned 50–50 by Wallenius and Wilh. Wilhelmsen. There is some arm's-length cooperation between EUKOR and WWL. Briefly, WWL has "slot" charter agreements with other carriers, NYK for example, but this does not work particularly well in times with high pressure on capacity, when carriers want to prioritize their own customers and no carrier wants to help another, unless they make more money by doing so. For WWL and EUKOR, the situation is slightly different, however, in that both companies would be willing to help its sister company. In reality, this is still a little difficult, especially when an arm's-length business relationship is required by the competition rules. This might change if the two companies were to merge.

The ranking among the biggest ro-ro car carriers is:

1 NYK
2 EUKOR
3 Mitsui O.S.K. Lines (MOL)
4 WWL

---

[4] Ro-ro, or roll-on/roll-off, ships are designed to carry wheeled cargo such as automobiles, trailers or railroad cars.

[5] Wallenius Wilhelmsen Logistics is partly Swedish (Wallenius), partly Norwegian (Wilhelmsen). The company owns 80 percent of EUKOR (Korea) and, when EUKOR is included, it is the world's biggest player in this segment. If EUKOR is not included, the largest company in this sector is Japan's NYK.

5 Kawasaki Kisen Kaisha (K Line)

6 Höegh Autoliners

(Source: Drewry Shipping Consultants, 2006)

Some traditional Norwegian lines – such as Fjell Line (Olsen & Ugelstad) or the West Africa Line (Leif Höegh & Co.) – are part of larger integrated shipping companies and may not have received the attention they need – managerially and in terms of capital – to succeed as modern liners.

Information technology (IT) can of course play an important role when it comes to creating a strategic advantage. This is particularly well illustrated by container liners. Maersk Line had problems with the effective integration of Ned-Lloyd when it acquired the company. IT has been blamed for a significant share of the problems related to the acquisition.

Orient Overseas Container Line (OOCL), for example, seems to have an effective approach to IT. Systematic investment in IT seems to have given OOCL a strategic advantage. It is important that IT should play its part in driving the firm's strategy, rather than solving ad hoc problems in hindsight. A better offering to the customer is key – and IT will inevitably be part of this.

Management – perhaps the very top executive cadre, in particular – will have to be ready to invest in IT to build a strategic advantage. This requires patience, as will be the case with the investment to build any new capability (including paper trading).

PASSENGER SHIPS AND CRUISE SHIPS

The classical passenger lines – once so prominent – are now more or less extinct. Instead, we have many passenger and car ferries, and also high-speed, multi-hull ferries. There is no doubt that these represent important – and stable – segments within shipping. Sales of tax-free goods often add to the attractiveness of this business. The cruise ship business has also evolved, with steady and impressive growth over the past decade, and heavy industry concentration. This business seems to be only remotely similar to most other shipping businesses, in that it is based on passenger demand patterns – typically a function of people's vacation habits. There are two major players in this segment. The biggest is Carnival, which has several brands, analogous to major hotel chains. These include Holland–America Lines, Princess Cruises, Costa Lines, and Cunard. The second-largest player, Royal Caribbean International, has two major brands – Royal Caribbean International and Celebrity Cruises.

The shipbuilding side of this type of business is of course critical. There are only a handful of shipyards that can undertake this specialized kind of ship construction. Placing orders at the right time is key. The trends in ship financing for cruise ships have a lot in common with other parts of shipping.

Branding plays an important role for cruise shipowning. It can signify that the company has a strong, coherent strategy, perhaps vis-à-vis financial market stakeholders, as opposed to run-of-the-mill consumers. And branding has a part to play in many segments of specialized shipbuilding – Seaspan and Danaos, for example, have strong brands vis-à-vis the financial markets.

REEFERS

This is a specialized ship market segment, primarily focused on the freight of fresh fruit and vegetables, meat, and fish. The freight is typically refrigerated, and the speed of this type of ship is relatively fast. With the advent of container ships, and specialized containers that can be cooled, the reefer freight segment has fallen on very hard times, with the result that it is no longer seen as a major shipping segment. Many reefer owners have organized themselves through pools – the most prominent of which is Seatrade.

OFFSHORE SHIPS

The two major market sub-segments of this business are anchor-handling and platform supply ships.

- Anchor-handling: these ships, with strong propulsion and pulling power, need to relocate land anchors that are used to position offshore oil drilling rigs. This market has seen strong growth with the increase in offshore drilling activities.
- Platform supply ships: these are used for the transportation of containers, various fluids, pipes, etc., from supply bases onshore to permanent offshore installations. There has been a surge in demand for these ships, in line with the increase in fixed offshore oil exploration installations.

While there clearly is an efficient market for offshore supply ships, this market is nevertheless specialized, and probably too small to be fully efficient.

LNG/LPG CARRIERS

Liquefied natural gas (LNG) carriers are large ships that carry natural gas over long distances. Most of these are built as part of larger, capital-intensive projects, with terminals on both the shipping and receiving ends. They are usually employed on long-term charters. Few LNG carriers would operate in the open spot market.

Liquefied propane gas (LPG) carriers, on the other hand, are relatively smaller and operate from refineries to various consumer installations.

The markets for both types of carrier are relatively specialized, although increasingly competitive.

CHEMICAL TANKERS

These are specialty tankers, with many parallel systems (segregations) of tanks, pumps, and loading/unloading pipes. The tanks are either specially coated or made of stainless steel. These tankers operate in networks between chemical plants and special-purpose tanker terminals. The market for this type of ship is specialized and heavily competitive, with relatively few companies active in this field – the most prominent companies include Stolt-Nielsen S.A., Odfjell, Jo Tankers, and Tokyo Marine.

Murphy and Tenold (2008) have made a study of the strategies of the main shipping company players in the chemical tanker segment, from 1960 to 1985, and point out how two Norwegian-originated companies (Stolt-Nielsen and Odfjell) became winners – through innovation combined with first-mover advantages, fleet structure, and good timing.

RO-RO SHIPS AND CAR CARRIERS

This ship segment is growing fast. It has evolved partly from traditional liner ships, partly from bulk-carriers with removable decks for the transport of cars. Today, these ships are highly specialized and usually have adjustable decks that can accommodate not only cars but also buses, trucks, earth-moving equipment, defense materials, etc. This segment is dominated by five groupings, which organize their ship services as routes, with regular sailings covering the entire world. The major automotive companies have long-term contracts with these charterers – indeed specialty liner services. The industry is heavily concentrated, with five major players. The largest grouping is Wallenius Wilhelmsen Logistics with its part-owned Korean affiliate EUKOR, followed by the three largest Japanese companies – NYK, Mitsui-O.S.K. Line and K. Line – and Höegh Autoliners.

VERY SPECIALIZED SHIPS

This category has a mix of ships that operate in small, specialized markets, with no atomistic competition. Five examples of very specialized ships are:

1 General self-unloaders: these are used for cargo that generates dust, like coal or ferro-alloys.
2 Cement carriers: these are highly specialized, closed, self-unloading ships built for the handling of bulk cement, which generates a lot of dust. While most self-unloading ships use a belt for unloading, cement carriers are increasingly employing pneumatic unloading.
3 Juice/wine tankers: these are relatively small ships focusing on specialized trades. The market is competitive.

4 Crane ships: these specialized ships are used for heavy lifting in the construction of new offshore installations. Again, this is a highly specialized market in which P. Heerema is a leader.
5 Offshore dredging: even more specialized, these ships are used for dredging in sand and/or rock, to enlarge harbors and develop new offshore building facilities, etc. Van Oord is a leader in this business.

CONCLUSION

In this chapter, we have reviewed the major shipping markets – wet, dry, and containers. We have also discussed a number of more specialized shipping markets. The major dry, wet or container markets are more or less atomistic, with perfect competition prevailing, as economists would say. Three major segments of shipping are therefore mature businesses. For specialty markets, such as the cruise market, reefers, offshore, or other specialty ships, these niches are a far cry from the major atomistic shipping markets. However, many of these too are maturing fast. A key question therefore is: for how long can one enjoy a specialized non-mature market context?

3   Shipping freight rates

Shipping is a precarious business. Factors such as rising oil prices, economic booms and recessions, and so on, can seriously impact the industry; there are also, of course, differences between geographical areas. And, as we know, economic development goes in cycles. During times of recession, we see too many ships and too few cargos, which results in falling freight rates. In the past, during economic booms, we saw the opposite effect – capacity could not be added fast enough to meet demand – and freight rates rose. While new capacity is perhaps becoming less of an issue, assessing where shipping rates stand and where they are going remains of key importance. The successful shipping companies will be those that can develop strategies not only to survive but also to prosper during economic swings. Anticipating market swings, rather than expecting particular market developments, is critical.

FREIGHT MARKETS

The freight markets dropped dramatically from September to November, 2008. Figure 3.1 illustrates the movement for the dry bulk markets as indicated by the Baltic Exchange Index. The fall has been faster, steeper, and longer than ever experienced before. Further, it should be noted that larger ships generally seem to face relatively larger amplitudes in charter rates than smaller ships. A Capesize bulk carrier would thus receive relatively higher top rates than, say, a Handymax bulk carrier, but the daily freight rates it receives would also fall relatively lower. Similarly, Figures 3.2 and 3.3 are examples of typical movements for bulk carrier freight rates and tanker freight rates, respectively, and indicate both radical falls in spot market rates as well as rather pessimistic outlooks for the spot market freight rates for most ship types.

Baltic Dry Index

FIGURE 3.1 Bulk freight rates
Source: Bloomberg.

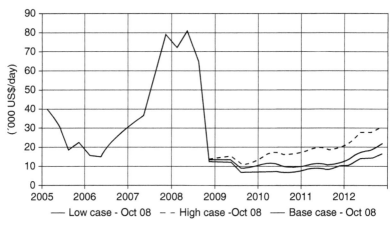

FIGURE 3.2 Panamax bulk carrier earnings
Source: Marsoft, 2008a.

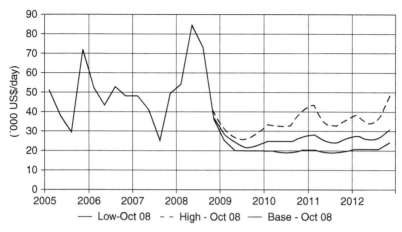

FIGURE 3.3 Suezmax tanker earnings
Source: Marsoft, 2008b.

GLOBAL DEMAND VS. SUPPLY

The integration and growth of global economies over the last few years
has resulted in an incredible increase in the demand for shipping
relative to supply. This has fundamentally changed the supply-and-
demand balance, which has governed shipping to date, creating
exceptionally strong markets for a relatively long period. As I noted
in Chapter 2, much of today's global shipping boom stems from growth
in China, particularly from raw material imports to support Chinese
infrastructure and manufacturing. But, since the fall of 2008, we have
seen a slowdown in China. Figure 3.4 provides an overview of iron ore
imports to China, and a breakdown of this by major exporting countries of source, of which Australia and Brazil are by far the most
prominent. Shipping growth is also fuelled by the container shipping
industry, which supports the export of products manufactured in
China (Hale and Hale, 2003).

Demand, however, rarely exceeds supply for long; rather, there
tend to be relatively short peaks of prosperity in the freight markets,
followed by longer slumps. Shipbuilding technology has exacerbated
this phenomenon – huge capacity is now available for building new

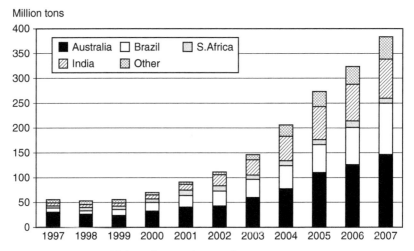

Million tons

FIGURE 3.4 Chinese iron ore imports by source, 1997–2007
Source: Simpson, Spence and Young Shipbrokers, 2008.

tonnage – and fast. And, as indicated, ample financing is available. Banks still appear eager to give loans; indeed, they are often seen as effective drivers of new shipbuilding activities. This combination of shipbuilding capacity and available financing shortens peak periods further and thus dampens freight rates. In general, this is unfortunate for the shipping industry, since supply tends to outstrip demand. The result is long periods of depressed freight markets (Stopford, 1997). Well-consolidated companies have the luxury of being anti-cyclical. To illustrate, they might buy modern second-hand tonnage at depressed prices. Because of their financial strength, they can be less dependent on the banks. Companies in this category may continue to grow until too much managerial complexity kicks in. It is thus still possible to be small and to play the market successfully.

Until Fall 2008, it was almost a truism in shipping that supply and demand for shipping activities should ideally be more or less balanced. It is important to view current trends in light of the extraordinary level of over-capacity. The rates that we saw in the last four or five years, until mid-2008, have dropped dramatically. Ship capacity utilization was exceptionally high until then – this tight picture was key to explaining the exceptionally high freight rates. There are many attractive opportunities in such an environment, but not all are sustainable. The question of which opportunities should cause a major strategic redirection must be analyzed and discussed, keeping in mind that the difficult structural problems of the 1980s seem to have returned. Newbuilding capacity is growing fast as well. The lack of demand, relative to supply, can be expected to last.

In order to develop better strategies, shipping companies must focus on understanding the underlying factors that affect global economic growth, supply and demand. It seems to have been a tradition in the industry to focus more on the supply side – availability of ships, shipyard capacity, and so on. However, experience has shown that it is the *demand* side that counts the most. The development of world trade and economic activities are key. With a better understanding of crucial underlying factors, management should be able to forecast more accurately those that will truly matter for their company and, therefore, be in a better position to manage risk and reduce the cost of capital. Because of this focus on managing risk and reducing the cost of capital, shipping has effectively become more aligned to financial management. However, the need to have an in-depth understanding of a series of basic underlying issues raises the question of how much complexity management is able to handle.

An interesting "complication" resulting from this alignment with financial management is the issue of turnaround time for investments: nowadays there is less available. More than ever, time means money, and, consequently, there seems to be a quicker "flip" regarding committed capital. Often, this means that competent in/out financial management is becoming more important.

SO, WHAT DRIVES SHIPPING RATES?

The answer is simple – the utilization ratio between supply and demand. But, the chief driver is demand, and it is particularly important to understand movements – or turning points – on the demand side. It is critical that shipping executives take a long-term view so that they are not distracted by short-term noise. Understanding the key factors that might impact demand can yield important clues about movements in shipping rates. I should, of course, hasten to stress that the supply fact will be key too – with too much newbuilding on order, so that supply will outstrip demand and rates will come down.

Commodities
There are, of course, strong interdependencies between freight rate markets, above all, for crude oil, coal, steel, and grain. But as we shall see, these major commodities are market setters for their own broad shipping freight rate markets. All the major shipping markets can be classified as commodity markets.

Trade developments
Strong growth in trade, above all to and from China and India, coupled with the strong import propensity of the US and Europe, has an impact on shipping rates. However, a slowdown in Chinese demand for oil and other raw materials, for example, would be likely to send shipping rates lower. It is also critical to understand the impact of trade barriers on free trade. The failure to find a new comprehensive worldwide free trade agreement and the relative weakness of the World Trade Organization (WTO) are definite negatives. Because they are political, these issues are difficult to forecast, but can still be of major importance for the development of freight rates.

For China and India, shipping rates may be more than a function of supply and demand. In China, for instance, there may be future uncertainties, since most delivery of vessels built at Chinese yards is backed by refundable guarantees from China banks. Hence, a less amenable political situation may have a negative impact on shipowners as well as ship financing over the years to come. This is very different from a simple question of supply and demand.

Availability of finished goods
The availability of finished consumer goods and container ship rates tend to be functions of the general economic outlook. Rates are also

affected by the distance between the places where goods are manufactured and where they are consumed. With a strong economic outlook in consuming regions such as the US and Europe, and strong economic outlooks and competitive cost levels for manufacturing regions in Asia, particularly China, one would expect to see stability in container shipping rates. However, container rates have fallen sharply because of the heavy addition of container ship capacity, as well as due to the recent slowdown in the US economy.

Port congestion and delays

Port congestion and delays represent a true challenge. Australian ports, for instance, can inflict delays of up to a one month on bulk carriers exporting iron ore. To some extent, Brazilian and Chinese ports have suffered from the same problem. However, there seems to be a strong investment in infrastructure in Chinese and Asian ports in general. On the other hand, the infrastructure in Australian ports, and to some extent in European and US ports, including their access facilities (roads, railroads, etc.), seems to be lagging behind Asia. Australian port congestion has a particularly high impact on dry bulk freight rates – the flow of coal, as well as iron ore, has been significantly delayed. However, port congestion may also be challenging for the container shipping industry. Contrary to what is commonly assumed, future delays, particularly in container ports and terminals, may be more prevalent in the US and Europe rather than in Asia or China.

Shipping rates do, of course, go up when capacity is curtailed. A lot of ship capacity is taken up as a result of these delays, particularly in the dry bulk segment, which leads to higher freight rates. And this leads to the question of when port congestion will ease up. Is this a question of infrastructure only, or is it also related to labor relations practices? This may be a major factor behind the relatively low productivity in US container ports. Also, when will intracoastal sea freight in China ease due to improvements in land-based infrastructure? The lack of sufficient capacity in land-based transportation infrastructure in China has led to the growth of intracoastal trade and thus capacity utilization of dry bulk ships in this trade (with implications for capacity worldwide).

The effect of port delays on capacity and freight rates

From Figure 3.5, one can see that there is a strong link between the general movements of the Capesize dry bulk freight rate and harbor congestion. Much of the congestion, as I have discussed, is in Australian harbors. Obviously, this has had a strong impact on the de facto available bulk carrier ship capacity and has also led to strong rate increases. We can observe a close correlation between bulk carrier rates and bulk carrier harbor congestion.

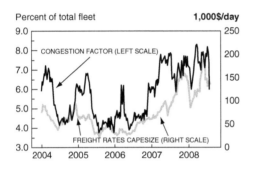

FIGURE 3.5 Port delays
Source: R.S. Platou Shipbrokers
A.S., Oslo, 2008.

Newbuilding and scrapping

New shipbuilding prices, in particular, are impacted by the price of steel. Many shipyards, as well as major owners, have started to hedge against rising steel prices to safeguard themselves against skyrocketing newbuilding prices. However, hedging practices in this area are not yet common. Recently, some signed newbuilding contracts have built in price escalation clauses linked to steel prices.

Let us examine the newbuildings order book relative to the existing fleet ratio (see Figure 3.6). We might want to claim that the volume of new ship construction must be commensurate with the growth of world trade – or better – for shipping values to stay high. And we see that a high percentage of the bulk carrier fleet – 60 percent – consists of

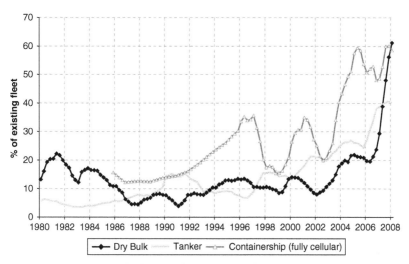

FIGURE 3.6 Order book-to-fleet ratio (dry bulk, tanker, and fully cellular containership fleet)
Source: Marsoft, 2008a, b, c.

newbuildings. For tankers, it is only 40 percent. So, do we expect world trade to grow about 40 percent over the next few years? Not likely. Thus, overcapacity – and falling rates – would be the result.

The rate of newbuildings on order relative to ships in the water – provides a measure of the imbalance between supply and demand that can be expected in the marketplace. We see that this is particularly serious for dry bulk ships and container ships. If we focus on the dry bulk ships on order and further break out the newbuilding orders of Capesize bulk carriers relative to existing ships, the result is a stunning 100 percent! So, it is no wonder that the Capesize bulk carrier segment was the hardest hit in terms of the drop in daily freight rates. A reduction in newbuilding orders relative to the existing fleet, say, due to cancellations, delivery delays, scrapping of old ships, etc., might contribute to improvements in the freight markets. But this will undoubtedly take time.

The fleet employment (utilization) rate for each particular ship segment is a significant driver for the actual daily freight rates that can

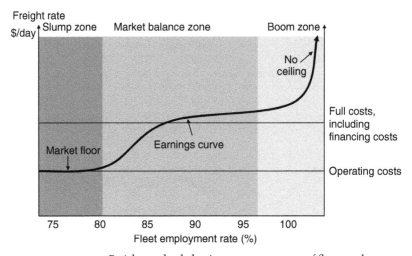

FIGURE 3.7 Freight market behavior as a consequence of fleet employment rate

Source: Dr. D. Jessel, Howe Robinson & Co.

be achieved. With high fleet utilization, the rates tend to go up – and vice versa. Figure 3.7 illustrates this.

Let us apply this to the Capesize bulk carriers. The daily freight rate as of June 2008 was more than US$200,000 per day. By the end of November 2008 it was less than US$4,000 per day, which is *less* than the typical operating costs of approximately US$8,000 per day. The owners might expect that rates would come up somewhat – the 1-month forward rate was US$7,600 per day (end of December 2008) and the 3-month forward rate was US$12,000 per day. Still, many owners decided to anchor their Capesize bulk carriers. As of the end of November 2008 an estimated 200 Capesize bulk carriers were anchored – out of an overall fleet of approximately 850 Capesize bulk carriers, i.e., a fleet utilization rate of approximately 71 percent.

The full cost of operating a Capesize, including financing costs, might be around US$20,000 per day. (The cost of a five-year old Capesize was approximately US$150 million in December 2007. By the end of November 2008, the cost was approximately US$50 million. The full cost estimate of approximately US$20,000 per day would be based on the former price.)

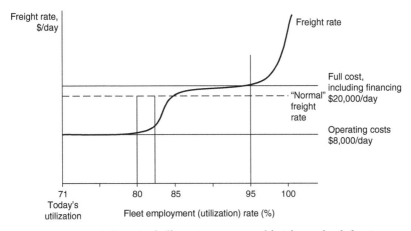

FIGURE 3.8 Capesize bulk carriers – expected freight market behavior

Consequently, one might expect the daily freight rates for Capesize bulk carriers to typically be between about US$8,000 and US$20,000 per day until extensive scrapping and cancellations/delays of newbuildings have taken place, which might, over time, bring the fleet utilization up (see Figure 3.8).

It should be noted that the *average* daily freight rates for Capesize bulk carriers were:

- for the period 1990–2003: US$17,000 per day;
- for the period 2003–2008: US$76,000 per day;
- for the period 2008–2011: US$17,000 per day (Marsoft estimate).

We thus see that, in years to come, Marsoft expects these rates to settle at a rate that is more or less similar to the last "normal" period, i.e., around US$17,000 per day.

Yet newbuilding activity remains relatively strong and new orders are continuing with high cost levels and long lead times for delivery. This is in the face of falling time charter levels for tankers and, above all, for bulkers. There seems to be a built-in expectation of continuing growth in world trade among many shipowners, which may explain the strong newbuilding activity. Or do shipowners fear being left behind and so feel they have to place newbuilding orders irrespective of the falling time charter levels for tankers? If so, this fear of being left behind seems to apply to all types of ship – bulkers and tankers – irrespective of rate differences. This may be analogous to the phenomenon of irrational exuberance described by Shiller (2000).

When the freight market is high, the newbuilding market will correspond to it. Second-hand ship prices will also be high, some say at a higher level than warranted by the high freight levels and new-building price levels. This could be termed an "asset bubble." An empirical study by Adland *et al.* (2006) tested this, based on the years 2003–2005. They found no evidence to support the existence of an asset bubble. Second-hand ship prices were in line with what would be expected, given freight rate levels and newbuilding price levels. Therefore, one can assume that freight rates, second-hand prices and newbuilding prices are relatively highly correlated and that these markets are indeed efficient.

It is, therefore, even more important for shipping executives to follow the movements of the markets and gain a keen understanding of them. It is particularly important to develop strategies that yield additional flexibility in the face of market developments. For instance, when ships are taken on time or bareboat charter, an option to purchase should be built into the contract in the event of rising markets, so as not to pay out high time or bareboat charter rates for nothing. An exit strategy should also be incorporated in the event of the market falling, so that the shipping company is not burdened with owning a ship with a heavy financial burden. Wholly owned ships can always be sold, providing funds for payments of time or bareboat risks. Sales of vessels may not make sense, however, if the ships are locked into long-term charters and the agreed rates are higher than the market.

Adland *et al.* (2006) have developed a simulation model for the probability distribution of future freight spot rates for VLCCs, as well as for future fleet size in terms of the number of VLCC ships, conditional on present spot rates.[6] The supply side of the simulation is estimated, based on actual available data. The contracting behavior as well as scrapping is estimated stochastically, as is the demand side. The authors claim that the model can be used not only to forecast the development of VLCC spot rates, but also for evaluating risks regarding ship financing, or for assessing freight derivatives portfolios involving VLCCs. Marsoft, considered by many as the world leader in ship freight rate forecasting, has a future tanker freight market simulation that might be utilized for similar purposes. However, the results of the model, relative to Marsoft's estimates, seem to indicate that Marsoft's results yield better predictability.

Forecasting movements in the market is never easy. Experienced shipping executives may, at times, feel that they have a better gut feeling than the forecasters. Several prominent companies have thus traded against the market and often ended up losing money. Recently, the market has fallen, while many seasoned experts had predicted that it would remain relatively strong. One seasoned shipping executive said, "It is better to be lucky than smart." In general, when one trades against future developments of the market, it is easy to lose money.

Perhaps, therefore, the forecasting challenge may not be so much a question of understanding the more conventional market cycles. We all know that downsides and upsides will probably average out over the long term. However, the recent positive market cycle seemed to be of a different kind. Its upside was sustained for a variety of reasons linked with excessively strong demand.

The paradigm for forecasting market cycles may thus have changed. The extraordinary growth in demand in the markets for shipping services until mid-2008 seemed to be abnormal in both strength and length. The question we must now ask ourselves is how long are we likely to stay in the slump before we enter another market upturn?

---

[6] Very large crude carriers (VLCCs) are ships with more than 200,000 dwt capacity for large quantities of crude oil.

As of November 2008, we have seen large-scale scrapping of ships. Psychologically, it is difficult for a shipowner to scrap ships that are less than fifteen years old. Instead, they typically prefer to anchor the ships, which would mean maintaining their class status. Deep lay-up is a more dramatic alternative, which involves abandonment of classification status, maintaining only a skeleton crew on board, etc. The eventual re-commissioning of these ships tends to be more expensive, and they often end up being scrapped in the end.

FUNDAMENTALLY A COMMODITY BUSINESS

It is important to recognize that shipping has always been – and is likely to remain – fundamentally a commodity business. Ship capacity issues, linked to the recent strong market situation, are perhaps not that different from what we saw in the early 1980s. At that time, excess capacity in every sector, coupled with the shipyard sector's increasing ability to deliver ships faster, led to a depression in all shipping sectors that made even diversification unhelpful. In short, there was nowhere to hide. It should also be observed that when markets come down to very low levels, volatility tends to be low – indeed too low to make trading very interesting. Chartering – with an option to buy – can of course be attractive during these periods, and it provided a great upside during the 1980s because these types of options were significantly underpriced. Perhaps we might even see an emerging market based on systematic options pricing. But, needless to say, sensing what options to buy is close to impossible during strong market periods.

Figure 3.9 shows that real commodity prices (adjusted for inflation) have entered a major bullish phase approximately every thirty years. These upswings have lasted about ten years, and then they have been followed by a twenty-year period of roughly stable and declining real prices. However, it is important to bear in mind that past performance is not always a good predictor of future performance. Steep price increases are usually triggered by extraordinary events that lead to sudden supply shortages and increased demand. The two world wars and subsequent reconstruction resulted in a demand boom for

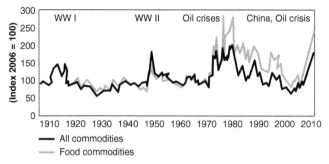

FIGURE 3.9 Major bull market every thirty years? Commodity cycles
(index 2006 = 100)
Source: "Commodities: Scarcity or Abundance," *UBS Research Focus*,
Zurich, August 2006, p. 53, since updated.

commodities that could not be met with existing supplies. The beginning of industrialization in the middle of the nineteenth century and the oil crisis in the 1970s had similar effects on commodity prices. The formation of cartels, such as the Organization of Petroleum Exporting Countries (OPEC), can have an impact too. The rise of new global players, such as China, India and other highly populated emerging markets, have prompted another long-term increase in commodity prices that began around 2001.

While shipping markets are not directly comparable to many other commodity markets, we should remember that commodities such as oil and ore have a profound impact on shipping rates. So these long-term cycles, with upswings lasting a certain period of time every thirty years, are important. If we apply this observation to the current situation, it suggests that reasonable shipping rates could last for several more years. The China boom, with its impact on strong demand, is still having a major effect.

Changing patterns of trade also impact freight rates, of course. Raw material imports to China imply longer trade routes, as do finished goods exports from China to the US and Europe. A new pattern of trade has emerged that also has led to higher freight rates.

Shipping rates are also interrelated with the financial markets. When charter rates are good, financing is readily available, and liquidity is abundant. Risk and return on cost of capital seem favorable, as long as the freight rate levels remain good. These can quickly turn unfavorable, however. When freight rates go down, liquidity dries up.

We can see from Figures 3.10, 3.11, and 3.6 that something dramatic started to happen after 2002. Before then, the freight rates remained relatively stable, and they were relatively low for bulk carriers, tankers and container ships alike (Figure 3.10). The rate of growth of trade, which in the end dictates demand – and therefore freight rate developments – was also relatively stable and relatively low for bulk carriers and tankers at around 2.5 percent. For containers it was much higher – almost 8 percent. After 2002, we see that growth in world trade shot up dramatically for dry bulk and that it continued to do so for containers (see Figure 3.11). For newbuilding orders, relative to

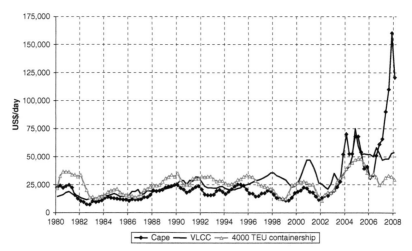

FIGURE 3.10 Vessel earnings (Cape, VLCC, and 4,000 TEU – one-year time charter rate)
Source: Marsoft, 2008a, b, c.

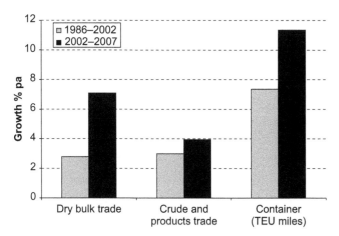

FIGURE 3.11 Rate of growth of trade (measured in tonne/mile or TEU/mile terms
Source: Marsoft, 2008a, b, c.

existing fleet (see Figure 3.6), we see a similar picture, with 2002 apparently being a break point.

For an experienced and traditionally successful shipping executive, the question might be, "How can so many who were more or less right for twenty years or so, be so fundamentally wrong for the last five years?"

Many within shipping were used to an industry with relatively small changes and relatively narrow ranges between the various ship segments in the industry. But suddenly, in or around 2002, the industry changed. All past plans went out of the window and there has not been any downward trend since, with the exception of the very recent uncertainties around credit risk and a US-based recession. The world changed. China's economy has undoubtedly had a lot to do with this.

There seem to be two fundamental new consequences, or realities, for shipping companies:

1 How has forecasting – i.e., outlook on the development of rates – changed? It is important to note that rates seem to have developed at a steady pace with only modest growth before 2002, but that these rates took off after this point (Figure 3.11). Let us now group these huge shifts.

- The pre-2002–post-2002 changes have been most dramatic for dry bulk.
- By contrast, the changes have not been so dramatic for tanker trades.
- For containers, the change seems to represent a basic continuation of a trend that started some years earlier.

2 A key question now is, what can we learn from this? We might expect fleet capacity to catch up with demand – see the newbuilding order activities relative to the existing fleet (Figure 3.6). We could compare the implications of this in terms of shipowners' expectations about growth with the rate of growth in trade indicated in Figure 3.11. Are the shipowners' growth expectations realistic or too optimistic? Can we expect a more normal demand–supply balance to be re-established? And would this have long-term consequences for freight rate developments? My own assessment confirms this – ship newbuilding may simply be coming out at too high a pace to allow rates to remain this high.

So it seems clear that when rates go up (primarily due to demand) – and stay up –shipowners place a lot of newbuilding orders. The banking sector has traditionally been willing to finance such a newbuilding boom. However, when all these newbuildings are delivered, rates fall due to over-supply. There seems to be a lag of about three years between peaks in newbuilding orders and the fall of rates. With the strong container order books we saw a few years ago, the rates currently seem to have fallen. Will we see the same thing happen when it comes to tankers and bulk carriers? These questions now seem to be being asked in the banking sector, with considerable reluctance to finance new newbuilding projects.

All this confirms the old dictum that it pays to buy ships during rising markets. This seems to be as valid today as it has always been. But did owners who bought ships just after 2002 have foresight, or were they just plain lucky? And with the high price of new ships that still holds today, could it be costly to own ships, given the potential for a considerable fall in their residual value after the market has dropped?

Let us look once again at the developments in rate of growth of trade between 1986 and 2007 (Figure 3.10). If we consider the pre-2002 period, we see that the container segment is at the top before 1997, higher than the tanker segment. The tanker segment is in the middle for growth in volume of trade and the dry bulk segment enjoyed the lowest growth in volume of trade during this period.

This all changed for the post-2002 period. The changing growth patterns – with the relative lack of growth of the tanker business, the relatively higher growth of dry bulk, and the dramatic growth in the container business – should have consequences for shipping companies' portfolio strategies. The container business, for one, is certainly relatively much more important now.

When considering the freight rate developments of the past, can we find any similar time periods in recent history from which we might learn? Perhaps we can. Container and tanker markets rose to a high in around 1980–1, only to fall sharply in 1981–2. The same was true, to a lesser extent, for bulk carriers. After these markets fell, they slumped at low levels for almost twenty years. What were the reasons for that fall? First, there was an increase in crude oil prices; second, there was an accompanying slowdown in world economic growth.

The same set of issues may be at work today. Until recently we saw a strong increase in the price of raw materials, particularly iron ore, as well as crude oil, and we are facing a slowdown in world economic growth too. We could also add the potential negative impacts of higher environmental compliance/pollution prevention costs on world growth. Rates may fall also again.

Figure 3.12 provides a picture of the rates for tankers, bulk carriers, and container lines, 1960–80. Note that container lines largely did not exist then; conventional liner rates are provided instead. We see a lull in the rates – particularly for tankers from 1974 – which led to a prolonged tanker crisis from 1974 to 1978. At the same time, it has been reported (Tenold, 2006, p. 110) that tanker newbuilding orders had risen to 80 percent of the overall tanker fleet by 1974. (As we saw in Figure 3.6, the tanker newbuilding orders relative to existing fleet are

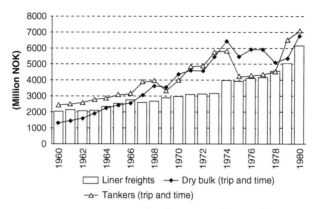

FIGURE 3.12 Gross freight earnings by vessel type, 1960–80 (million NOK)
Source: Statistisk Sentralbyrå, Historisk Statistikk 1994, table 22.8,
reproduced from Tenold, Stig, *Research in Maritime History* No. 32,
"Tankers in Trouble: Norwegian Shipping and the Crisis of the 1970s
and 1980s," St. John's, Newfoundland: International Maritime Economic
History Association, 2006, p. 110.

in the region of 60 percent today.) Also, as we have noted, the world
economy went into a recession, and higher oil prices led to lower
growth in oil shipments.

In light of all these developments, what can we learn in terms of a
better understanding of the outlook ahead?

First of all, we notice that there was a strong newbuilding order
to existing fleet ratio in the mid-1970s. There is similarly a strong
newbuilding order backlog today (see Figure 3.6). Is this possibly an
indication that rates may be about to fall once more, even relatively
soon, as we saw in the 1970s?

Second, it was primarily the combination of orders of expensive
newbuildings, and the failure to secure charters for them, that seemed
to cause problems for many shipping firms during the tanker shipping
crisis of the 1970s. A recent study by Tenold (2006, p. 110) shows
that it is this combination, rather than factors like the fleet portfolio
composition, that was the prime cause for the shipping crisis at that
time. An important lesson for us now would be only to order new
tonnage if we are able to secure a longer-term charter.

MARKET FORECASTING

We know that classical shipping markets follow cyclical patterns. To achieve a meaningful return on capital investments, investors need to be present over long periods of relatively low earnings interspersed with shorter periods of stronger earnings. An alternative to this would of course be to go in/out during the peaks, totally avoiding the lean periods – while appealing, this is hard to pull off in practice. Figure 3.13 illustrates a typical shipping market freight rate development cycle over time.

An understanding of this type of cyclical freight rate pattern is critical for shipowners. But for those firms who use steel, this type of cyclical pattern is not necessarily the best basis for strategic decisions because firms using steel work in capital markets where stability and predictability of earnings are critical. For many of these shipping firms, a stable income stream, ideally portraying stable growth from an upward moving market, would be essential to attract financing and capital. Because of this desire for stable dividend patterns, achieved through longer-term commissions and contracts, there is often more predictability and more exit possibilities for firms that use steel than for firms that own steel. Shipowners are more vulnerable to the inherent market risks – but then again, these are the risks that they are paid to take.

Studies have shown that shipping rates, notably with respect to the tanker freight markets, tend to show higher volatility when

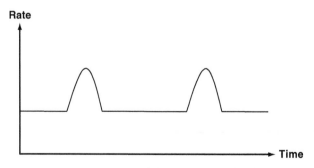

FIGURE 3.13 Typical shipping market freight rate development

markets are high (Adland and Strandenes, 2007). This is an important factor to reckon with when it comes to dealing with the parts of one's fleet portfolio that show particularly high utilization rates. There is also empirical evidence that delays, such as those created by port congestion, are relatively more important for dry bulk markets than for tanker markets – another important reality (Adland and Strandenes, 2007).

When it comes to market cycles in shipping, one should remember that shipping is a relatively mature industry, with the expectation that cyclical patterns of the past will continue into the future and be relatively "normal," such as depicted in Figure 3.14. What happens if this turns out not to be the case? For instance, what happens if the cycle does not flatten out as it approaches the top, but extends and climbs even higher? Or, alternatively, what if the bottom of the cycle does not lead to a flattening out and the market continues to decline? Figure 3.14 illustrates the potential of these developments – often deemed unlikely, according to conventional wisdom in the industry.

How might these discontinuities impact strategy? We know that, traditionally, for shipowning firms, buying and selling steel – that is, ships – is critical. Shipowners try to buy low and sell high. This asset play strategy may no longer always be valid – the market

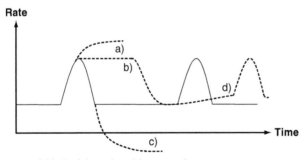

a) Market(s) continue(s) to go up!
b) Strong market(s) continue(s) to last (longer)!
c) Slump market(s) continue(s) to fall!
d) Slump market(s) continue(s) to last!

FIGURE 3.14 Abnormal shipping market freight rate developments

may simply not recover in the foreseeable future. Instead, a strategy based on having the lowest operating costs may become more important. A low breakeven point will always be an advantage, particularly in weak markets. Attention to costs and breakeven points may thus become more accentuated for shipowners if the anticipated regularities of the shipping markets fail to materialize.

Shipowners will, of course, also operate in special segments of the financial markets. Long-term ship financing will still require commitment to income streams, but uncertainties about the residual value of ships may trigger refinancing during downturn periods. Many banks may be lenient when it comes to granting payment extensions to shipowners and hesitant when it comes to triggering defaults on loans. They may even allow the shipowner simply to make interest payments without providing a down payment – all to facilitate the continuing viability of a given ship project until the next market upswing. In/out decisions may be key when it comes to working with banks and financial institutions to salvage bad loans. And, in the end, everything is based on an understanding of industry cycles and freight rate expectations by shipowners and bankers alike.

What are Marsoft's contributions? First, Marsoft attempts to provide a better understanding of the shipping markets, so that shipowners and others can make better in/out and long/short decisions. Predicting turning points in the market is particularly important for this.

Second, the banks can benefit from Marsoft's services when it comes to risk management, particularly to obtain a better estimate of a shipping client's likelihood of default. This can help banks to develop a relationship with shipping companies that may have fallen on hard times. Potential losses may be recovered, at least in part, through patience, cooperation, and problem-solving.

A well-formulated contract dealing with long-term credit facilities might benefit shipping companies, giving them the flexibility to suspend down payment installments on loans for up to a year. This will help them cope with the effects of market downturns and a (hopefully) temporary inability to service the debt.

Market forecasting does have an important role to play. My sense is that many of the shipping companies in existence today would find it very hard to survive a sustained 50 percent downturn in rates – and corresponding ship values. But this is exactly the risk the industry is facing right now – we can expect a meltdown of the markets over the next three to five years. Shipping strategists need to ask themselves what kind of bets they want to place today. Do they want to place bets on the return of the strong markets that have been creating winning strategies until mid-2008? Several rational forecasters highlighted what they perceived to be downside market developments during these years, but have been proved wrong. Perhaps they overlooked the potential upsides that we have actually enjoyed over the same period. In the end, they may have been correct.

Marsoft recently issued a new dry bulk base case. This shows, in essence, a long depressed period, perhaps as severe as the one we saw in the 1980s. This raises the question of how one can gain the acceptance of the decision-makers in the shipping industry for this type of outlook. How can this be done so that shipping firms can focus on what they perceive as exceptional short-term opportunities, while remaining prudent? The ship supply realities indicate exceptionally strong newbuilding orders. And, new cost-competitive shipbuilding capacity is being added in China, Vietnam, and elsewhere. The demand realities will be based primarily on regaining growth in China.

SHIPPING FREIGHT RATE FORECASTERS

In a commodity market, the innovators are consulting research firms, such as Marsoft, which forecasts ocean market freight trade developments for bulk and wet cargos, containers, and second-hand tonnage. Their customers are primarily shipowners, who need a better understanding of when to go in or get out, when to go long or short, etc. The banks that handle ship financing also represent an important customer segment.

Marsoft is perhaps strongest at forecasting broader scenarios in the markets, while customer relations-oriented firms are needed for day-to-day movements. Consequently, one would assume that Marsoft's forecasts would be complemented by individual data gathering by each type of specialized firm when it comes to customer relations, particularly for issues such as port congestion, delays, etc.

Shipbrokers may also provide forecasting services for shipowning firms that are concerned with timing, when it comes to new ship acquisition investments as well as for negotiating the best possible freight deals in the markets and/or with their customer relations-focused counterparts. The customer of a shipbroker would be partly the shipowner, and partly the company that would need tonnage for transportation – say, an oil company or an ore provider. The broker is in the middle and the customer relationship will be a balancing act.

Shipping markets tend to be atomistic markets, exhibiting more or less perfect competition. The price offered for the freight service determines (in large measure) who gets the deal – the lower the offer, the better the chances. There are many suppliers, with very little concentration in the shipping industry sector. Further, there are many sources of demand for shipping services – again with relatively little concentration on the demand side of the industry. All in all, these tendencies underscore an atomistic or highly fragmented pattern, with much supply and demand. Finally, the various ship types – basic oil carriers as well as bulk carriers – are usually more or less similar, i.e., interchangeable, which further adds to the commodity orientation that is used to describe shipping markets and services. Ships vary enormously in terms of size, speed, age, etc. Nevertheless, there is a strong correlation between the freight rates for various ships. For instance, a falling market for very large ships pushes freight rates down for categories of smaller ships, although usually with a lag. In addition, rates for newer ships tend to fall, along with rates for similar types of older tonnage.

The key to success for shipowners operating in the classic atomistic shipping markets is to understand better the importance of timing in their decisions, and above all, to learn to anticipate turning points in the freight rate market. Companies that provide forecasts for the freight rate markets, particularly when they focus on forecasting turning points, are in high demand. Forecasting alternative scenarios for various shipping markets is very difficult. Nevertheless, there are a number of organizations in the forecasting business: Marsoft is one of the leaders and others include Jefferies & Company, Inc., Maritime Strategies International (MSI), China Ship Economy Research Center, and Drewry's.

When creating market scenarios, Marsoft takes a multitude of factors into account, which shape both supply and demand sides. A range of scenarios are developed – the base case, high case, and low case – for each of the main bulk size categories, the main oil carrier categories, and the main container ship categories. These scenarios can serve as an effective and convenient base when developing detailed forecasts that factor in specific port delays, etc. This information is useful to both shipowners and banks in the business of financing ships on a long-term basis. Banks will also find this information useful in helping them adhere to the Basel II Accord, an international standard that banking regulators can use to inform regulations about how much capital banks need to put aside to guard against the financial and operational risks they face.

When considering market forecasts, it is useful to distinguish between the basic model, the underlying assumptions that go into the model, and the resultant forecasts. The assumptions will drive the model and determine the specific outcomes. Although Marsoft utilizes leading analysis houses worldwide, various economic experts, and available resources from a broad set of sources as the basis for its assumptions, it does not always come up with accurate forecasts. For example, it underestimated the development of the shipping markets to and from China, particularly with respect to the dry bulk markets. However, subsequent testing of Marsoft's basic model, putting in assumptions about China that were more realistic on a post facto basis, confirmed that Marsoft's model was indeed rather good. The key point is that to get accurate forecasts, it is essential to fix meaningful assumptions.

While Marsoft's model provides realistic general scenarios for freight rate developments, based on a consistent set of data inputs, its forecasts have been less reliable when it comes to predicting day-to-day fluctuations in the dry bulk market. Marsoft thinks that demand developments are responsible for short-term movements, but their analysis is only quarterly, and so misses some of the volatility inherent in monthly, weekly, or daily movements. It pays particular attention to iron ore freight developments and the detailed, exact, and exhaustive real-time congestion data from large ports, particularly those in Australia, but also in Brazil and China. In the end, it is really up to the individual shipowners or operators to add their own data intelligence to improve the forecasting scenarios.

Increased emphasis on locking in strong rates
There may be an increase in time charters relative to relying on spot markets during periods with very high rate levels. Time charter rates are not usually route-dependent, i.e., rates are not higher on some routes than on others. This may not always be the case for trip-charters, where there may be rates depending on the routes. In general, owners and operators today seem to want to secure tonnage at almost any cost, so as not to run the risk of being left out, again perhaps analogous to Shiller's (2000) irrational exuberance. The actors may feel that they must act as if there is a bubble in the market.

More financially oriented players
Many new financially oriented players have come into the industry. The financial sector has provided easy financing, with very low cost of capital for capacity expansions. Funds for new projects have been reasonable and readily available, from financial institutions as well as from new groups of individual financial investors that see the shipping sector as offering interesting investment possibilities. Newbuilding projects have particularly benefited from this. But is this resulting in too much supply? Interestingly, some traditional players in the shipping industry are exiting. But, as we have seen, factors exogenous to shipping, such as

the sub-prime real-estate financing crisis, can have rapid dampening effects on the prospect of new ship financing.

Perhaps some shipowners will end up going directly to investors rather than via traditional banking channels – not just to get access to liquidity but also to save on financing costs.

Currency fluctuations

Currency developments for dollars, Euros, the BRIC currencies (those of Brazil, Russia, India, and China), and others can be of major importance for ocean shipping, and can lead to sophisticated hedging/put-call options, in/out financial engineering-based activities, etc. Currency conditions are clearly related to newbuilding contracts but also to chartering activities. One way to diminish currency exposure is to take a ship's newbuilding financing and its charter rates in the same currency. The basic forecasting of currencies is difficult, but it is a critical part of the chief financial officer (CFO)/competent financial management function. Cost of capital can differ widely with different currency rates, depending on inflation pressure and devaluation outlooks. It can be tempting – but risky – to finance a new ship in a speculative currency.

Liquidity

Forecasting of liquidity is an important part of the overall portfolio planning for shipping firms. Good liquidity represents a buffer. The quantity of liquidity reserves becomes a function of the risk-taking propensity of a firm's management. To have sufficient liquidity to be active in the derivatives markets, particularly in the FFA market, and an understanding of the impact of liquidity on exposure to counterparty risk is still important.[7] So far, the issue of liquidity has not been a

---

[7] The forward freight agreement (FFA) offers shipowners, ship operators, charterers, and traders a means of protecting themselves against the volatility of freight rates. Broadly defined, the FFA takes a position in a futures (paper) market as a substitute for a forward cash (physical) transaction.

large constraint when it comes to the development of the FFA derivatives segment.

It should be pointed out that the banking sector's willingness and ability to provide peak liquidity through new financing to the shipping sector is not solely a function of the strength of the shipping markets. It is also a function of the banking sector's general willingness to provide new financing, which in turn will be affected by exposure to large losses in general, such as the sub-prime real-estate crisis in the US in the latter part of 2007.[8]

A large liquidity reserve also builds trust in a company. For instance, even if one seemingly unrelated financial sector runs into trouble, such as the US housing sub-prime market, effects on financing within the shipping sector can be handled.

Biases surrounding randomness and uncertainty of data

Forecasting the markets for shipping, as Marsoft tries to do, is not easy. As we can infer from the previous discussion, the wrong assumptions can clearly impact the accuracy of the forecasts. We should also bear in mind that the world truly seemed to change in 2002, with regard to shipping. The key challenge now is how to interpret these newer step-functions, without the pre-2002 stability. How do we forecast now, and how do we use those forecasts and judge their precision?

There may be no clear answers to these questions. What does seem to be clear, however, is the need to be prepared for uncertainty – i.e., through scenarios rather than single-point forecasts. There are also some genuine biases when it comes to dealing with randomness and

---

[8] A humorous account of the heightened conditions for ship financing can be found in a limerick by Ken Low of Seaspan Ship Management, which won third prize in *TradeWinds'* Limerick Competition, 2008:

> *There once was a banker, a friend*
> *To all shipowners he'd lend*
> *But when he asked for credit*
> *His boss said, "Forget it!"*
> *"With sub-prime, there's no more to spend."*

> Source: Tradewinds, *Volume 19, Number 11 (March 14, 2008).*

uncertainty, well articulated by Taleb (2004). He raises the key question of whether we may at times be taking our beliefs and the quality of our knowledge a little too seriously. Taleb claims that there is a human tendency to underestimate randomness and that we need to distinguish between charlatans (his characterization) and genuine visionaries. Success is sometimes the result of pure luck – being in the right place at the right time – which must not be mistaken for skill, superior ability, or rare insight. This type of luck cannot be replicated because it is obtained by chance.

So we may have some real problems of deduction, i.e., trying to deduce future patterns for shipping markets from the expectations we have based on the past. There is a bias toward survivorship, whereby we view the wisdom of the winners through the lenses of the survivors. When we concentrate on the relatively few winners and ignore the many losers, past events always look less random than they actually were (hindsight bias). These reservations, set out elegantly and convincingly by Taleb (2004), do not represent a reason for not employing forecasting analysts, like Marsoft. The Marsoft approach can help insightful practitioners alleviate insecurity; its data can be used to develop insights/methods for dealing with doubts about which way the shipping markets may be going, thus improving the chances of success.

Skills do count, but probably less when it comes to highly random environments, such as shipping markets, than when it comes to others (e.g., dentistry). Although one should always be as prepared as possible, of course. These are all aspects of cultivating security, so that the shipping markets can be handled with healthy skepticism. During economic booms, in particular, it is important to bear in mind that most shipping markets are fundamentally mature markets. And during prolonged down cycles, it is perhaps important to remind oneself that there will eventually be an upside. Cultivating skepticism must not be mistaken as cultivating an unwillingness to make decisions.

While Marsoft is good at explaining the past, a fundamental question to ask is what the predictive power of its approach might be, given the fundamental changes that are taking place in the industry. There are many non-traditional factors that, taken together, seem to call for a different mode of predicting future opportunities, in contrast to the more traditional approach followed by Marsoft, which is looking at a detailed base case scenario for shipping market development. In particular, the post-2002 period led to a call for a different approach to market rate forecasting. By failing to predict the strength of the recent strong markets adequately, Marsoft may, in fact, have led shipowners to make exit decisions too early, leaving money on the table.

CONCLUSION

For all types of shipping organizations, the common denominator for success remains a good understanding of the key factors that drive shipping rates, both directional and key turning points. A good understanding of the shipping markets remains critical and good forecasting is key. Factors associated with the demand side may be particularly significant. World trade movements and the strength of the world economy are important, but so is an ability to understand movements in other essential underlying factors. An opportunistic instinct and the ability to move fast when the markets are changing are also musts. Above all, the post-2002 era has led to a different outlook concerning these issues.

4 Shipping industry clusters

In this chapter I primarily discuss financially oriented maritime clusters. However, it could be argued that logistical/port clusters could also be legitimately discussed under this heading. Consequently, I shall cover this – albeit briefly – at the end of the chapter.

European national shipping industry cluster policies came about in response to the emergence of ships flying flags of convenience after World War II. A ship is said to be flying a flag of convenience if it is registered in a foreign country for purposes of reducing operating costs or avoiding government regulations. While European nations, such as the UK, Norway, the Netherlands, etc., were the dominant owners of shipping fleets, measured in terms of dead weight tonnage, at the time, the emerging low-cost flags of convenience gradually took larger shares of ownership. Here it should be kept in mind that shipping is essentially global, i.e., not country dependent, when it comes to the ships themselves.

The cluster policy came about in response to this development, and to re-establish European competitiveness. Porter (1998) defines a cluster as "geographic concentrations of interconnected companies, specialized suppliers, service providers, firms in related industries, and associated institutions that compete but also cooperate." The focus is thus on assembling relevant competences for doing shipping business in a cluster. The ships themselves can of course be run under a different flag. Other important works, with direct reference to the shipping industry's clusters, are Wijnolst, Janssen, and Sødal (2003) and Wijnolst (2006).

PRIME GLOBAL SHIPPING CLUSTERS
While it will always be difficult to reach a general agreement about what would constitute a major global shipping cluster – and it would be

hard to come up with commonly agreed measurable criteria – my sense is that many leading shipping executives might agree on the following:

- Oslo
- Singapore
- New York
- London

These places are prime shipping cluster centers, with top class services – banks, insurance, lawyers, suppliers, shipbrokers, etc., – where executives can talk shipping, network, and generate enormous cross-sharing of ideas.

The cluster concept could be considered paramount. If an average size shipping company wants to succeed, it will be critical to be part of such a network. Take such an average shipowner, with five to ten ships, and with little or no explicit competitive advantage or strategic superiority. As part of a strong shipping cluster he would have access to information, finance, competent staff, etc. Socially, too, the owner and his family would be part of the cluster. Such a company might not even survive if not located in a strong cluster.

An interesting example is John Frederiksen, who regularly used to hold social network gatherings, soliciting information from brokers, financiers, shipyards, suppliers, etc. – "eating, drinking and sleeping shipping." He expanded his mastery of networking to London and then New York. Had he been based in, say, Edinburgh or Vancouver, he might have been less likely to succeed in shipping (although as a great entrepreneur, he was bound to have succeeded in some other sector).

There are, of course, prominent shipping companies such as A.P. Moller-Maersk, Teekay, and Seaspan that are not located in a cluster. However, these are large companies, and can build their own internal professional networks, without having to draw on the open network that a cluster offers.

If the Norwegian government continues its present economic policy toward shipping, then Oslo could diminish in relative importance. A similar argument might also hold for London.

SECONDARY SHIPPING CLUSTERS

It is difficult to draw a clear distinction between what might be considered prime and secondary clusters. However, I'd like to propose the following:

- Rotterdam
- Shanghai
- Dubai

Shanghai is probably still a long way from Hong Kong in terms of representing an effective full-blown cluster. Dubai and Shanghai might be trying to follow a similar approach to Singapore – but the largely government-driven master strategy for building an effective shipping cluster strategy may be less pronounced or consistent. Some clusters are out of balance – much of the ship finance for Shanghai is done through Hong Kong, for instance.

Peter Shaerf (2008) a strong proponent for New York, cites the following reasons why New York is a powerful and effective shipping cluster:

- abundance of capital and liquidity, with over twenty leading investment banks, two large stock exchanges, and a vast private equity community;
- the home of over 250 shipping companies and an abundance of maritime professionals;
- excellent, affordable arbitration with over 100 maritime law firms.

PERHAPS LESS SUCCESSFUL SHIPPING CLUSTERS

Once again, I propose a subjective list of ports in this category:

- Tokyo
- Hamburg
- Limassol
- Vancouver

These centers may have too narrow a focus. Hamburg, for instance, is strong on ship financing and container ships but is still not a full-blown shipping cluster. Government policies can also have an adverse impact on a center's effectiveness. In Vancouver, the government put in place an impressive tax incentive package for shipping companies to attract activities from Hong Kong in the wake of the China takeover of the formerly British colony. But it let it fade over time, and eventually there were no further government initiatives. Go/stop government policy negatively impacted the development of an effective shipping cluster.

THE ORIGINS OF NATIONAL SHIPPING CLUSTERS

The first national shipping cluster to emerge, in 1996, was the Dutch maritime cluster policy, which later went on to become the European standard (Janssens, 2006). The report to establish the Dutch cluster had been published two years previously in 1994 (Peeters and Wijnolst, 1994). Before then, the focus had been on maintaining a Dutch flag fleet, manned by Dutch nationals, and promoting the development of modern, specialized vessels, all under the Dutch flag. The report, in contrast, recommended creating a competitive cost level for Dutch shipowners, and a national shipping policy that would maximize "added value for the Dutch owners" and "employment in general, not only by Dutch seafarers." The aim was to maintain and increase maritime activity levels in the Netherlands. It was established that only 30 percent of the added value of the shipping sector could be attributed to activities at sea, whereas 70 percent of the added value was created on shore, directly and indirectly. Traditional shipping policies had focused more or less solely on the sea dimension, not on the overall cluster picture.

In 1997, almost immediately after the cluster policy was introduced, the private Dutch Maritime Network was established, partly funded by the government. There was a coordinated effort between the public and private sectors in shipowning, shipbuilding, and maritime equipment to strengthen the country's maritime cluster. Political lobbying was undertaken to ensure a reasonable economic policy toward maritime cluster industries. There was a keen sense of the tradition that the Dutch shipping industry had grown from.

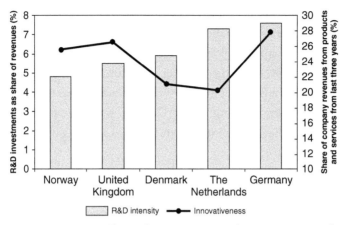

FIGURE 4.1 Share of revenues invested in R&D compared with level of innovativeness in five national maritime industries
Source: Jakobsen (2006, p. 48).

Following the Dutch maritime cluster, similar national clusters were established in relatively short order in Norway, the UK, Denmark, Germany, and elsewhere. The Dutch and the Danish clusters were particularly successful, looking at "where they have been able to achieve" in bringing relevant shipping competencies together.

One factor one might assume would be important for the success of a national shipping cluster would be its degree of innovativeness, as a consequence of the level of investment in research and development (R&D). This does not seem to be quite so straightforward, however.

From Figure 4.1, we can see that Norway invests relatively little in R&D, compared to the UK, Denmark, the Netherlands, and Germany. However, the amount of innovativeness – the ability to create new business through commercialized inventions – coming out of the Norwegian cluster may be higher than the UK and Dutch clusters, and more or less on a par with the Dutch and German clusters. There might be a stronger interrelationship among key elements in the Norwegian cluster, more eclectic cross-fertilization/cross-dissemination, among shipowners, ship design innovation firms, shipyards and ship equipment suppliers. The issue of innovativeness in clusters has a lot to do with the availability and movement

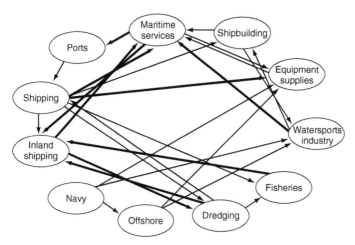

FIGURE 4.2 Personnel mobility within the Dutch maritime cluster
Source: Janssens (2006, p. 108).

of talent from one element of the cluster to others, or as Seely Brown and Hagel (2005) put it, "open" innovation.

In Figure 4.2, we can see how the movement of people in the Dutch maritime cluster takes place. Flexible human resource policies and interrelationships among entities within a cluster seem to be a critical factor in enhancing innovativeness. Regrettably, some trade union policies tend to be at odds with this.

Many of the ships controlled by Norwegian shipping do not actually fly a Norwegian flag; instead, they sail under various flags of convenience, including that of the Norwegian International Ship Registry (NIS), which provides a number of advantages when it comes to taxes, crewing, etc. Thus, a major issue has to do with the maintenance of the Norway-based headquarters for various shipping companies. A key problem area is the high level of personal taxation of owners and senior executives. Without liberalization here, it is doubtful that the Norwegian maritime cluster will continue to exist in its present dominant form. A recent reversal of favorable taxation for shipping companies, in September 2007, has also added doubt about the long-term viability of the Norwegian maritime cluster.

Clusters are almost by definition focused on specific national state entities. But shipping clusters might increasingly be viewed as

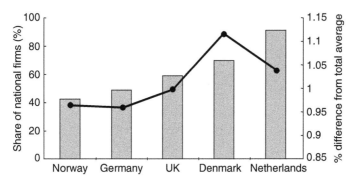

FIGURE 4.3 The relationship between preferences for keeping headquarters in the home country and satisfaction with public policy
Source: Jakobsen (2003, p. 21).

global. We know that ships can be registered in countries other than that of the cluster nation, and that shipping is one of the most international industries. Customers are found everywhere. Hence, and particularly with the emergence of technologies to enable networks, relevant competencies can be brought together from all over the world – they do not have to be physically located together. In view of this, the nation-based cluster concept may be somewhat less relevant in shipping. Still, it is important to have a local shipping milieu allowing face-to-face contact among professionals, particularly when it comes to the strategic side of shipping companies. The location of headquarters for shipping companies within clusters then becomes critical.

Figure 4.3 indicates that shipping companies headquartered in Norway have the lowest share of "want" compared with other companies that choose domestic headquarters. Shipping companies headquartered in the Netherlands score the highest want, while Germany, the UK, and Denmark fall in between. There seems to be a relationship between the public policy index and the propensity to be located in one's particular home country except, perhaps, in the Netherlands. The undisputed success of the Dutch maritime cluster policy can explain why there is nevertheless such a relatively strong loyalty toward maintaining the headquarters in the Netherlands, despite a relatively weak public policy index. The opposite can be said about Norway. The Norwegian maritime cluster policy does not seem to have been as effective, resulting in a relatively high degree of willingness to relocate. Several Norwegian-born shipowners and companies have done so, including Fredriksen, who has relocated much of his shipping to London, Bermuda, and Cyprus; Kristian Gerhard Jebsen, who runs Gearbulk from London; and Westfal-Larsen, which operates National Bulk from Singapore.

CLUSTER COMPOSITION

Let us briefly review what might be a reasonably complete activity list of what a maritime cluster might encompass – see Figure 4.4, which illustrates the European Union maritime clusters. Maritime clusters are wide-spanning, with seven main areas and thirty two sub-areas.

The concept of the shipping cluster has migrated from Europe, and become important in other parts of the world, most notably Singapore. In general, many of the European shipping clusters, as well as the Singaporean one, seem to have become very efficient. The Norwegian shipping cluster, on the other hand, seems relatively less efficient.

Category	Sub-category	Incl. (ex)
Manufacturing	4	Shipbuilding, repair
Transport	3	Shipowning
Resources	3	Fisheries, oil and gas
Service and other operations	8	Brokers, finance
Leisure and tourism	3	Cruising
Public sector	6	Education, unions
Research	4	Universities, towing tanks
7	32	

FIGURE 4.4 Maritime clusters (European Union)
Source: Andersen and Wojnols (2006, p. 8).

Looking at Singapore, we can see that the maritime industry has grown substantially in recent years. This has been spearheaded by a focused approach from the government on many levels, for example, the Singapore Maritime and Port Authorities (MPA), tax incentives, education programs offered by institutions such as Nanyang Technological University (NTU), and the establishment of foundations, such as Singapore Maritime Training Foundation (SMTF).

Another overriding reason for choosing Singapore as an Asian base is the country's political stability. Singapore is second to none in terms of offering a progressive environment for businesses, the availability of people of various types, relevant talents – as far as both quality and quantity are concerned – and proximity/connectivity with the entire region and indeed the world at large. For the maritime industry, this means a community of shipping specialists, covering the entire span of activities: a world-scale port; customers; shipbuilding and related industries; shipowners (including the container liner APL – ranked number eight worldwide); traders; maritime law firms; shipbrokers; financiers; etc. On top of this, Singapore has some of the most progressive and proactive government agencies in the world. This can create challenges to innovation-oriented firms, which tend to remain firmly located when they were initially established. Professionals may not feel much incentive to move: Carl Bro is still in Copenhagen, Skipsteknisk in Aalesund, and Marsoft in Boston and Oslo. Why does it seem to be so hard for them to relocate to Asiatic locations?

This cluster, within the physical confines of Singapore, suggests that networking is comprehensive and efficient. It yields clear economic benefits to the players in the cluster, including:

- dealing with some of the shortages of qualified labor for senior seafarer positions, as well as for specialists in shore positions;
- facilitating the transition within parts of the industry from a predominantly private to a more corporate culture;
- facilitating the transition from a more reactive, at times even secretive, corporate culture to a more proactive, open, industry culture.

FINANCIAL SUPPORT FOR SHIPBUILDING

Finally, let me discuss financial support of one aspect of the shipping industry – shipbuilding – a governmental activity that does not fit neatly into the concept of shipping clusters. Shipbuilding subsidies are now forbidden within the Organization for Economic Co-operation and Development (OECD). Still, there seem to be many national shipbuilding policies, supported by some specific national governments, which might lead to special arrangements in terms of shipbuilding price discounts, special financing, etc. This type of support is increasingly provided via favorable financing. Sadly, this can lead to an increase in protectionism and ultimately be a threat to free world trade movements. It may not be a beneficial development for the shipping industry in general.

I have already pointed out that it is difficult to carry out individually driven governmental fiscal policies. The EU, for instance, is regulated so that fiscal policies cannot be used to transfer "economic burdens" from one country to another. Interest rates, used to keep inflation under control and to stimulate growth, are more or less determined for the entire Union. Budgetary fiscal soundness is called for, to ensure balance in each country's national budget. Still, there are some opportunities for national governments to influence the conditions faced by industries and corporations. The primary one relates to taxation. Corporate tax rates differ widely from country to country and some industries are granted particular tax preferences within some countries. Further, personal tax rates, wealth taxation, inheritance taxes, etc., can differ, making some industries more attractive than others because the executives who run them are offered lower taxes in some locations. As we know, many shipowners also own their firms. The interface between personal taxation and corporate taxation thus becomes particularly important in shipping. This may be one of the reasons why so many shipping entrepreneurs live in London.

Subsidies are still prevalent in many industries. They can take the form of investment in large new projects, or so-called investment stimulants such as more favorable financing, guaranteed lower interest rates, introductory tax breaks, etc. These factors play an important role in many Asian countries.

Lastly, customs barriers still prevail in places. Some countries still use trade tariffs to attempt to boost their own economic regions at the expense of other countries, although this practice is becoming less and less accentuated.

Even though there seems to be general agreement among nations on a world order base to minimize local idiosyncrasies, there is no doubt that these still play a very important role, which is increasing in importance. This can impact business in significant ways and can be critically important for some types of corporations, affecting their potential success or failure.

MARKET CAPITALIZATION OF SHIPPING FIRMS' STOCK PER CLUSTER

The distribution of public companies' market capitalization for each shipping cluster globally is also significant, in that it indicates where the capital supporting the world's leading public shipping companies comes from. As Figure 4.5 shows, by far the most capital is generated by the US, underscoring the importance of New York as a cluster.

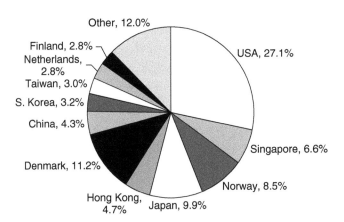

FIGURE 4.5 Global market capitalization
Source: Shaerf, AMA Capital Partners (2008, p. 6).

Denmark (Copenhagen), Japan (Tokyo), Norway (Oslo), and Singapore follow. Together, these five leading clusters account for more than 60 percent of the equity capital supporting the world's public shipping companies.

GLOBAL CLUSTERS VS. NATIONAL CLUSTERS

Clusters like those in Singapore and Copenhagen are becoming increasingly global. The Danish maritime cluster is one of the most successful. Several prominent, dynamic and successful Denmark-based shipowning firms are headquartered there, including A.P. Moller-Maersk, Clipper, Norden, Torm, and J. Lauritzen. All of these are more or less international, however, with significant operations outside Denmark.

When it comes to research-based innovations, innovators are global and could be located almost anywhere. Customers are also global, and the infrastructure is focused on the global side of the value chain. In view of this, perhaps we should take a more global point of view when it comes to developing clusters. Admittedly, countries are competing to have fleets registered in their domains. This would mean the advent of tax incentives and possibly other financial benefits, coupled with political stability. However, people availability and education could be sourced from several locations in order to keep costs low. Connectivity within the marketplace could also be sourced from any location. A national cluster policy would be inadequate, as it is important for the interface with the customers to take place at each key local point – face-to-face, not on a virtual basis. Time differences, for instance, are important. Strictly national clusters would not be well equipped to cope with this.

The Norway-based company, Jotun, is an example of a player within a global maritime cluster environment. The company is head-quartered in Sandefjord, Norway, and is one of the world's largest providers of marine paints, among other types of industrial and decorative coatings. Interestingly, the marine paints are manufactured in the Middle East, Southeast Asia, China, South America, and other markets such as Japan on a joint-venture basis. This means that Jotun's activities in Norway, as part of the Norwegian maritime cluster, represent less than 10 percent of what it is doing to serve the global maritime industry. Research, manufacturing, and marketing are carried out globally, to serve the global shipping cluster. Another example would be the global ship classification business, where DnV holds a 17 percent global market share (Jakobsen in Wijnolst, 2006, p. 42).

Innovation firms are of course important. Research leading to innovations – based on speed and attracting talent – is related to cluster thinking. Employees and personnel policies thrive within clusters. Eclecticism seems to be critical to innovation. Consider, for instance, the many innovations in ship equipment and new ship designs that have emerged in connection with the offshore supply shipping industry in Norway. This innovative reality is clearly facilitated by Norwegian maritime cluster thinking.

Clusters are inarguably important for creating an innovative atmosphere, i.e., stimulating innovation-focused companies within the maritime industry. Competencies around the general strategic management functions seem particularly key. Also, in order to attract ownership of tonnage, to build the trading/chartering-type firms within the shipping industry, or to attract operations crewing companies, and/or firms that pursue an innovation-based strategy, it is important to be cost competitive. As such, a country will have no choice but to be consistent when it comes to financial policy vis-à-vis the shipowning industry and other key shipping firms. The parameters and competitive conditions are indeed global.

PORT/LOGISTICS CLUSTERS

The largest port in the world is Rotterdam, followed by Shanghai, Singapore, Hong Kong, Antwerp, and Hamburg. These might be considered as port/logistics clusters with not only berths and loading/unloading facilities, but also warehouses, roads, trans-shipment services, repair shops, ship chandlers, hotels, restaurants, etc. We can indeed label these large, international part facilities as clusters too.

CONCLUSION

Clusters can be either national or global. We have seen several examples of attempting to establish national clusters to strengthen the competitiveness of the maritime sector. This has often taken place with considerable government support – particularly in terms of tax relief. Tax advantages are key for national shipping clusters. The challenge for the national public sector is to develop additional advantages, beyond tax-related ones. The Netherlands and Denmark seem to have been particularly successful in Europe, as Singapore equally has been in Asia. Some actors or firms would, however, be more meaningfully classified as part of global clusters, such as the marine paints cluster with Jotun, or the ship classification cluster with DnV. Many shipping firms would fall increasingly into this category too – although the location of such firms' corporate headquarters might preferably be in strong national shipping clusters.

Part II Strategic archetypes in shipping

5   Specialized strategies   *page* 79
6   Owning steel   112
7   Using steel   142
8   Operating steel   170
9   Innovating around steel   175

5   Specialized strategies

Traditionally, ship ownership has been at the center of what a shipping organization stands for. The very essence of successful shipping companies has often been linked with the number of ships under management and the amount of tonnage that the company owns. But there is now a marked trend away from the focus on owning steel. Shipping is no longer a traditional industry with set ways of operating. It has become a new and, for many, an even more exciting reality, offering many new opportunities.

Because of the influx of new capital, the industry is no longer characterized as it used to be by often relatively small-scale family firms. Publicly traded companies and professional managers have been increasingly replacing the privately held shipping companies and shipowners of the past. And they need to be relatively large scale to compete in the global economy. With this new corporate culture, and public capital, comes a focus on the integrity, timeliness, and accuracy of financial reporting. The traditional shipowner's focus on control is becoming less pronounced and, in general, the results seem to have been positive. Seaspan, for instance, emphasizes its strong corporate governance with an independent board of directors. It further estimates that its cost of capital for newbuilding is around 15 percent less as a professionally run public company than it was before 2005, when it was privately held. For Seaspan, this has become a critical success factor.

Overall, it is probably fair to say that competition in the shipping industry is extreme. It has always been very competitive – a true approximation of a worldwide "perfect" competitive market situation. It is also global (Bhagwati, 2004; Wolf, 2004) and there is strong competitive transparency and high connectivity, in the sense that ships can be used in most trades and by most shippers in a largely interchangeable way.

Further, as we discussed in earlier chapters, the industry is highly capital intensive and cyclical, and opinions differ about the predictability of cycles and the reliance that can be placed on forecasting.

CONSOLIDATION

As equity markets put more pressure on publicly owned shipping companies to improve their performance, the standard response has been to consolidate, especially in segments such as container liner shipping. Why? Shipping companies wanted global coverage to maximize their buying power. With size, they gained more flexibility, which meant that they could move their assets (ships) around to take advantage of fluctuations in supply and demand. Also, the sheer size of these major global players has been enough to deter would-be competitors from entering the market. But more importantly, they have been looking for financial results to meet shareholders' expectations – and they have, until recently, been able to come up with alternative financing based on large-scale fleets.

However, alternative financing based on large-scale fleets has been less easy to obtain until recently. Many ship-finance banks are no longer willing to sign up for large credit facilities, then attempt to syndicate these obligations as a separate second step. Some banks have found themselves stuck with obligations that they might have wanted to sell to other banks, but have been unable to do so because of the general credit crunch.

This move toward consolidation, and the rising importance of risk and revenue management, has produced a group of more competitive players – new talent from outside the industry – to fill more top management positions. There are fewer and fewer traditional shipping specialists left. All of this has resulted in a group of more competitive corporate players in the shipping industry.

Times are changing and so is shipping.

BEYOND CONSOLIDATION: SPECIALIZATION

So what options remain for shipping companies? Are there any truly new strategic innovations for success, beyond focusing on scale, to

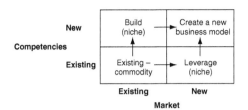

FIGURE 5.1 Conceptual model for shipping strategies
Source: Lorange (2005, p. 23) and Chakravarthy and Lorange (2007, p. 45).

minimize costs? In my opinion, progressive shipping companies are adopting a number of new strategies.

In a recent book (Lorange, 2005), I proposed a conceptual scheme for shipping business strategies, which, although not discussed extensively here, is nevertheless fundamental to developing shipping business strategies within any of the four business archetypes I have identified. Figure 5.1 is a brief recap of this basic business model.

We thus might take as a starting point the fact that most shipping business activities tend to be more or less commodity-based, with atomistic competition (multiple actors).

There are two fundamental options for creating strategies that are less commodity-based, or more niche-oriented.

1 To move into new markets, using one's existing know-how. There are many examples of this. Most shipping is already based on global markets, requiring a global scope, so this strategic move may not create a niche. For some, however, this can be a realistic option. The specialized dredging firm, van Oord, for instance, transplanted its approach to dredging harbors in the Netherlands to dredging and building artificial islands in Dubai and elsewhere.

2 To develop new technical or commercial technology. The development of pollution-friendly, self-unloading bulk carriers, say, for a cement or coal truck, would be an example of this.

To develop new business models involving a combination of these two options is rare. However, I.M. Skaugen provides an example. Skaugen, through its 50/50 joint venture with Teekay, Skaugen PetroTrans, has a capability to undertake freight barging on major rivers. Most of Skaugen

PetroTrans' operations are in the US. Skaugen also has a capability to move liquefied propane gas (LPG) and other chemicals, based on its know-how with relatively small gas/chemical carriers, Nordpool. Much of this trade has taken Skaugen to East Asia. Further commercial contracts have been nurtured in China – investing in gas tank manu-facturing, shipbuilding, and pleasure boat building. By combining this new technology in new markets Skaugen has been able to establish a strong shipping business on major Chinese inland waterways.

SPECIALIZATION TRENDS: DECOMPOSITION

For shipping companies that aspire to be the global winners, special-ization may be the answer – and not just specialization, but rather, a decomposition of the value chain. In the past, the typical shipowning company owned various types of ship and undertook inherently associated functions, such as buying and selling ships, financing operations, chartering (often through in-house chartering and finance departments), and promoting innovations in ship design (often via their in-house technical departments). Crewing was also done in-house. When it came to buying and selling ships, shipowners were tough negotiators with a focus on buying low and selling high. However, as I argue throughout this book, this type of integrated shipping company is likely to become less and less prevalent in the future.

Today, with national borders opening up, deregulation in the industry, lower transaction costs, and the growing importance of cap-ital markets, more and more shipping companies are identifying one aspect of the value chain to focus on – e.g., owning ships, using ships, operating ships, or innovating around ships. Some companies are more heavily involved in innovative activities, such as ship design, finance and/or trading innovations. Other specialist firms might focus on pursuing the lowest possible costs, attempting to achieve scale advan-tages in owning steel. Still others might develop customer scope via trading, focusing on brands, service, etc. A fourth option is to focus on operating innovations through the best possible pool of employee talent, the effective running of ships, or attempting to achieve the lowest crewing and running costs. This emphasis on managing only one aspect of the entire value chain has resulted in more outsourcing of the other aspects of the chain's activities, including, at times, ship-owning itself. By specializing, shipping firms define their own core activities and, by extension, those commodity-based activities that can be outsourced.

Historically, many shipping companies have specialized, but without this aim of decomposing the value chain to determine which core activities they should choose to focus on. In the past, shipping companies might have specialized around ship types. Leif Höegh & Co., for example, had separate organizational entities specializing in the liner business (West Africa Service, sold in 1990); bulk carriers for wood products; ore-bulk-oil carriers (OBOs) and tankers (subsequently sold to Teekay); forest product carriers (Gorton); reefers (Cool Carriers); car-carriers (Höegh-Ugland, HUAL); and liquefied natural gas (LNG) ships. Its portfolio has since been significantly sharpened to involve only car-carriers (Ugland was bought out) and LNG carriers. In 2006, the company was restructured into two separate entities – Höegh Autoliners and Höegh LNG – with a common holding company (Leif Höegh & Co. Limited). The ship management expertise is maintained in Höegh Fleet Services. The focus remains on shipping. A.P. Moller-Maersk merged its car-carrier fleet with Höegh Autoliners in 2007 and presently holds a 30 percent ownership share in HUAL.

Bot *et al.* (2001) argue for additional business specialization, which they call "winning through slivers," "... a kind of horizontal consolidation that is, at the same time, both narrower and more wide-ranging than anything that has been tried thus far." Essentially, sliverization is based on companies finding one sliver of the business that they are best at and then broadening out, through outsourcing, across other sectors beyond the sliver. For instance, the large tanker shipping company, Frontline, used to own and trade tankers. The ships were spun off to Ship Finance International Limited and Frontline took them back on long-term charters. Since then, Frontline has specialized in chartering and trading, and Ship Finance International on shipowning. A similar refocusing has taken place at Teekay. Seaspan is an example of a company that focuses only on shipowning. This kind of specialization is greater than what typically occurs in local, regional, or even national economies. Companies that pursue this type of strategy deliver a specialized product or service that is economically viable at a global level.

As national borders continue to blur, there is a clear trend toward dispersing the components of the shipping value chain to specialized firms. This has been made possible by enablers like information technology, which have produced lower transaction costs for the specialized firm.

Industries also often seem to be increasingly splitting the ownership of major capital-intensive assets from the more multifaceted operation of assets. Hotel chains, restaurants, and airlines are obvious examples of this. We are also seeing splits leading to new types of organizational focus in other fields. Hagel and Singer (1999) report on similar developments within the newspaper, credit card, and pharmaceutical businesses. More recent examples include IBM and Volvo. IBM has transformed itself from predominantly a manufacturer of computer equipment to a much more service-driven organization. Its PC manufacturing has been taken over by Lenovo of China and Hong Kong. Volvo developed its new S70 cabriolet with Pininfarina, which subsequently took a 60 percent interest in Volvo's car manufacturing plant in Uddevalla, Sweden. Volvo, however, continues to handle the marketing of the S70.

DECOMPOSITION AND NATIONAL MARITIME CLUSTERS

How does the concept of national maritime clusters fit with the refocusing of the shipping industry into specialized entities? The government tax breaks that several European nations have provided, particularly Denmark, seem to have a direct impact on shipowning companies. A reasonable fiscal national policy is important for attracting shipowning companies to sail under a country's flag. The location of shipowning activities is a global undertaking, however, where cost matters highly. Thus, tonnage will perhaps be controlled by cluster nations in the future, while the ships themselves run under flags of convenience. Seaspan, for instance, is headquartered in Hong Kong; its management resides to a large degree in Vancouver, Canada; but its ships are registered in the Marshall Islands. The CEO comes from Shanghai – but is now a Canadian citizen. On top of this, its stock is listed on the New York Stock Exchange, a major source of its equity – all in all a truly transnational, even global, picture.

Although one can expect that countries providing the best financial services will become strong candidates for shipowning, it is not clear that strong clusters will necessarily develop simply because of such strong financial policy/tax lenience focused on owning ships. More is required. Singapore is a good example, catering to a strong cluster that promotes the maritime industry as a whole. This is the result of a highly focused approach from government, as well as from many private stakeholders.

EMERGING TYPES OF SPECIALIST FIRMS

How can we understand the emergence of specialist firms? Hagel and Singer (1999) describe four types of specialist firms, each focusing on a different aspect of the value chain – customer relations, product innovation, and infrastructure. Figure 5.2 illustrates the critical success

Archetypes of specialist firms / Strategic focus	Infrastructure / Owning steel	Customer relations / Using steel	Operations / Operating steel	Product innovation / Innovating around steel
Economics	Scale	Scope	Costs	Speed
Culture	Costs	Customer	Team – we, we, we	Employees (individuals) – me, me, me
Competition	Scale	Scope	Professionalism	Talent

FIGURE 5.2 Four archetypes of specialist firms
Source: Adapted from Hagel and Singer (1999, p. 135).

factors for each specialization in terms of economics, culture, and competition. I have added a fourth specialization – operations – which is particularly significant in shipping. The critical success factors for each of the four archetypes are unique.

We can deduce from Figure 5.2 that what Hagel and Singer (1999) call customer relations firms would focus heavily on scope. Although they have clear links to one or more of the other archetypes, their competitive driver is customer focus. Prototypes of this in shipping are ship operators, trading firms, shipbrokers, etc. But container liners also fall into this category. Here, as we know, the global network required – serving customers at many locations, often worldwide – is capital intensive. In contrast, asset intensive infrastructure firms focus on scale and strive for the lowest possible costs; for them, size/scale advantages are core drivers in the competitive battle. Shipowning firms are prototypes of this archetype. Hagel and Singer talk about product innovation companies, which focus on speed and attempt to attract the best employees. Having the best talent is the competitive driver for ship engineering design firms, ship research, market forecasting firms, etc. My fourth (additional) archetype is operations firms. These focus on operating ships in a cost-effective way with respect to crewing, maintenance, etc. Cost-focused professional teams are central here.

Hagel and Singer set out general trends but, as we have observed, we are now seeing these trends in the shipping industry. Some firms are focusing relatively more on infrastructure, such as owning ships, with a heavy focus on size, scale, and low costs. For them, in/out and long/short decisions are key. Other firms might be relatively more focused on customer relations to develop strong bonds with their customers via scope, brand name, operations, service, etc. A third category of players may focus more on product innovation, where speed of innovation may be particularly critical. In the shipping industry, this could include specialized consulting firms, market forecasting, and research firms, etc. A fourth type of shipping firm might focus on cost-effective ship operations, including low-cost crewing, maintenance, etc. Figure 5.3 gives an overview of the different types of

Archetypes of specialist firms / Strategic focus	Infrastructure / Owning steel	Customer relations / Using steel	Operations / Operating steel	Product innovation / Innovating around steel
Commodity shipping	Bulk owners, tanker owners, container owners, e.g., • Seaspan • Suisse Atlantique • Danaos	• Freight tracking FFAs; share trading; chartering • Liners, e.g., Maersk Line	Low-cost crewing-based operators • V. Group • Thome • Wallem • OSM	Market forecasters Marsoft • Clarkssons Research • Ship designers • Anti-pollution
Specialized (niche) shipping	Special ships • Heerema • van Oord	Tailored to specific customers • Heerema construction • Maersk contractors	Specialized operators	Technical consultants • Carl Bro • Skipsteknisk • Heerema Engineering
Critical success factors	• Low costs • In/out • Long/short	• Relevant service to customer	• Cost efficient • Quality	• Commercially valid/necessary

FIGURE 5.3 The specialist movement within the shipping industry

shipping specific specialist firms. The power shift toward more specialized shipping seems to have been at the expense of the more fully vertically integrated generalist shipping corporations. A drive toward benchmarking – comparing oneself with the best firm in class globally – as well as added requirements for transparency contribute to this development in specialization.

Note that container liner companies fall into the customer relations category. As this specialist movement gains momentum, many shipping companies are taking a more aggressive approach to mobilizing their resources by splitting up their formerly integrated businesses into owning steel, using steel, operating steel, and/or innovating around steel. Let us now discuss these in more detail.

OWNING STEEL VS. USING STEEL

Owning steel (owning ships) entails owning very similar assets – a ship is a ship. For a shipowner, it might pay to aim at standardization of its fleet. General Maritime, for instance, primarily owns Aframax and Suezmax tankers, enjoying the benefits of relatively similar designs, with common spare parts for engines, and other auxiliaries, more standardized operations and maintenance, etc. Seaspan follows a similar policy, aiming for scale benefits. It owns twenty three identical 4,250 TEU container ships.

In contrast, for customer relations firms that use steel, such as trading firms or shipbrokers, the focus is on scope or closeness to the customer. This can take many forms. One is the classical shipbroker who attempts to build a bridge between diverse stakeholders, such as companies that need freight services and shipowners (for freight chartering); between shipyards and shipowners (for new ship construction); or between several shipowners (for purchase and sale of ships). A second is traders in FFA markets, focusing on getting stakeholders together to commit to future freight paper trade. A third is container shipping lines, focusing on freighting goods for several shippers via scheduled services. With the emergence of more and more global customers, one would expect these activities to be located primarily where the customers are. Brokers tend to be local and liner organizations are built up around networks of local offices.

Seely Brown and Hagel (2005) indicate that owning steel could be analogous to what they call "push systems." These are characterized by a top-down, centralized, often rigid managerial approach for meeting previously specified tasks, and applying a corresponding longer-term managerial behavior. We can often see this when it comes to planning for ship acquisitions. Operating steel would fall into this category – running ships is a matter of top-down discipline. In contrast, for using steel Seely Brown and Hagel (2005) talk about "pull systems," which are characterized by a more bottom-up, often modular design. In shipping, this is seen with various types of specialist groups, such as ship operators, brokers, traders, etc. These connect a diverse array of participants not only in shipping, but also in financial sources and other operators. Product innovators fall into this category – bottom-up driven credibility. Seely Brown and Hagel (2005) indicate that pull systems create totally different, more bottom-up oriented, corporate business model realities, compared to the classic top-down push systems of shipowning. The differences between the four archetypes are summarized in Figure 5.4 – two are bottom-up oriented and the others top-down oriented.

As many shipping companies have traditionally been linked to owning steel, a certain sentimentality often surrounds shipowning. However, since industry forces are calling for shipping companies to become more focused and more specialized, how do they overcome the emotional elements of shipowning? In my opinion, there are at least six key reasons why the classic integrated shipping company should now be revised. An understanding of these forces might reduce emotional dysfunction.

1 **Different time horizons**. The time horizons for owning and using steel are different. Owning steel usually demands a long-term focus – a shipowner will need to stay in the business for at least one business cycle. A lot of liquidity is required to be able to stay through a full business cycle, making the risk profile relatively high. Given the fact that you need to stay in for the entire cycle, the entire cycle must be considered. Some owners may attempt to get in and out so that they can benefit from peaks in the cycle. This implies a shorter time horizon, and requires less liquidity. This does not mean that shipowners will not play on the short-term market. Clearly, if the market is in a slump, they may want to keep ships open or enter into short-term charters until things improve. However, shipowning generally takes a longer-term, full-market-cycle point of view.

   In contrast, using steel demands a shorter-term focus, with almost constant adjustments based on long- and short-term aspects of the business cycle. One must enter and exit much faster. It is also important to be able to eliminate the losses associated with certain positions that are not working – stop–loss management is key – and play on a narrower percent of the cycle, whether it is an upturn or a downturn. This trading approach requires less liquidity than shipowning – or even ship

Characteristic/ key factors	Shipowning owning steel/push systems	Trading/brokerage using steel/pull systems	Operating operating steel/pull systems	Product innovator innovating around steel/ pull systems
Demand side	Demand can often be somewhat anticipated by understanding the forecasted shipping markets	Demand is highly uncertain	Demand is very predictable – based on ships available	Demand is uncertain – where are innovations needed?
Locus of process	Top-down processes • Centralized control • Specific procedures, manuals • Tightly coupled functions, to become a project	Bottom-up processes • Decentralized control • Open-ended procedures, manuals • Loosely coupled functions to become a project	Top-down processes • Centralized controls • Clear benchmark standards	Bottom-up processes • Random opportunities • Breakthroughs
Resource focus	Physical and financial resource centric	People centric	Very cost conscious people	Key creative people
Participants	Participation restricted (few participants); "the shipowners"	Participation open (many, diverse participants)	Participation restricted	Participation open
Efficiency or not?	Focus more on efficiency	Focus more on novel approaches, serving the customer	Efficiency	Creativity
Options	Limited number of major options, i.e., choice of ship types	Novel approaches to value creation all the time	Operations of key classes of ship types	Novel, creative
Culture	National	Global	National	Global

FIGURE 5.4 Owning steel, using steel, operating steel, innovating around steel
Source: Adapted from Seely Brown and Hagel (2005, p. 88). Columns three and four have been added.

operations – and the risk profile is lower. A similar argument can be made for specialist firms engaged in innovations.

For container liner companies, closeness to the customer, flexibility, and rapid adaptability are key. Admittedly, container liners are capital intensive too, but need heavy investment in the customer interface – i.e., land transportation, computer-based tracking services, storage, and marketing – rather than capital intensive ship investment.

2 **Different key dilemmas**. Steel owning implies the efficient running of ships, as well as asset-play timing, i.e., attempts to buy low and sell high. An in/out long/short focus is important. The unit of transaction is a ship. Similarly, operating ships implies a focus on efficiency and a scale-driven approach. In contrast, the use of steel implies financial understanding, chartering, marketing, trading with freight derivatives, and negotiating contracts in a more flexible way – not necessarily based on a ship as the unit of transaction. Liner operations, too, are based on working with the customer. The customer-based network is key here, rather than the ownership of ships per se. Accordingly, the number of liners outsourcing ownership rose from 23 percent to 52 percent over the ten-year period 1997–2007 (Clarkson's Research, January 2008).

3 **Lower transaction costs**. In the past, many aspects of the different types of shipping activities were integrated in order to be able to offer a package to the customer and to develop a sense of corporate power by having a shipping firm that covered all bases. Nowadays, however, this no longer has to be so. The various customers can now access specialists directly, and there are few transaction costs between the various specialist entities. There may be little or no long-term competitive benefit in exclusively controlling parts of the business that might have been integrated into a larger firm in the past. Consider A.P. Moller-Maersk's ownership of the Lindø shipyard. Admittedly, this yard is the source of ship innovations, which can give A.P. Moller-Maersk a temporary advantage. For instance, it is believed that the design and delivery of the world's largest container ships, the 15,000-plus TEU

Emma Maersk class, have given the company at least a one-year competitive advantage in which it can operate exclusively with this unique tonnage. Still, it is not a competitive necessity to own a shipyard. Interestingly, the Lindø shipyard is now building a series of bulk carriers for Greek owners, while the major shareholder of A. P. Moller-Maersk, Danish magnate Mærsk Mc-Kinney Møller, has ordered two bulk carriers at a Korean shipyard.

Or consider the Greek-based container-owning shipping company, Danaos. This firm also owns one of the world's largest IT services businesses, which provides information technology (IT) solutions for shipping firms. The IT business is free to find clients anywhere, and is not a competitive necessity for the container shipowning business.

Clipper, the Danish–Bahamas diversified shipping firm, has also undertaken a similar type of diversification, owning Glomaris – a leading software firm focusing on financial reporting, with many shipping firms as clients.

It would seem paramount for an innovation-based specialist firm like Marsoft – a world leading forecaster of tanker, dry bulk, and container ship freight rates – to be independent from shipowning as well as from trading, chartering, and operating. Independence is the only way Marsoft and other forecasters will be perceived as providing truly unbiased analyses and advice. For this reason, it is rare to find ship-brokering firms going into shipowning. These firms have incentives to avoid conflicts of interest with their shipowning clients.

Likewise, ship operating firms must be seen to provide similar types of crewing and maintenance services for all of their clients. If a ship operating firm owned ships, this would no longer be the case. If it were active in using steel through trading or chartering activities, the same lack of true independence and equality vis-à-vis all clients would be jeopardized.

4 **Financing**. The financing function takes on different forms with specialization. For shipowning, the emphasis is on securing the lowest cost of capital. Cheap financing makes ships less expensive, and so more competitive. Obtaining the cheapest possible financing is only possible

if one or a series of ships are financed on the basis of long-term charters. In contrast, for the trading or chartering – use of steel – firm, the focus will be on securing reasonable financing – often in the equity market – based on a relatively steady, ideally growing, cash flow from this type of operation. Securing public funds can be accomplished more easily if based on the normally more steady cash flow pattern that can be achieved for this type of specialist firm, which contrasts with the less predictable cash-flow patterns associated with classic shipowning firms.

There are, of course, variations. Seaspan, for instance, a major owner of modern container ships, has all its ships on long-term charters to solid liner operators, and in a sense leverages itself on the strong reputation and balance sheets of its charterers, and its ability to produce relatively stable cash flow expectations, a condition for Seaspan's predictable and generous dividend policy and frequent equity offerings in the open investor market. However, this means Seaspan foregoes the chance to make more opportunistic use of some of its ships to play the market, with potentially large financial gains. Reaching such a stage would imply an even larger size for Seaspan – say 100 ships, as opposed to today's 65, and a lower pay-out ratio of its profit dividends, say from today's 95 percent to 70–5 percent.

Financing needs are less of an issue for innovation-based specialist and operating-specialist firms than they are for the former two specialist archetypes. Financing requirements are associated with having enough working capital to cope with payroll and accounts receivables/payables. Again, the specialist focus will also help to secure inexpensive financing.

5 **Management focus**. Perhaps the biggest driver for specialization is the focus it puts on management. Managing too many unrelated activities at world-class standards can be difficult, if not impossible. Trying to do too many tasks well will exceed the cognitive limits of most people; different aspects of the value chain require different competencies, relationships, etc. By focusing on fewer activities, the chances of excellence increase, as does competitive advantage and the firm's chances of success.

A winning shipping company today must be world class. This implies doing one type of shipping business absolutely superbly, through specialization. A minimalist approach is called for. Bureaucracy, slowness, unnecessary hierarchy, etc., must be minimized.

6 **Culture: global vs. national**. An in-depth discussion of key aspects of achieving an international culture is outside the scope of this book. However, a global culture is critical for trading-related shipping activities, including container lines. Turf issues and organizational silos lodged in various regional offices can easily create competitive disadvantages. For innovation-related shipping activities, the focus is similarly global. Technological and commercial innovations will almost always be global in scope.

Shipowning and ship operations, on the other hand, are based much more on national culture. The headquarters culture in shipowning is dominant. The same can be said of ship operations, when processes and systems reflect the parent country.

In other words, the various elements of the shipping business require different skills or competencies with their own critical success factors. From a cognitive point of view, it is becoming increasingly difficult – perhaps almost impossible – to continue to link the various sides in a single organization. Specialization means consistently doing well in all functions – focus, speed, minimalism – all key to success in today's shipping world.

Owners and users: a symbiotic relationship

Pure shipowning asset players often seem to have a symbiotic relationship with a complementary set of companies that use and operate steel in the relatively short-term world of commercial chartering and trading. Short-term players benefit by shifting capital intensity to shipowners and taking advantage of chartering margins and trading opportunities. An example, already referred to, is Frontline, a publicly traded company controlled by John Fredriksen that trades and charters in very large crude carriers (VLCCs) from Ship Finance International Limited, another publicly traded Fredriksen-controlled company, which focuses solely on owning ships. The latter has developed a leasing model for the ships it owns.

During difficult years in the shipping industry, such as the 1980s, there is generally not a lot of money to be made from owning steel. Shipowners might not even break even, particularly when depreciation charges are applied to each shipping project. In the last four to five years, however, the strong shipping markets and the exceptional appreciation of second-hand ship values has made shipowning very lucrative. In the longer run, however, one would expect owning steel to become neither more nor less attractive than using steel. The two shipping activities will always be complementary.

Do you need ships at all?
A good margin, based on a low investment, is, of course, a great business. But, where do the margins come from? Do you need ships at all to take advantage of particular opportunities? The freight derivatives market can play an interesting role here. It eliminates the need to have a presence in the physical shipowning market. Instead, gains are realized from trading. Thus, the market, in effect, expands, and actors can have management control without ownership.

In other words, you can either be a great commercial manager and earn money by chartering ships and trading against Contracts of Affreightment (CoA) or the spot market – or you can essentially do the same thing by investing in a long-term charter derivative on the one side and a spot market derivative on the other. By trading in the derivatives market, you avoid many of the practical issues associated with owning ships, such as demurrage, port delays, and so on.

This arbitrage opportunity also lends force to the point that the business skills involved in owning steel are very different from those involved in using steel. The using steel business segment is run by traders, while the owning steel segment is run by managers.

Reality is often somewhere in the middle

While I argue for a clear delineation between specialist archetypes, such as owning steel and using steel, I do realize that in reality both types of activity can take place within the same corporate entity. Nevertheless, when owning steel and using steel are found within the same firm, each archetype should have a clear and separate focus – i.e., a longer-term focus on owning versus a shorter-term focus on market trading. This dichotomy, however, should not be taken too far. While separating the two sides is vital, allowing them to live side by side, within the same corporate entity, can make a lot of sense. Consider J. Lauritzen. While this firm owns many bulk carriers, they are all being traded in the markets. A using steel paradigm dominates for both its bulk carrier and its product tanker businesses. The owning steel dimension is subordinate to the using steel dimension. In contrast, the opposite is true for J. Lauritzen's fleet of small gas carriers. Here, the focus is on long-term ownership, based on long-term charters and industrial relationships. Owning steel drives this part of the business. The result is that Lauritzen's portfolio strategy has now become complicated, with large business entities in both the owning steel as well the using steel business segments.

FREDRIKSEN'S FRONTLINE AND SHIP FINANCE INTERNATIONAL LIMITED

Let us consider an example of how a shipping group might be split into two archetypes. Frontline and Ship Finance International Limited are both controlled by John Fredriksen, reputedly the world's leading shipowner. Frontline concentrates on running ships, chartering, etc., while Ship Finance owns the ships. Both companies are listed on the New York Stock Exchange. Frontline was taken over by Fredriksen in 1996, and Ship Finance was established in December 2003. Both companies are separately quoted, but the latter started out as a subsidiary of Frontline. Ship Finance raised US$580 million through a bond loan in the US market, at a fixed interest rate of 8.5 percent. This allowed Ship Finance to take over most of Frontline's debt of US$1 billion, which was collateralized in its fleet, and to buy all forty seven of Frontline's VLCC tankers. Frontline then chartered the tankers back at a rate of US$25,575 per day, on long-term charters for the life of each ship. It was further stipulated that if Frontline were able to obtain a higher rate than the charter arrangement with Ship Finance in the market later on, Ship Finance would receive 25 percent of the profit.

Frontline was initially the exclusive customer of Ship Finance, and the board of directors of the two companies is largely the same. Thus, Ship Finance – with initially only one customer, Frontline, although today it also has other customers – does not have the same diverse customer base or independence from its customers as, say, Seaspan, which has several major container liner operators as customers (Hause and Stavrum, 2005).

Investing in ship assets or shipping company stocks?
An interesting question is whether an individual or a shipping company might simply invest in shipping company stock rather than in ships themselves. In order to gain positive benefits from the fluctuations in the shipping markets, one might purchase shares when the shipping market is down and sell them when the market is high. Again, there is a trend away from actually owning ships to owning stocks in shipping firms. One example is Awilco, owned by the A. Wilhelmsen family of Oslo, Norway. Awilco used to be a traditional shipping company owning primarily tankers, but also bulk carriers. It recently sold its offshore supply business to China Oilfield Services Ltd (COSL) for US$2.5 billion (Ng, 2008), with a total of eleven rigs in its portfolio (delivered and on order), both jackups and semi-submersibles.

In addition, Awilco follows a more fundamental mode of investments in stock – listed companies – most, however, within the shipping and offshore segments.[9] For this, it utilizes its knowledge about the underlying shipping markets and decides where it can get the best return, i.e., owning steel or owning shares. Awilco has invested in several companies exposed to the container and dry bulk markets. Its experience has been that it can take positions in these companies before the majority of the institutional investors discover that the underlying markets are performing in a positive or negative way. They reckon that there are relatively few investors worldwide with this in-depth knowledge of the shipping and offshore businesses. Further, the major investment banking houses may not have dedicated as much analytical power to following the shipping sector as they have to other industry sectors.

Each prospective publicly traded shipping company needs to be carefully analyzed, taking into consideration the unsystematic risk associated with the stock – the Sharp coefficient. Awilco feels that owning a portfolio of shipping stocks is an attractive business platform for the company and a way to obtain information about a broad array of shipping companies through discussions with investment officers.

As a result of the financial crisis in the latter part of 2008, shipping company stock prices have fallen dramatically. The bulk carrier companies have experienced the most severe drops. Even for companies such as Seaspan, which is exclusively in the business of owning modern container ships, all on long-term charters, the drop in stock prices has been significant – from a level of over US$30 per share as late as August 2008, to less than US$8.50 per share on November 15, 2008.

In addition to owning and using steel, J. Lauritzen owns shares in shipping companies. Some of these shares represent

---

[9] Awilco has interests in several other business segments, including a 20 percent share of Royal Caribbean Cruise Lines (RCCL), Miami, which now has thirty five large cruise ships, and ownership of hotels and supermarket plazas, primarily in the Baltic countries and Moscow. In addition, the company is very cash rich, after the sale of its offshore platform business. These issues are not discussed here, although they are central to Awilco's portfolio strategy.

investments that are attractive purely from a market-based point of view. The decisions to make these types of investments rest with the executives who run the bulk carrier or the product tanker businesses. Indeed, this may be seen as an extension of the using steel trading focus. J. Lauritzen is also accumulating shares in companies that may become takeover candidates later. The decisions to make these types of investments are made at the top of the firm, by the chief executive officer (CEO) and chief financial officer (CFO).

This evolution toward more paper trading in the shipping industry has been accentuated by the emergence of derivatives and futures trading and the materialization of the International Maritime Exchange (IMAREX). Clearly, it is easier to enter and exit the stock market and/or the futures trading market than to purchase and sell ships. What's more, deals can be smaller. Rather than investing in an entire ship, one can invest in many shipping companies, and/or in ship cargos, which spreads the risk further.

As shipping firms become more focused or specialized, shipping stocks that represent particular niches are becoming more readily available. These allow the investor to diversify risk on their own, rather than investing in traditional shipping company stocks, where the shipping company may already have made attempts at risk diversification.

It is interesting to note, as an aside to investment in shipping stocks, that many shipping firms are family controlled, meaning that they are usually traded lightly and have little liquidity. Thus, they do not necessarily yield maximum value in the stock price.

There also seems to be a potential relationship between paper-based forward trading through forward freight agreements (FFAs) and shipping stock movements. By closely observing a firm's exposure to FFAs, and relating this exposure to the forward market for a particular type of FFA, one might anticipate that the actual stock price for this individual shipping stock might move up or down. Some specialized traders/brokers are focusing on this opportunity for arbitrage – reminiscent of sector asset management.

Investing in shipping funds

A variation on individual investments in shipping company stocks would be establishing specific funds for investing in shipping, say, with asset play in mind. Marsoft, for instance, took the initiative to invest in the so-called Diogenes Fund in 1995, with Lehman Brothers as the key financial underwriter, and Harvard Investments Trust as the major investor. The aim of the self-liquidating US$75 million was to make the most of the investors' desire to make money in a promising shipping market. It targeted tankers as investment vehicles, and successful asset plays – executed between 1995 and 1998 – led to a high degree of success for the fund. Marsoft withdrew in 1998 and Lehman Brothers took over, at which point most of the fund was liquidated. To iterate one of the mantras of this book, in order to achieve the asset play objective successfully, timing decisions for both entering and exiting are critical. The timing was excellent for the investors in Diogenes – both in terms of entering and exiting. A market outlook, with particular focus on the market's turning points, can be particularly useful here.

OPERATING STEEL

Ship operators represent the third specialization archetype. These are companies that provide crews to run ships and provide day-to-day ship maintenance. These firms usually have bases in countries like the Philippines, India, and/or Eastern Europe. They also run training programs for developing the appropriate competencies of the crews. The raison d'être for such firms is to be able to offer cost-efficient operations for ships.

Several shipowners have abandoned crewing their ships themselves and rely instead on established ship-operating firms. Fredriksen, for instance, does not crew his own ships, but uses five different ship-operating companies. This allows him to keep tabs on the relative performance of each, in terms of cost as well as performance.

The largest ship-operating companies are V. Group, Thome, Denholm, Wallem, OSM, and the Schulthers Group.

INNOVATING AROUND STEEL

Shipping firms that focus on innovation represent the fourth specialization archetype. These could be forecasting consulting firms, such as Marsoft; some of the research units within traditional ship brokerage companies, such as Clarkson, R.S. Platou, Fearnleys, etc.; or specialized ship consulting firms, such as Carl Bro, Vik & Sandvik, Skipsteknisk, etc., which specialize in developing tailored ship designs on demand. Major ship classification entities, such as Det norske Veritas (DnV), are also sources of innovation, as are specialty software firms, such as Danaos or Eniram, engine manufacturers (Sulzer, B&W), and propeller manufacturers (Lips-Wärtsilä). Finally, shipyards can drive innovations through an interactive process with shipowners. The Lindø shipyard, mentioned earlier, had a major role in the design of the world's largest container ship series, the Emma Maersk class, providing solutions to power transmission and hull design, and built all six ships.

In the past, integrated shipping companies tended to deal with the innovation side of the business in-house, through their own technical departments and chartering organizations, which provided the marketing inputs. These in-house attempts were often rather "homemade." Specialists can often deliver better quality innovation services, especially when they have a customer-focused culture, mission and capabilities.

EXAMPLES OF SPLITTING OWNING AND TRADING

Apart from the four main archetypes I have identified – owning, using, operating, and innovating around steel – there are more examples that illustrate the split between owning and trading.

Kommanditgesellschaft investment funds (KGs)

These German tax advantage funds bring together many smaller independent investors to buy single ships, which are then chartered out to owners or container liner companies that use them on their routes. This large source of funding and cost-efficient investment mechanism is the backbone for financing much of the growth in the German-owned container ship business. KGs provide a way for smaller investors to take part in shipownership. Indeed, this represents a specialized function focused only on owning steel.

Public companies that own ships

Seaspan and Eagle Bulk are examples of companies that are focused entirely on shipowning. They follow business approaches that are analogous to aircraft leasing companies, in that they provide relatively inexpensive ship capacity to operators. A low cost of capital – the ability to secure relatively inexpensive ships – is a key factor for their success. They are able to achieve this by securing long-term charters for their vessels, with relatively secure long-term cash flow patterns. This enables them to attract new equity investors, whom they invite through new equity offerings. By putting the ships on medium- to long-term charters, they are able to minimize or avoid spot market exposure. A new breed of similar companies includes Double Hull Tankers – a spinoff of OSG; TK Gas Partners – a spinoff from Teekay Shipping; and Ship Finance International – the shipowning spinoff from Frontline. All of these entities own ships that are on long-term charter with their former parents. This allows them to focus on shipowning.

Public companies that focus on shipowning provide a way for investors to participate in shipowning by investing in tailored ship stocks. In addition to offering a solid, steady yield, investors may hope that their stocks become "growth stocks." Public companies of this type – Seaspan is a good example – have indeed experienced rapid growth recently.

Pools

Pools provide a single marketing (chartering) organization for a group of shipowners. Examples include Tanker International, the Heidmar Group (owned 50 percent by Morgan Stanley and 50 percent by J. Economos), and Seatrade. By taking care of the marketing and trading side, pools allow shipowners to focus on shipowning. Pools are specialized and large enough to provide economies of scope.

These examples, and others, lend further credence to the notion that there is an emerging difference between owning, using, operating, and innovating in the shipping industry. For marketing/trading and innovation activities, the focus will be more on scope – to offer superior customer service. This is in contrast to the exploitation of cost and scale benefits associated with owning and operating ships, usually by larger organizations. All four types of organization can create value, of course. The key is how to achieve the benefits from each specialized archetype, i.e., exploration benefits (scope) and exploitation benefits (scale), as they relate to short-term versus long-term foci, and achieving low costs versus high innovation.

DEVELOPING A CLEAR STRATEGY

The first step in developing a strategy for a shipping firm would be to analyze the industry's value chain to determine where the most promising opportunities might be, now and in the future. Whether the firm owns, uses, operates, or innovates around steel, a clear and understandable strategy is a key factor for success. This involves several facets:

- Focus on a specialized archetype, with a clear and minimalistic understanding of the critical success factors. It is essential to have systems and processes for this.
- Realistic planning processes must exist within the firm, to ensure that a particular specialist shipping strategy can be developed. This will be different for each of the four archetypes. The relevant line managers should have a clear understanding of the priorities for the particular archetype of shipping that they are now part of, and be involved in the planning process, to make sure that there is clear ownership of the strategy from the line. They must have personal incentives to ensure this. Too often, planning processes are general and do not reflect the chosen shipping business archetype – this can lead to an endless amount of paper and numbers, without clear managerial ownership.

- Shipping is very much a matter of acting on opportunities as they arise. The largest mission of the planning process, for any one of these four shipping business archetypes, is to develop a strategy of preparedness, so that when opportunities present themselves, decisions can be made with speed. Some planning processes overlook the issue of preparedness, by failing to focus on likely decisions. Projections and forecasts are based on general extrapolations rather than on the key issues for individual archetypes. The unintended effect is to create slowness and a lack of focus in the shipping organization.

- Key executives need to demonstrate enthusiastic ownership of strategy. The competences that are required will differ for each of these archetypes. It is important for a management team to understand what is key for their specific area. Enthusiasm and self-confidence are important, but must be consistent with understanding what truly matters in each given context.

- In the past, shipowners, with an integrated value chain behind them, held a position of power vis-à-vis shippers, or customers. The balance of power now seems to have shifted the other way. With the emergence of the specialist firm, customer satisfaction has become vital. For each of the four archetypes I have identified, it is critically important to understand what customer satisfaction means. Speed? Service? Lower costs, at the expense of speed and service? Or a one-stop-shop service – shipping, truck or train transportation, IT-based support, terminal services? Identifying what type of value or service customers are looking for is essential.

It follows that the meaning of "brand" varies from archetype to archetype. Branding is linked intimately with scope, i.e., strong relationships with key customers. Companies want customers to associate the brand with quality, reliability, excellent service levels, etc. Branding will be particularly important in shipping segments that focus on establishing strong customer relationships – brokerage firms and traders like Clarkson, R.S. Platou, Cargill, etc., and cruise shipowners like Carnival and Royal Caribbean, which represent heavily branded products.

In certain segments of specialized shipowning, branding can signify that the company has a stronger, more coherent strategy, for example, vis-à-vis financial market stakeholders, than run-of-the-mill consumers. Seaspan or Danaos are strongly branded vis-à-vis the financial markets.

- When it comes to using steel, branding signifies strong customer relationships. In container liner shipping, Maersk Line, COSCO, OOCL, etc., set the standards for service and reliability vis-à-vis specific customers-cum-container shippers. Steel owning firms, like Seaspan, represent reliability, efficient cost structures, a modern fleet, etc. For innovators around steel, the brand will represent quality and innovation. Marsoft, for example, stands for quality of products, integrity, and professionalism. For ship operators, such as V. Group or Thome, the brand will stand for cost efficiency and quality.

SIX STRATEGIES FOR STAYING CLOSE TO THE CUSTOMER

The shipping industry does not have a strong tradition of customer relations in any of the four areas I have identified, particularly when it comes to owning ships. Shipping is not Nestlé, Unilever, or Wal-Mart. To a large degree, this is both natural and understandable, given that most of shipping is a commodity business. But it cannot last: as we have discussed, the balance of power is swinging toward the consumer and it will be critical for all shipping firms to develop a better consumer understanding. This holds true despite the general commodity nature of shipping. The following six areas of focus might help shipping firms develop this competence and fight the notion of accepting their commodity status.

1 **See business opportunities not yet obvious to others**

To be part of the marketplace and stay close to customers, the shipping firm depends on having several key executives who keep a broad, external focus. An eclectic, international profile will help ensure that a broader perspective is maintained and new ideas are generated about how to spot new business opportunities. In short, the dynamic shipping organization must "lead the market," not "be led by the market" (Kotler *et al.*, 2000 – or, as Baron Nathan Rothschild said in the eighteenth century, "The time to buy is when blood is running in the streets" (quoted by Shaerf, 2008).

This can be particularly difficult in shipping, where the market mechanisms play such an important role. But it can be a mistake for shipping organizations to sit back and say, "The market dictates it all, so there is nothing for us to do in terms of creating non-commodity niches." On the contrary, customers are individuals, and they matter – a proactive vision, not a "me too" attitude, is critical. The firm must find new ways of thinking outside the box. How can it do this? How can it better understand what customer-centricity means? There are several ways.

Let us take Gearbulk. This firm has become the market leader in shipping cellulose from South American producers – primarily from Brazil – Aracruz, Votorantim, Suzano, and others. The contacts they have with each firm and specific individuals within each organization are key to their success. By staying close to these individuals, Gearbulk is able to identify new opportunities that can be developed into shipping contracts.

2 **Meeting places between problems and solutions**

It is essential for shipping company executives across organizations in the supply chain to be able to hold extensive dialogues with each other to find better solutions for their customers. For example, a shipping company may want new insights about innovative unloading equipment to improve their logistical approach for a customer. Non-obvious outside sources, such as shippers with particular transportation needs, might be brought into the discussion. The dialogue could also involve the shipping company's technical experts. The key here is to bring together a broad set of people from both sides of the table – suppliers and customers – to listen to and try to understand each other. Brainstorming without a set agenda often produces great results.

Clearly, this will work best where solid relationships based on trust already exist. Non-intuitive solutions can often follow.

Again, let us consider Gearbulk. Traditionally, many of the ships in its fleet were equipped with gantry cranes – but these are expensive. As a result of broad dialogue among many people, a new generation of bulk carriers is being equipped with simpler cranes, probably at a significantly lower investment.

For the shipping company, it is important to be able to argue for solutions that have anticipated value for the client. In order to maintain trust, it is critical to maintain a level of sophistication "appropriate" for a given customer. It is particularly important for the shipping organization to be humble, not arrogant – to work with customers effectively and not belittle them. But how can the company do this?

3 More experimentation

It is important to aim for far-reaching solutions and to attempt to bring them to light rapidly. This could be accomplished through more innovative prototyping – by moving faster, one learns faster, even from initial setbacks. The dynamic shipping firm must make decisions based on creativity and personal interaction, so that experience building can take place faster. One must practice "failing early to succeed sooner." Or, as Tom Erik Klaveness (2003) says, "Put one toe in the water at a time – nothing is called failure." In line with this, he pointedly says, "Turn all stones, but don't analyze the issue to death."

Team pressure is created by doing, which also means trying to simplify – to make sure that the central, often difficult, issues are grasped. Simplification also implies avoiding excessive data analysis and market testing ad absurdum. The excessive use of software support packages, with their strong analytical capabilities, can ironically become a barrier, in the sense that they can induce a senseless trial and error attitude. Instead, how can more systematic, true learning take place?

4 More systematic learning

As Klaveness said, there should be no such thing as failure – everything that is acted upon is a learning experience. Top management must encourage the organization to take action and to learn from it. They must avoid stigmatizing executives associated with occasional setbacks. Initiatives must be praised, and not lead to punishment if they do not work out as intended. The style of the CEO will be central to building a learning organization. For example, the head of Norden's bulk shipping division left a leading shipping firm to join the company, and he says his present tasks are truly stimulating because the CEO has given him his full support and "space" to be creative. To give positive reinforcement – praise – is vital (and very hard for many). Management also has to know how to encourage employees to develop their curiosity and be willing to try unconventional new approaches. The question is how?

5 **Juxtaposing traditional and radical business views**

Shipping is generally a traditional, some would even say largely non-intellectual, business. The emphasis on the laws of the markets can easily discourage unconventional thinking. The established truths of the industry, however, must be challenged. There can be no sacred cows. Unfortunately, in many shipping companies, the opposite is sometimes the case: "We are used to doing things our way." Non-intuitive solutions are often inspired by lead customers. It is key to listen to these customers, not to treat them arrogantly or distantly. An openness and a willingness to try what they might suggest are important. Only then will true "thinking outside the box" lead to better solutions for all. To return to Gearbulk and the successful development of its Brazilian pulp business, this was achieved by listening to and working closely with a few key individual players. Traditionally, Gearbulk has served Brazil's largest family-owned firm, Aracruz, for years, covering its shipping needs for transporting cellulose from Brazil to the rest of the world. Gearbulk developed special purpose ships with gantry cranes for this task. Similar business was subsequently developed with Suzano and Votarantim. As a result of Gearbulk's extreme customer focus it now dominates this shipping trade.

6 **"Not invented here" syndrome**

I have already noted that it is important to avoid a "we know best" attitude and silo thinking lodged in organizational fiefdoms. Homegrown or home-biased organizational cultural structures and processes must not be allowed to get in the way. In shipping companies, it is particularly important to make sure that the project-based nature of value creation – linked to the customer – is preserved. This implies, for example, that charterers should not be isolated from the operating organization. All key members of the organization should be part of the team that meets the customers. Leif Höegh does this, with an integrative project focus, for each of its two business platforms, and so do others. Local information must not become a power base. For instance, the chartering department must not "own" relevant customer information – it must belong to the entire organization. Finding new ways of serving customers depends on broad information sharing within each business area.

These six principles should help to create a customer-driven, commercially focused shipping organization, even in a commodity-oriented industry. One must learn to see shipping organizations in this light by actively developing a customer-centric, commercially focused culture. In this respect, the appointment of the ex-CEO of Carlsberg – the consumer-centric brewing giant – to head A.P. Moller-Maersk is interesting. More customer focus, with more speed and agility – and less bureaucracy – may be what this world-renowned shipping giant is looking for. Nevertheless, a better organizational culture alone will not generate dramatically increased commercial results. To do that, it will be important to ensure that there are internal entrepreneurs among the key executives and that the CEO and the board of directors are key initiative takers for creating economic value in the shipping organization.

The emergence of specialized shipping firms – focusing on any of the four archetypes I outlined earlier in this chapter – implies that planning, leading, staffing, and managerial focus must be tailored to the given archetype. Close proximity to the customer creates a decisive advantage – customer insight is key. There is no one right way to run a shipping firm but focusing on key concerns will be critical for success.

STOLT-NIELSEN

A recent example of a major shipping company that has split itself up into distinctive activities is Stolt-Nielsen, a global company with significant operations in various maritime-related industries. Through its wholly owned subsidiaries, Stolt Tankers & Terminals and Stolt Tank Containers, Stolt-Nielsen is one of the world's leading providers of globally integrated transportation services for bulk liquid chemicals, edible oils, acids, and other specialty liquids. The company's wholly owned subsidiary, Stolt Sea Farm, produces and markets high quality turbot, sturgeon, sole, and caviar. The company employs more than 4,700 staff in twenty three offices around the world. The company's main businesses include:

- Stolt Tankers & Terminals (ST&T) – the leading provider of bulk liquid transportation and storage using a global network of sophisticated parcel tankers and terminals. World-class manufacturers and users of specialty chemicals, food-grade oils and solvents, acids, and other specialty liquids around the world use ST&T to meet their transportation needs. The tank storage terminal segment is particularly profitable. Other operators are Odfjell and Vopak.
- Stolt Tank Containers (STC) – the leading global provider of logistics and transportation services for door-to-door shipments of bulk liquid chemicals and food-grade products. STC operates the world's largest fleet of stainless steel ISO tank containers, with over 22,000 units in service.
- Stolt-Nielsen Gas (SNG) – recently established (August 2007) to explore opportunities within the liquefied petroleum gas logistics industry, building on the good reputation of the other Stolt-Nielsen businesses.
- Stolt Bitumen Services (SBS) – focuses on the delivery of bitumen logistics services to its global clients. Based in Asia-Pacific, it combines the use of bitutainers, bitumen tankers, and bitumen storage terminals

to provide its customers with an integrated and complete distribution service.

- Stolt Sea Farm (SSF) – the world's leading turbot producing company, which, as stated earlier, also focuses on marketing high quality sole, sturgeon, and caviar.[10]

Focused on five specialized business segments, the likelihood of business success is enhanced – with each organizational entity now more likely to master the unique critical success factors applicable to each particular business.

CONCLUSION

There is a clear tendency toward specialization emerging in the shipping industry. The critical success factors are different for each of the four archetypes – owning, using, operating, and innovating around steel – as are the portfolio strategy implications. While shipping firms of the past were integrated, there was an initial trend toward splitting firms into specialized divisions. This has been taken a step further, to the establishment of specialized firms. Some companies have activities in two or more areas but they must have an overriding portfolio strategy to cover this meta-balance. Each of these four different types of specialization is unique, requiring unique understanding and focus.

[10] Adapted from Stolt-Nielsen's website.

6 Owning steel

Owning steel – owning ships – has been seen as the ultimate, most prestigious aspect of the shipping business for a long time. The integrated shipping firm had many types of ships with fully integrated services – i.e., an in-house chartering department for customer relations, an in-house technical department for spearheading technological innovations, and an in-house crewing department for seafarer staffing. But, as we have seen, the market is shifting away from the classic, integrated shipowning of the past. Today, shipowning is much more specialized, focused on owning one type – or, at the most, a few types – of ships, and not integrating with the other functions. In this chapter, I explore this new world of shipowning.

COMPETITIVE FOCUS: MUST-WIN BATTLES

Financial understanding, to secure the lowest cost of capital, represents the most critical success factor in shipowning. This means:

- Having a reasonable level of equity. Raising new equity capital in the market as the company expands becomes key. A reasonably strong share price is important – with a low share price, new equity can be expensive, and the dilution effect on existing owners of issuing new equity can be significant, leading to downward pressure on the stock price. A steady dividend payout policy will help keep the stock price up. (This is assuming that the company's earnings might actually be at a sufficiently high level to allow for this.)
- Being able to access the debt market in the most cost-effective way. This assumes that the company has a modern, effective, standardized fleet.
- The banks will want to guard themselves against huge drops in second-hand ship values due to obsolescence. It helps if the ship has an adequate long-term charter.

- Financial understanding, which includes a focus on tax considerations. By allowing firms to take advantage of the tax benefits that might result from the depreciation of a ship, an even lower cost of capital might be secured.
- Good purchase timing and acquiring new ships at a reasonable price are critical. Orders should be timed when shipyards' bookings are low. Ordering a series of identical ships will result in a lower newbuilding price per ship.
- It follows that it will be critical to have an effective network approach with various charterers, as well as with various banks. By engaging in alternatives, the shipowner might secure a better charter, as well as better financial terms, with a lower cost of capital.

CUSTOMERS

The customers for shipowning firms are customer relations-focused firms – users of steel. For instance, a shipowning company such as Seaspan has major container shipping lines as its customers – COSCO, China Shipping Corporation, OOCL, A.P. Moller-Maersk, Hapag-Lloyd, CSAV, K. Line and Mitsui O.S.K. Line. For Seaspan, it is essential to understand the particular strategies of each of these companies, including what types of ships they might need (TEU size), by when, and their policy about owning vs. chartering ships. Seaspan sees itself as a direct strategic partner for its customers, not simply a service provider. There are no brokers involved as intermediaries in their relationships. Seaspan's credibility in this role depends on its financial and operational strength.

Companies that own bulk carriers and/or tankers usually have major oil, ore or trading companies, such as ExxonMobil or Shell, BHP Billiton or Rio Tinto, Dreyfuss or Cargill, as customers – with the latter taking ships on time charter from the tanker or bulk carrier company. Some shipowning firms also do their own chartering and so deal with the market as a customer. It is a matter of definition whether one would call the market or another customer relations firm the customer. Under all circumstances, it is important that the shipowning firm fully understands the movements of the markets, and bases its negotiations with its customers on this.

There are also asset-owning firms that work in specialized niches. One example is Heerema, which owns a series of ship cranes, offshore oil pipe laying barges, etc. Heerema used to own the majority of shares in a heavy lift shipping company, which it elected to exit from because it felt that the business was about to become too commodity oriented. For these types of companies, the customers are typically infrastructure contractors. In the case of Heerema, some of the contractors would be sister companies, such as Heerema Construction. Another example, A.P. Moller-Maersk, which owns a number of jack-up rigs, has a sister organization – Maersk Contractors – as its major customer.

As we have discussed, it is essential that shipping firms understand what contributes to customer satisfaction and develop a sense of power by being able to deliver along these dimensions. For the ship-owning firm, this may mean that they can offer relatively modern ships, relatively safe ships when it comes to oil spillage (double hulls), relatively fast ships, relatively low costs of operation to the charterers, standardized ships, etc.

ECONOMIES OF SCALE

Lowest possible costs will determine the shipowning firm's success, in the end. Therefore, as previously noted, owning ships implies a focus on economies of scale to keep costs low. Owning a series of ships with more or less the same design can lead to significant savings on a number of dimensions. Spare parts, for example, will be the same across the series, which will result in lower costs. Also, when a yard is able to build an identical series, they benefit from the learning curve effect, which leads to lower costs. Crewing is also simplified with a series of identical ships – the crews can be easily exchanged as required. And, above all, when it comes to financing, considerable potential savings can be made when a series of more-or-less identical ships is being put onto the ship financing market. Thus, modern shipowning implies having several ships of more or less the same design to maximize the benefits of various economies of scale. We have already seen that General Maritime and Seaspan do this. Also, as previously noted, another advantage for large companies is that they can achieve advantageous financing terms from lending institutions (low margins and low cost of capital) based on the size of their balance sheet and historical corporate performance, rather than on the merits of a specific project.

FINANCIAL UNDERSTANDING

To ensure the lowest possible cost of capital, competent financial understanding also plays a critical role. A reasonable expected return on a given project, relative to the risks, is a prerequisite for investors, banks, and other financial institutions, for them to give the lowest cost of capital. Therefore, an understanding of available financial markets and their cyclical patterns is essential for efficient long-term ship financing.

A reasonable and stable long-term interest rate will also be advantageous. Therefore, it is important to have an understanding of expected movements in interest rates – a function of inflationary pressure, general levels of need to support the growth of an economy, etc. The same can be said about currencies – their relative strengths are linked to interest rate differentials between them – also key for ship financing. Financing of new shipping projects is always difficult during economic downturns, particularly if the banks see the firm as financially weak from being, for example, highly leveraged. Too much tonnage taken in on time charter by liner companies or shippers such as steel companies, with a steady fixed drain on cash flow, can also make efficient ship financing difficult during downturns. Conversely, bulk carrier and tanker owners, and charter-vessel operators like Seaspan, try to charter out tonnage at the peak of the market to secure revenue during a potential market downturn.

During the latter part of 2007, we saw a dramatically different picture of ship financing – more expensive and harder to achieve. This was the case for all types of shipping, including container ships. The banks' inability to sell off some of their shipping obligations to other banks contributed to this. While profitability was again positive for the container liner industry in 2007, after a difficult 2006, tanker markets fell sharply at the end of 2007 and bulk markets continued to be very strong. The tighter picture of ship financing in 2007 was related to the credit crunch; its impact on many lending banks, especially in Germany, led to particular challenges, even problems, when it came to financing tanker and container ship projects.

According to Shaerf, the tightening credit markets have led to higher prices of debt, with fees to banks increasing sharply (Shaerf, 2008, p. 19, 20, and 22). Banks have found it increasingly difficult to syndicate loans. With increased spreads and long-term funding only available at a premium, several banks – above all, German – have withdrawn from lending to shipping (or significantly reduced lending) due to overexposure to the sector. Shaerf expects that this will have an impact on supply, and debt will cost more and have more restrictive covenants as well. The end result is likely to be fewer financial transactions.

In order to obtain a reasonable cost of capital, it is also important to understand the basic requirements and expectations of the financial markets, particularly in order to deliver a steady (and ideally increasing) dividend for companies with funding in equity markets. By providing reasonable yields, it can be easier for a company to obtain more reasonably priced equity capital from the market, which contributes to keeping the cost of capital down. Of course, overall financing must be reasonable. Major US-listed shipping companies, such as Seaspan and Teekay, have enjoyed situations where the asset value of their ships is higher than the book value of their companies, making it relatively easy to raise inexpensive equity capital. They have had an impressive growth multiple of their stocks, based on stable cash flows and dividend payouts.

There are a number of financial strategies that a shipping firm can employ. They include:

- Asset securitization for particular ships in the fleet.
- Issuing investment grade bonds – in contrast to low-grade "junk" bonds.

- Tapping new banking sources, e.g., Chinese banks, so that there is an efficient portfolio of lead banks, which ensures strong competition for deals.
- Issuing new equity. One might also issue convertible equities, i.e., loans that can be turned into equities later. Reasonably priced new equity requires planning for reasonable dividend levels, as previously discussed.
- Interest rate swaps. Swaps should be exercised so that the interest payment commitment, say, on long-term financing, is locked in to avoid too much exposure to interest rate fluctuations. This is a critical issue for firms like Seaspan.
- Hedging – for example, when it comes to currency types. To ensure steady income flows from time charters, it is crucial that expenses for long-term financing, operations, etc., are held in the same currency – if not, it could be seen as deliberate speculation. The treasury function will be key here.

Let's look at an example of understanding shipping and financial markets. In July 2004 Castle Harlan Inc., a private equity firm, paid about $663 million to buy Horizon from Carlyle Group, which had acquired Horizon fifteen months earlier for $300 million. Castle Harlan then put more debt onto Horizon's balance sheet, and took it public, through an IPO, in September 2005. The stock price has tripled since the initial IPO. Another interesting example is K-Sea Transportation. In 1998, Furman Selz, a private equity investment firm (that subsequently merged into Jefferies Capital Partners), engineered the leveraged buyout of New York-based domestic tug owner Eklof Marine. Cleverly renamed K-Sea Transportation (a play on the name of the CEO, Tim Casey), the company was loaded with significant leverage. In 2004, Jefferies took the company public through a tax-advantaged vehicle, the Mater Limited Partnership. Jefferies retained control of the general partner and five years later took part of the general partner public. While business has grown steadily for K-Sea, the returns have been phenomenal and clearly the shareholders have benefited from clever financial engineering and the use of astute leverage.

These examples illustrate a keen sense of timing, as well as clever use of the capital markets – in other words, competent financial management. Similar types of finance-driven deals have been done by General Maritime and others. Deals that did not come off, such as those spearheaded by GSL or Seacastle, should also be mentioned (*TradeWinds*, 2007, p. 50). Competent financial management can allow a company to ride shipping cycles without suffering catastrophic losses in a market downturn.

DEMAND VS. SUPPLY OF NEW SHIPS

As we know, the strong shipping markets until mid-2008, along with the availability of inexpensive financial funding until the latter part of 2008, have clearly played a role in stimulating the massive ordering of new ships. Additionally, there might be an element of irrational exuberance (Shiller, 2000), partly driven by a fear of being left behind.

A solid understanding of shipping markets and their cycles is a key factor to being a commercially successful owner. Critical decisions are centered on entry/exit (when to order ships, when to charter them in, when to charter them out, when to sell them) as well as long/short (whether to go for long-term or short-term charters). A long-term view of the shipping cycle is key. The success of the so-called asset play – i.e., making money on buying and/or selling ships at the right moment – depends on an understanding of the full cycle. Asset play strategies make less sense if undertaken alone and are best combined with the cost-effective running of the ships.

Shipbuilding capacity is a critical factor of ship availability. Figure 6.1 provides an overview of new container ship supply relative to expected growth in demand. As we can see, supply has far exceeded demand over the last few years, and this imbalance is expected to continue until 2010. Figure 6.2 indicates the same for tankers.

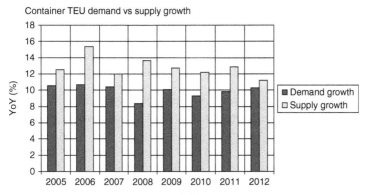

Container TEU demand vs supply growth

FIGURE 6.1 Container supply/demand balance
Source: Marsoft (2008c).

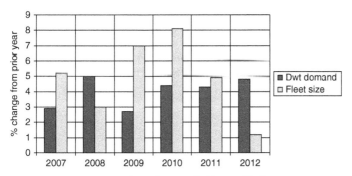

FIGURE 6.2 Crude tanker supply/demand balance
Source: Marsoft (2008b).

Segmentation of ships on order

The Singapore-based consulting firm, Worldyards, provides a web-based analytical system, giving information on 280 active merchant shipbuilding yards worldwide. This source provides details about order books, type of ship, yard, shipowner, approximate price per ship ordered, approximate dates of ordering, and delivery, etc. It also provides delivery schedules on an aggregate basis for various ship types. Further, it provides a ranking of the twenty largest shipbuilders in the world, by dead-weight tonnage (dwt) on order. As of 2007, the world's three biggest shipyards, with a combined market share of 26.8 percent, measured in dwt delivered, were:

1. Hyundai Industries (Korea): 43.1 million dwt = 14.1 percent worldwide market share.
2. Universal (Japan): 21 million dwt = 6.9 percent market share.
3. Daewoo Shipbuilding and Marine (Korea): 18 million dwt = 5.8 percent market share.

Worldyards also provides information about developments in technology and ship design in a monthly newsletter, and news for each of the major shipbuilding nations.

The segmentation of ship types is interesting. One may roughly classify the more capital-intensive ships (in terms of cost per ton) as specialized ships, built in Western Europe, vs. ships that are relatively less expensive per ton, such as standard design dry bulk carriers, crude oil carriers, and container ships, built in Japan, Korea, or China. A more detailed breakdown of ship categories can be found in Figure 6.3.

According to Worldyards, twenty one major categories of ships can be identified, with 113 sub-categories. The sign (•) indicates generally less sophisticated ships, in terms of value per dwt, typically built in Asia. Many of the new ships primarily operate in commodity markets, i.e., where adaptation to the world market rate conditions is key – I have indicated these with (♦). Ships in other categories operate in niches, although in practice it is difficult to make a firm distinction between niche and commodity ship segments.

If we look at shipbuilding in a high-cost country like Germany, we can see an increase in activities over the last five years (see Figure 6.4). This underscores that there is also room for niche-oriented, high-value shipbuilding. A similar increase in activity levels can be found in Norwegian shipyards, with a heavy focus on specialized offshore supply ships, and in Finland, with a focus on large passenger ships.

Let us now look at the order books for new ships, in terms of billions of Euros, by country of control (Figure 6.5).

	Category	Number of sub-categories	Low price per dwt (•)	Commodity (♦) or niche?
1	Bulkers	11	•	♦
2	Containers	10	•	
3	Semi-liner tonnage	4 (including ro-ro)		
4	LNG	4		
5	CMG	1 (including gas)		
6	LPG	7		
7	Combination carriers	2 (including OBO)	•	♦
8	Crude tankers	6	•	♦
9	Product tankers	7	•	♦
10	Product/chemical tankers	5	•	
11	Chemical tankers	6	•	
12	Specialized tankers	2		
13	Specialized cargo	6 (including reefer)		
14	Car carriers	2	•	
15	Heavy lift cargo	3		
16	Passenger ships	3		
17	Offshore	17		
18	Barges	2		
19	Dredgers	10		
20	Service/misc. vessels	6 (including crane vessel)		
21	Naval	1		
21	**TOTAL**	**113**		

FIGURE 6.3 Segmentation of ship types
Source: Worldyards (2007).

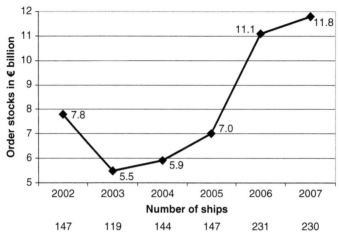

FIGURE 6.4 Shipbuilding activities in Germany
Source: Schulz (2007 p. 82).

	Ships	Value (€ billion)
Japan	644	36.9
Germany	963	33.5
USA	126	21.5
Greece	430	18.8
Norway	317	16.9
Denmark	246	12.4
China	211	12.1
Italy	174	11.1
South Korea	130	6.7
Hong Kong	130	6.0
Others	2015	88.2
Total	**5386**	**264.1**

FIGURE 6.5 Ships on order per country (of control)
Source: Schulz (2007 p. 83).

Figure 6.5 shows Japan in the lead, followed by Germany, the US, Greece, and Norway. The relatively high level of orders coming from Germany is surprising. This can largely be explained by the strong dominance by container ships owned in Germany (Figure 6.6). A significant reason for this is the particular German tax advantage that wealthy individuals might benefit from by participating in the Kommanditgesellschafts (KGs), i.e., limited partnerships for each

	(TEU millions)
Germany	1,157
China	261
Japan	235
Taiwan	187
Switzerland	172
Greece	161
Denmark	142
Singapore	140
South Korea	115
USA	81
Others	848
Total	**3,499**

FIGURE 6.6 Container ships in existence by
country of ownership, 2006
Source: Der Spiegel, No.8, (2007, p. 81).

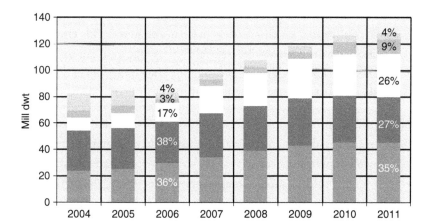

FIGURE 6.7 Shipyard capacity by country
Source: Marsoft, presentation at IMD, August 2007.

ship. This provides highly cost-efficient equity capital to German owners, who typically put these KGs together and then operate the ships.

As far as shipyard capacity is concerned, much of the new expansion comes from Southeast Asia. Figure 6.7 gives an indication of this,
with a likely increase in capacity from 2006 to 2011 of around 50–
60 percent. Internal sources indicate that China's share of the world

market is already significantly larger than indicated here, more or less on a par with Korea and Japan. However, several orders have been booked in China with "greenfield" yards, where capacity is not yet fully in place. There is a lot of discussion in the industry today about whether all Chinese yards will deliver as promised.

Figure 6.8 indicates the capacity growth by the major shipyards in Korea, Japan, and China. We can draw several implications from Figures 6.7 and Figure 6.8.

- China has become an important shipbuilding nation over the last five years, and its relative prominence is expected to increase. Before that there was effectively a Japanese–Korean duopoly in shipbuilding that had an effect on newbuilding price. The entry of China has brought more competition. Newbuilding price increases have slowed since.
- We see relatively stronger growth in capacity for the leading Chinese yards, relative to their competitors in Japan and Korea. This growth assumes that the currency differential between the local currency and the US$ does not widen, since newbuilding prices are given in US$. The development of labor costs can also impact this trend.

Newbuilding prices tripled from 1985 to 1995. Initially Japan and Korea were the dominant players. Subsequently, China developed a significant shipbuilding capacity. This seems to have had a moderating effect on newbuilding price increases. Needless to say, the significant rise in ship freight rates from 2002 also led to substantial increases in newbuilding prices. Figure 6.9 illustrates this.

Shipbuilding

There have been huge technological developments in shipbuilding, with countries in the Far East in particular accounting for increases in productivity. Initially, Japan led the way toward more productivity in shipbuilding, taking over from many of the traditional European shipbuilding nations. Then Korea took the lead, and today this country has some of the most productive shipbuilding companies in the world. Now, increasingly, China is emerging as a huge shipbuilding nation.

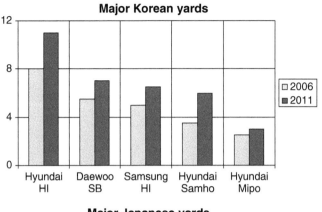

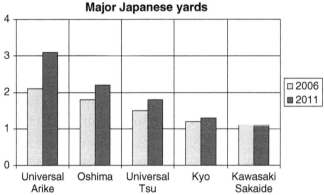

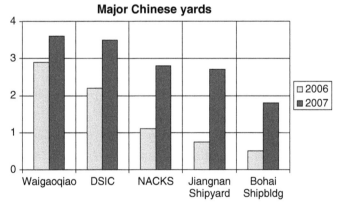

FIGURE 6.8 Major yards: capacity growth – ships delivered
Source: Marsoft, Presentation at IMD, August 2007.

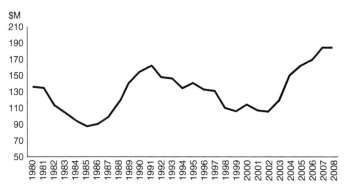

FIGURE 6.9 Newbuilding prices
Source: China Ship Economy Research Center Presentation, Beijing,
April 18, 2008.

China's aim is to become the number one supplier in the world by 2015, if not earlier – according to some statistics, it is already there.

Today, it takes approximately ten to eleven months to build a very large crude carrier (VLCC) super tanker, down from thirteen months in 2005. Similar figures for a 5,000 TEU container ship are eight months, down from ten months. Added yard productivity and throughput mean that shipbuilding capacity has been dramatically increased. One can speculate that this might lead to shorter peaks in shipping markets, due to the fact that excess demand for ships will now be met relatively quickly by the rapid increase in newbuilding capacity.

Damen shipyard, in the Netherlands, offers a good example of why a strong customer focus is particularly key when it comes to innovation strategies in shipping.

The company focuses on building ships that can be standardized in design, so that long series of similar ship types can be built. Damen has been particularly successful in building tugs and today is the world leader in this market. The hulls are built in low-cost countries, first in Poland, then in Romania, and now in Vietnam. The ships are mostly finished at the yard in the Netherlands. Thus, Damen can deliver a state-of-the-art product at a competitive price.

What characterizes Damen above all is a relentless focus on marketing and catering to the customer. When orders have been booked, delivering the ships represents a controllable challenge. Internal capacity constraints are not allowed to limit the company's activities.

This strong market and customer focus are key characteristics of most innovation-oriented companies in the shipping sector, ensuring that business is created, and then focusing on high-quality implementation and delivery. The opposite has too often been the case in the past. A capacity and production-oriented focus has led to too much focus on constraints, rather than bringing in innovation-driven new business. Many European shipyards regrettably slipped into this category, with the disastrous result that they had to go out of business (de Jong, 2000).

BALANCE BETWEEN SUPPLY AND DEMAND

A key question has to do with the balance between the expected availability of shipping capacity and the demand for shipping services. As Figure 6.1 indicates, the percentage of increase in supply has been outstripping demand for the last few years, and this is expected to continue until 2010. New ship ordering behavior, indicated in Figure 6.8, gives a good indication of the supply side, i.e., shipping capacity. But how does this match with the demand side for the three major ship categories? In general, one can question whether all these newbuilding orders will become realities. Given the recent difficulties of ship financing, there may be significant cancellations. Some newbuilding contracts may also be sold at bargain prices.

Figure 6.10 provides a more detailed picture of this, broken down for dry bulk, tankers, and container ships. There is some oversupply, but not excessive, in dry bulk. This imbalance is more accentuated for tankers. Supply and demand are out of balance for container ships, but are expected to even out in the future.

As already noted in Figure 6.1, a balance between supply and demand is not to be expected before the end of 2010. In the years up until then, oversupply – at times heavy – is expected.

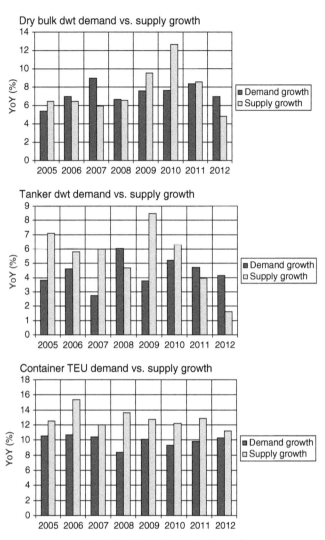

FIGURE 6.10 Matching demand and supply
Source: Marsoft (2008a, b, c).

In general, one can expect all of these major fleet segments to consist of relatively modern tonnage by 2010, with relatively little need for renewal from then on. The order books are clearly much higher than would be expected from analysis of the increase in demand. Based on this, freight rates, newbuilding prices, and second-hand prices can be expected to come under pressure. It should also be remembered that the new ships coming on stream now have higher productivity than older ships. Additionally, single-hull tanker replacement activities will dwindle after 2010. Following a recent oil spill, South Korea banned single-hull tankers from 2010 onwards. However, other Asian countries have refrained from joining the international convention requiring double-hull tankers by 2010. Some sources therefore expect single-hull tankers to be in operation until at least 2015.

The data point to oversupply and a fall in ship freight rates, as well as in newbuilding prices and second-hand prices, can be expected. Furthermore, levels for shipbuilding will fall, particularly after 2010.

CONTAINER SHIPS – NEWBUILDING ACTIVITIES
Figure 6.11 is an extension of Figure 6.1. It shows that the top twenty liner operators, apart from Evergreen, have relatively aggressive new-building programs. The industry leader, A.P. Moller-Maersk, also looks relatively conservative.

The competitive dynamics, when it comes to newbuilding, seem to be changing, with price leaders and price takers playing different roles. Traditionally, price leaders were major shipping firms placing orders for a large fleet of ships at reasonable rates, but they no longer seem as prominent in this role as they were some years ago. Actually, in the second half of 2007, we witnessed an unprecedented explosion of orders, which smashed historical record highs. In the span of four months alone contracting for new tonnage matched the total tonnage contracted in each of the previous three years. Most of the tonnage is for mega ships (12,500 to 13,300 TEU).

Interestingly, liner companies (large and small) account for a mere 25 percent of the recent mega ship newbuilding activity, while charter-vessel owners (like Peter Dohle, MPC Group, C.P. Offen, Nordcapital, B. Rickmers, Seaspan, Danaos, etc.) account for 75 percent. German interests account for 55 percent of the total, most of which is on a speculative basis (in contrast to Danaos, Seaspan, B. Rickmers and MPC Group, which have all arranged for a long-term charter).

#	Operator	Total existing TEU	Total existing Ships	Order book TEU	Order book Ships	Percent of existing
1	APM-Maersk	1,952,956	540	384,835	82	19.7
2	Mediterranean Shg Co.	1,241,361	378	593,724	57	47.8
3	CMA CGM Group	903,013	380	651,124	78	72.1
4	Evergreen Line	623,719	176	108,596	10	17.4
5	Hapag-Lloyd	497,814	140	133,045	16	26.7
6	COSCO Container L.	441,014	142	414,482	63	94.0
7	CSCL	431,718	139	249,037	40	57.7
8	APL	402,857	125	261,090	39	64.8
9	NYK	398,277	119	226,832	41	57.0
10	MOL	356,466	112	176,027	33	49.4
11	Hanjin/Senator	354,227	85	316,324	41	89.3
12	OOCL	351,298	82	134,210	21	38.2
13	K Line	310,166	94	168,956	35	54.5
14	Zim	291,017	114	290,164	41	99.7
15	Hamburg-Sud Group	281,268	121	173,371	38	61.6
16	Yang Ming Line	274,281	83	188,684	31	68.8
17	CSAV Group	265,948	89	152,863	23	57.5
18	Hyundai M. M.	226,979	51	155,098	19	68.3
19	PIL (Pacific Int. Line)	173,832	111	95,631	29	55.0
20	Wan Hai Lines	143,943	84	56,780	21	39.4

FIGURE 6.11 Top twenty liner companies – new orders at March 10, 2008
Source: AXS-Alphaliner, May 22, 2008.

Today, liner companies prefer to let independents arrange the financing and chartering of mega ships for a period of eight to twelve years. In this way, they do not have to carry the ships on their balance sheet, while they have secured long-term employment.

Conversely, this is a great way for charter vessel owners like Seaspan to expand their fleet, secure steady cash flows and achieve advantageous finance terms from lenders and equity markets.

In a hot market, like 2007, some owners signed newbuilding contracts with yards on a speculative basis (without having charter agreements from a liner company) but were able to capitalize quickly on that as liner companies rushed to secure contracted tonnage and offered advantageous terms. In falling markets, the reverse might hold true and some speculative contracts may end up in financial trouble. This may be a reflection of the fact that the market is fairly saturated. The yards have relatively little need for additional orders and see little reason to give traditional price leaders a better deal. The fact that Maersk and Hapag-Lloyd have relatively small orderbook to fleet ratios is attributed to the fact that these companies tried to expand in 2005 via acquisition rather than through organic growth (newbuilding), and suffered a performance penalty in 2006 and 2007. Maersk lost market share after the acquisition and replaced its senior management, while Hapag-Lloyd is in trouble and a candidate for sale by its parent company (TUI) – several companies have negotiated for it, including APL. Given the financial trouble that these two companies have faced as a result of expansion, it is understandable that their focus on newbuilding has since withered. Evergreen, on the other hand, is the only company that has stayed away from ordering large ships and its market share is likely to fall in coming years. Many of the big companies may see it as advantageous to let other, smaller firms do the brunt of the newbuilding in anticipation of a falling market, as can be seen from Figure 6.11.

Container liner firms are being supplied with new ships owned by specialized shipowning firms, such as Seaspan, Danaos, or B. Rickmers. Let us consider Seaspan's newbuilding programs. Seaspan has entered into the purchase of ten 2,500 TEU vessels, to be built by Jiangsu Yangzijiang Shipbuilding Company in China. The contractual price is US$41,750,000 per vessel, to be delivered in March and June 2010. Two 3,500 TEU vessels have been ordered from Zhejiang Shipbuilding Co.

Seaspan has also ordered fourteen 4,250 TEU vessels, to be built by Jiangsu New Yangzi Shipbuilding Company. These ships, costing US$61,350,000 per vessel, are to be delivered between March and September 2009. Further, Seaspan has agreed to buy eight 8,500 TEU vessels, to be built by Hyundai Heavy Industries in South Korea. The latter are priced at US$122,500,000 per vessel, to be delivered between November 2009 and November 2010. Finally, in August 2007, Seaspan ordered eight 13,100 TEU mega container ships at Hyundai Heavy Industries and at Hyundai Sancho Heavy Industries, at a total cost of US$1.5 billion, i.e. US$187,500,000 per ship – to be delivered in 2010–2011.

All of these ships have already been placed on long-term charters to major container liners: the 2,500 TEU series to K. Line, the 4,250 TEU series to CSCL, the 8,500 TEU series to China Shipping, and the 13,100 TEU series to COSCO. Seaspan remains optimistic about the demand for container ships, confident that it can supply the major container liners with cost-efficient new tonnage, all chartered out on long-term time charters.

To what extent are size and economies of scale decisive factors? Or, is focus on a few specific trade legs, rather than going for size-driven volumes and market share, relatively more important?

Let us review the experiences of Maersk Line, which attempted to create larger entities and economies of scale.

Maersk Line acquired P&O Nedlloyd in 2005. The major rationale for the acquisition was to go for economies of scale and to develop an even stronger market share in the important Asia–Europe legs. But things did not work out as planned. Costs of integration were higher than expected and inadequate systems, particularly in IT, proved troublesome. In 2006, rates tumbled. Several liners were fighting for volume and market share and there was a resulting disaster in the container liner industry. Maersk Line lost money in 2006.

Then, from the end of 2006, A.P. Moller-Maersk initiated a change in policy. It withdrew ship capacity from certain trades – notably the transpacific route – and went for profitability rather than market share. Focusing on specific trades and withdrawing from others became

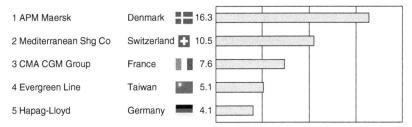

FIGURE 6.12 Market share (%) of the five largest container ship lines
Source: AXS-Alphaliner, May 22, 2008.

a trend for many liner operators. The results have been higher rates and profitability.

Maersk Line provides a good example of how a leading container liner company is adapting to new competitive circumstances in the container shipping segment. We know, from Figure 6.12, that Maersk Line's 16.3 percent market share is the highest in the world, more than 80 percent greater than its nearest competitor.

Maersk Line has developed a new strategic plan to increase the profitability of its business, built around several dimensions:

- Reduce staff, and increase productivity. Sales per employee are reported to be almost twice as high for COSCO than for Maersk Line (*Berlingske Tidende*, 23 May, 2008, p. 16).
- Modify the deployment of ships with a shift toward more routes with strong profitability and growth (i.e., more ships on Far East–Europe routes, fewer ships on Far East–US routes).
- Optimize container usage, particularly to secure return freight, avoiding the return of empty containers.
- Avoid port delays as much as possible.
- Save fuel costs by slow-steaming. According to Eivind Kolding, President of Maersk Line, fuel costs represent almost 50 percent of the line's overall costs today, compared to 10 percent a few years ago (*Berlingske Tidende*, 23 May, 2008, p. 17). What consumers want from operators is regularity. With slow-steaming, the liner company can bypass smaller harbors, and/or add an additional ships to a particular

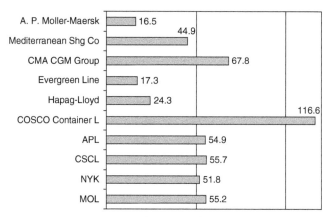

FIGURE 6.13 New ships on order as % of existing fleet (including ships chartered in)
Source: AXS-Alphaliner, May 22, 2008.

trade. COSCO, for instance, recently added a ninth container ship to its South Asia–Europe string, so that it can continue to meet customer demand while saving fuel costs by slow-steaming.

• Resist the purchase of new tonnage. Figure 6.13 shows how Maersk Line limits new ship ordering relative to its competitors.

In summary, the significant change in direction at Maersk Line was to focus on profitability rather than market share, when the potential benefits of going for economies of scale did not materialize. The moral of their story is, do what you do well, but do it better.

It is interesting to observe that scale – expanding to become more efficient and reduce costs – and scope – close customer relations – may be becoming more or less the same thing for some companies. Both Maersk Line and Gearbulk, for instance, are attempting to cultivate a door-to-door service, i.e., close customer relations, while facing huge capital-intensive asset requirements (special purpose ships, terminals, warehousing, land transportation, computer, based cargo trading, etc.) This implies that the focus on specialized strategies, scale-driven or scope-driven, may not be applicable in all instances. The effect of this is added complexity – seen in container liner businesses, but also in instances of industrial shipping (such as for Gearbulk, Star Shipping, etc.). The key question for these companies might be, are the expected returns large enough to justify the risks taken? One should develop the notion of being paid "per unit of risk taken." But when scale-related and scope-related factors form part of the strategy, this can imply lower returns, as Maersk Line's reduced performance in 2006–2007 demonstrates.

TIMING IS KEY

As noted, it is important to play the cycles right so that capacity matches swings in the ship freight markets. There are, of course, similarities between shipowning and other asset-intensive industries, such as paper, cement, steel mills, aluminum smelters, automotive plants, etc. Achi *et al.* (1996) have come up with a number of principles for investment behavior to better manage one's capacity in these basic industries. They state that in all of them, waves of mass investment inevitably drag down the profitability of the industry due to overcapacity and so lead to the next slump. Overinvestment in new ship capacity can lead to falling ship freight markets. The market will stay down, until supply and demand are once again in approximate equilibrium.

Financing is generally easier to achieve at the top of the market, which explains partly why a lot of ordering and fleet expansion is done at market peaks. From the lending perspective, margins are lower at market peaks when many banks compete against each other. Furthermore, a healthy balance sheet is an open invitation for equity capital (many IPOs take place at market peak). So from the financing perspective, it is easier to raise capital in strong markets, even though you might pay the penalty of higher newbuilding prices. Furthermore, many bulk, tanker and containership charter-vessel owners are able to secure advantageous long-term charter-out terms in high markets. A detailed analysis of the cost of capital and financing engineering should be done before owners decide to place newbuilding orders. Do they really want to expand or are they afraid of being left behind? By improving their timing when investing in new ship capacity, companies can smooth out these business cycles and moderate the impact they have on the firm's overall returns.

In fact, newbuilding programs should be managed in a counter-cyclical way, which is exactly the opposite of what most companies tend to do. It is psychologically difficult to go against mass movements in the industry, where Shiller's irrational exuberance effect (2000) – the fear of being left behind – definitely seems to be at work. But if companies get swept along and order new ships along with everyone else, the level of invested capital will be driven up. This, combined with the weak shipping markets that result, will make the return on capital less attractive.

On the other hand, investing in new capacity when the market is down can substantially enhance the company's return on capital and eventually its profitability. Companies that build aggressively when the market is up will fear the worst when the market is down. When that happens, it is tempting to acquire attractive second-hand tonnage, available at a considerable discount when people start to worry about oversupply. While this may be excellent thinking in theory, in practice it is hard to get access to cheap new assets. Many of the companies in the industry will have sufficient capital to be able to ride out lengthy periods of excessive capacity and low freight levels – and good second-hand tonnage may simply not be available. It is also difficult for potential buyers to gauge when the prevailing weak market conditions are near an end – so as to avoid buying too early.

Figure 6.11 shows that many of the leading container liner companies are currently avoiding investing in newbuilding for the growing container ship segments. Perhaps they realize that investing heavily when the segment is growing will tie up capital and make return on capital less spectacular. A.P. Moller-Maersk, for instance, is investing relatively less in owning container ships, taking them in on long-term time charter instead. As already noted, the number of ships owned by non-container lines is expected to grow to about 60 percent from today's 52 percent level – clear acknowledgement that the trend for specialization in shipping is set to continue.

Good timing is critical in ship acquisition, across all areas of shipping. There is no doubt, for instance, that major shipowners, such as John Fredriksen, have had greater success in buying second-hand tonnage than other unfortunate owners who overexpanded and were then forced to sell. Fredriksen's acquisition of B. Aaserød's fleet of ten VLCC tankers in 1999 is an example of good opportunistic timing.

OPTIONS FOR ADDING NEW SHIP TONNAGE

So how should a company add new ship tonnage? Through organic growth, newbuildings, acquisition of existing shipping companies, or purchasing second-hand ships? The answer is probably through all four.

- While organic growth might seem important enough to be a regular discipline for adding new capacity, particularly for large companies with large annual depreciation, it will still need to be tempered by the freight outlook cycles for ocean shipping.
- Newbuilding can be critically important, but also calls for discipline. Orders can be accelerated or decelerated, depending on the prospect of the ship freight markets. Large firms might undertake newbuilding with more regularity.
- Acquisitions of competing companies are attractive when the freight market is in a slump. John Fredriksen has been particularly good at this, with the acquisition of controlling ownership in Golden Ocean, Golar LNG, Northern Offshore, etc. Timing is critical for acquisitions. The price can be too high at the peak of the market – as we may have seen with Maersk Line's and Hapag-Lloyd's acquisitions in 2005 (Maersk took over P&O-Nedlloyd; Hapag-Lloyd took over CP Ships) – but buying when the market is low can be tremendously successful, as Maersk's happier assimilation of Safmarine and Sealand in 1999 demonstrates. Mergers and acquisitions also involve issues of corporate and cultural integration that can backfire seriously. Maersk and Hapag-Lloyd faced logistic problems, client dissatisfaction, loss of market share, etc., with their ill-fated acquisitions. Companies should either be well prepared for

integration before the merger happens or stick to acquiring smaller companies, as CMA CGM has done repeatedly with notable success.

● Attractive second-hand ships can be picked up when the market is down, or when companies face a liquidity squeeze as a consequence of having overextended their newbuilding activities, i.e., too much exposure when markets fall.

Adding new infrastructure calls for strong discipline. It will always be tempting to do the same as everyone else but flock mentality is likely to lead to bad timing and the wrong exposure.

SHIP SCRAPPING

Finally, there is a developing market for ship scrapping, as I discussed briefly in Chapter 3. Marsoft forecasts scrapping as a function of the freight rate levels in ocean shipping as well as steel prices. High freight rates mean less scrapping. The technological obsolescence that will follow from the ban on single-hull tankers from 2010 will lead to an increase in scrapping.

MACRO FACTORS THAT MAY IMPACT DEMAND FOR SHIPS

Global competitiveness is a key factor in world trade. I am not going to review world competitiveness here but refer readers to IMD's *World Competitiveness Yearbook* (2008), which gives a picture of globalization and world competitiveness changes, year on year. Page 13 of that publication gives the picture for 2008. For an interesting comparison of where countries measure today against ten years ago, see Garelli (2006).

The US takes a leading role in overall competitiveness but the picture is very different when it comes to shipping. For example, productivity in US ports and terminals lags well behind Southeast Asian ports, including Chinese ports. Liner companies cannot use state-of-the-art technology in the US terminals because practices are limited by union requirements. Expanding port capacity, which is sorely needed in both the US and Europe, can be delayed for years or even derailed completely by political interests and environmental concerns. In contrast, ship turnaround and operations are quicker and more efficient in Southeast Asia.

Shipping companies operating flags of convenience ships enjoy lower costs and competitive advantage. In 2007 Maersk decided to replace expensive Danish seafarers with cheaper international crews, as the company struggles to bounce back from the failure of its 2005 acquisitions and limit costs.

World-class skills are essential for competing in the global shipping economy. For instance, Singapore is very strong in terms of world competitiveness, and it has a strong shipping cluster – the same can be said for Denmark and Norway. This reinforces the importance of shipping clusters, as discussed in Chapter 4.

Owning, using, operating, and innovating around steel require access to different kinds of world-class skills. A key issue for operating steel is close proximity to relatively cheap labor. Many crews come from the Philippines, India, and countries in the former Eastern European bloc. Firms that use steel, like shipbrokers, are primarily found in North America, Japan, and Europe because closeness to key customers is critically important. Similarly, when it comes to innovating around steel, proximity to world-leading technical centers, typically in the US and Europe, will be key. For owning steel, there will be a focus on the lowest possible costs, financial skills, and tax advantages, where the world's economically leading countries are major players. There will thus be different key success factors for each type of shipping. The key cluster competencies and factors for owning, using, operating, and innovating around steel will not be the same. When discussing competitiveness, we need to be clear which type of shipping cluster we are discussing.

BARRIERS TO ENTRY

With the abundance of low cost capital available until recently, barriers to entry have been lowered. While scale is still important for shipowning companies, it is possible for relatively small companies to compete in the market. Many scale issues – negotiating a good purchase price, securing favorable financing, and a crewing organization that manages the fleet effectively – involve the effectiveness of particular ships. Beyond a certain minimum size, there may not be much scale advantage to gain except, as discussed, for financing and operating major series of ships.

CONCLUSION

Specialization may be the way forward for global winners. Companies may need to focus on two or three of these strategies and do them well, rather than trying to do them all.

For example, the acquisition of P&O Nedlloyd by Maersk in 2005 brought the latter indigestion, short-term losses, and loss of market share. In late 2006, the company decided to abandon the pursuit of market share at the expense of freight rate and focused instead on profitability, at least in the short term. This helped things turn around in late 2007, but not before management was replaced in the senior tiers of the company.

Investment may favor expansion in port terminal activity, as long as expansion is measured and coherent. A company cannot drive expansion uncontrollably because of its impact on terminal and ship capacity. Similarly, many liner companies opt to outsource logistic requirements to third parties to take advantage of cost savings (rather than maintaining an extensive, all-encompassing in-house logistics service).

Innovation in operating practices can boost the bottom line. At the beginning of 2008, the three top liner companies (Maersk, MSC, and CMA-CGM) created a cooperative precedent by sharing strings and slot capacity on the transpacific route, focusing on improving vessel utilization and profitability during the slump in US demand. This is in sharp contrast to developments in early 2006, immediately following the acquisition of P&O Nedlloyd from Maersk, when we saw companies trying to undercut each other by offering lower freight rates to their customers in pursuit of market share. That proved disastrous for most of the players in the industry.

Finally, competent financial management: most companies need to focus on achieving low cost of capital but some do it better than others. For example, many liner companies rely on chartering in tonnage from charter vessel owners (Seaspan, Danaos) who can obtain preferential financing terms and achieve lower newbuilding prices because of their relationships with select yards.

Owning steel, i.e., owning ships, is a matter of getting the timing right – acquiring them at a reasonable price, financing them at an acceptable cost, chartering them out at a favorable rate, etc. This calls for:

- Good forecasting of the markets, interest rates, etc., combined with an understanding of critical movements in essential underlying factors.
- Timing – above all, anticipating turning points in the freight rate market.
- A long-term view of the shipping cycle, its ups and downs and turning points.
- An opportunistic instinct – the ability to move fast when the markets are changing.
- Economies of scale – e.g., investing in series of ships of the same design when seeking new equity capital.
- Low cost of capital.
- World-class financial management skills.

7   Using steel

Trading in ships has traditionally been the domain of the ship broker-age business, with independent shipbrokers acting as the middlemen between shipowners and those with cargo to be freighted. Over the last few years, we have seen the emergence of ship freight derivatives trading – so called FFA trading. This is particularly prominent within dry bulk, but also has a smaller presence within the tanker business. There is no FFA trading within container shipping. Container liner firms do the job there – I discuss this later in this chapter.

Broadly speaking, trading is the principal focus for customer relations shipping firms – firms that use steel.[11] It includes stocks and shares, derivatives (FFAs), chartering of various sorts, and/or running ships with a special service focus – not commodity-based.

Key success factors for market-based and trading-driven shipping firms include:

- A short-term feel for the detailed movements in shipping markets, including specific turning points, is vital to spot in/out and long/short chartering opportunities as well as for seeing opportunities for equity and/or FFA derivatives trading, before they are obvious to everyone else.
- Equally vital is the ability to access relevant capital markets for one's own needs – based on a good track record, a good risk profile and, with luck, adequate capital. These markets look for a relatively stable return, and some growth in activities over time. Full exposure to swings in the freight market would not necessarily be attractive to financial investors.
- Management that has strong financial capabilities to assess its counterparties and a good understanding of the risks involved is key.

[11] I use steel to indicate all ships, including those made from aluminium, composites, etc., such as fast ferries and cruise ships.

In assessing counterparties' capabilities, it is crucial to ask if the firm will be able to live up to its obligations, above all in its ability – and willingness – to settle trade results if there are adverse market developments.

COMPETITIVE FOCUS: MUST-WIN BATTLES

Users of steel need to have a deep understanding of the shipping markets, that is, the various freight markets for goods such as oil, ore, etc., and the newbuilding and second-hand markets for ships. What are the key factors to secure competitive success?

- **In/out**. When do you enter the market? When do you get out? Experience and outlook, coupled with relevant market data, are critical factors. It is a truism that one would enter the market when it is expected to go up and exit when it is expected to fall. However, the ability consistently to judge the right timing is everything. To do this, one must keep track of underlying factors that might impact the market. While many have focused on supply-side factors, such as the availability of new tonnage, yard capacity, etc., there is strong evidence that demand-side factors, most notably those to do with levels of world trade, are of overriding importance.
- **Long/short**. Another key decision, again dependent on market expectations, is whether to go for a longer-term charter or to choose to employ one's ship in the spot market. With a rising market, one would stay in the spot market; with a falling market, one would attempt to secure a longer-term charter. However, in reality it can be difficult to implement such policies. For instance, who would grant a longer-term charter to a shipowner if market expectations were down? Unless of course, there were different market outlook expectations, you would turn this down. Alternatively, would a firm keep all its ships in the spot market, when the outlook might indicate a rising market – or would the firm's bankers insist on some longer-term chartering coverage?
- **Good shipbrokers can make the difference**. A broker and his team must be able to gauge how the markets are likely to develop to be

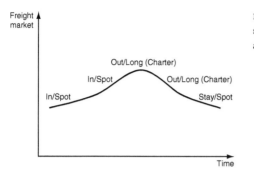

FIGURE 7.1 In/out and long/ short strategies (various market assumptions)

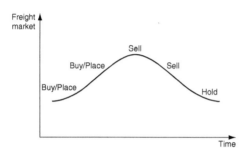

FIGURE 7.2 Buy/sell/place second-hand ships and newbuilding orders

able to initiate a chartering/trading policy along the following lines (Figure 7.1).

This is obvious when it comes to actors' behavior in relation to expected developments in the freight markets, but it is also true for the second-hand market for ships, and for the market for placing newbuilding orders (Figure 7.2).

While newbuilding orders have traditionally not been extensively traded, it is interesting to see how companies like Golden Ocean have been able to realize considerable profits by placing newbuilding orders at a suitable time, and then selling them when market expectations rise.

CUSTOMERS

Users of steel – or customer relations focused firms (Hagel and Singer, 1999) – consider their end customers and markets. However, because shipping is a commodity business, this is less visible than it is in other businesses. Nevertheless, the major customers of a leading container liner company are likely to be a wide array of manufacturers of finished goods, such as shoes (Adidas); food, pet food, drinks (Nestlé); consumer electronics (Matsushita); and so on. None of the leading container liner companies, such as A.P. Moller-Maersk, Hapag-Lloyd, Evergreen, COSCO, China Shipping, OOCL, etc., would be expected to have particular insights about the final customer in, say, the US or Europe. So who does understand the final customer? Perhaps logistics transport firms, such as Kühne + Nagel or Panalpina? Or freight parcel express firms, such as UPS and FedEx? Maybe. Let us go one step further: what about customer insight firms, such as Google or Yahoo, or even major banks, like Deutsche Bank (with their customer insight databases)? The answer there is probably yes.

Firms with in-depth information on consumer buying patterns hold knowledge that would be valuable to container shipping lines. However, container shipping lines seem to be content with understanding intermediaries rather than the final consumer. The challenge is to make container lines more consumer-oriented. It is interesting to note that A.P. Moller-Maersk appointed the head of Carlsberg – a strong consumer goods company – as its head in November 2007. A.P. Moller-Maersk owns the world's biggest container line, with a global market share of around 19 percent. Perhaps it is beginning to see this business as a true consumer business.

Another issue facing container liner shipping companies is that their key customers – major shippers like Wal-Mart, Nestlé, Nike, etc., – may dictate the establishment of certain routes to service their needs, even if they are not profitable for the shipping firms themselves. This can lead to a misunderstood concept of how to service customers. If customers have the power to dictate routes to shipping companies, the result may be excessive duplication of routes, risking the profitability of the entire industry.

Instead, container liner shipping companies may want to focus only on routes that are profitable for them. This may mean that one container line's customer ends up with another container line on another route – a route that would have been unprofitable for the first container line but is profitable for the second. In order for this to work, the key container shipping lines would need to view shipping routes as a global network, similar to what we find in the airline industry. It is still very important to attempt to maintain some sense of power vis-à-vis the customer. The issue of speed and service now vs. cost and later delivery may be the key to understanding how to establish this. But with the advent of skyrocketing bunker prices until recently, many container shipping lines are considering running their ships at slower speeds. A reduction from twenty five knots to eighteen knots can reduce bunker expenses by 50 percent – but the containers arrive a little later. Does the shipper truly care? Is the container liner shipping company losing bargaining power?

For commodity-type firms, on the other hand, one could argue that it is not the individual end customer but the market that is important. The movements of the dry bulk shipping market and/or the tanker market are representative of cost-driven customers. Trading firms, such as Cargill, see the ship markets as surrogates for individual cost-driven customers. Low cost performance is what the market – the customer – is looking for.

Another category of customer relations-focused firms is the highly specialized shipping firm in, for example, dredging freight of olive oil, wine, orange juice, etc. Although many of these niche players are shipowning firms, they are classified as customer relations specialists because their major focus is on customer service – the unique features of the ships that carry these specialized goods – rather than costs. A major consideration for such firms is assessing the likelihood of the eventual commoditization of the specialist shipping niche they are in. Other owners are likely to copy them. But how quickly will imitation become a problem?

THE IMPORTANCE OF BRAND

Branding plays an important role when it comes to customer-related shipping activities, such as container liner shipping. Maersk, Evergreen,

COSCO, Hapag-Lloyd, OOCL, and others all represent strong brands in container liner shipping, standing for quality, regularity, service, etc.

For the typical commodity type segments of the shipping business, such as bulkers or tankers, branding has a relatively limited role. What matters here is the ship. It must be of a certain minimum standard, but beyond this, the most important issue is delivering at the lowest cost. Branding is of little or no consequence.

FORWARD TRADING INSTRUMENTS

Let us now discuss in more detail some of the instruments (terms and concepts) available for forward trading in customer relations-focused users of steel.

Paper trading in shipping (FFAs) have become almost ten times bigger in the dry bulk segment than in the tanker segment – IMAREX estimated this to be about US$80 billion for bulk carriers by the end of 2007 and about US$8 billion for tankers by the end of 2007. Why the difference?

FFAs are typically used for hedging, but they can also be used for speculation. Klaveness is perhaps one example of a firm that might use FFAs primarily for hedging, while TMT is an example of a firm that might make relatively more use of FFAs for speculation. When it comes to using FFAs for speculation, one might appropriately use the word "bet," while the term "cash-settled trading instrument used to manage freight exposures" might be more appropriate to use when hedging.

Differences in industry structures between the dry bulk and tanker businesses can explain a lot. There is a relatively small number of oil companies that certify a number of tanker shipowners and then engage in freight contracts with them. There are some additional actors, notably oil traders, in the tankers market but the number is still relatively small.

In contrast, there are many more actors in the dry bulk market. There are numerous shipowners, and many operators act as middlemen and take bulk-carriers on charter. The number of actors demanding dry bulk tonnage is also much larger. The sheer number of actors meets a key condition for the development of an active FFA market.

Within the tanker segment, we see much more specialized tonnage than is the case for bulk-carriers, the design of which is much more standardized. This is a key determinant impacting the relative prominence in freight derivatives trading in the dry segment compared to the wet segment.

Differences in the typical ship structure between wet and dry might also play a role. For dry ships – bulk-carriers – standard firm charters specify that charter costs will be paid by the ship's owner. For tankers, on the other hand, the charters are settled through the much more complicated world-scale, which is affected both by bunker prices – now to be paid by the charterer – and by currency concerns – all to be calculated well after the time period that the physical shipping takes place. This is a much more complex way of doing business, and detrimental to paper trading in tankers.

Forward freight agreements – derivatives

What is a forward freight agreement (FFA)? An FFA is a contract where a buyer and a seller are committed for a given volume (tons or days) at a specified price for a specific route or basket of routes on a specific vessel. Essentially, it is a bet on the future value of one or more freight indices, set by the Baltic Exchange (or by Platts). The contract is for the difference between a trade price and a settlement price, where the trade price is at time t and the settlement price is at time $t+x$ and is based on the average daily index value, now typically over one month. For most of the standard trade routes, time charter average rates are now typically settled against the average for the entire month. This implies that there is less possibility for a particular shipping company to influence the market to support its own paper position. The freight index consists of inputs every day on six model trade routes by eleven independent brokers, monitored by the Baltic Exchange.

As noted, the basic bulk and crude oil shipping segments represent large global commodity markets. Both the tanker and dry cargo shipping markets are in transition toward becoming the platforms for large financial derivatives markets. Shipping freight derivatives trading is now an established market showing strong annual growth. There is a great need for an exchange as this market matures.

IMAREX is the only worldwide marketplace where freight derivatives can be traded, on the screen, between suppliers and demanders. The company is authorized by the Norwegian Credit Surveillance Authority (Kredittilsynet). To complement this, there are four clearing platforms for FFA contracts:

- NOS in Oslo
- London Clearing House (LCH) in London
- Singapore Exchange (SGX) in Singapore
- New York Mercantile Exchange (NYMEX) in New York – which does a limited amount of clearance in the tanker segment only.

One important task of an exchange like IMAREX is to provide *clearing solutions*. Strictly speaking, IMAREX might not be seen as an exchange, as it is not regulated like a typical exchange. Rather, IMAREX can perhaps better be seen as a trading screen, which clears through NOS Clearing ASA. There are also other trading screens, but none of them have taken off in the market as of the end of 2008. This means that – motivated by the pressure put on the performance of controversial companies such as Enron and others – credit approval is now more strictly monitored and set. Lack of transparency makes it increasingly difficult to judge whether shipping companies are bona fide counterparts in trades. Often, however, smaller companies enter the market with volatile earning patterns. Some of these firms would not even be qualified to get credits from the major oil companies. Hence, strong credit approval procedures and enforcement are essential. A clearing possibility increases the probability of matching deals, and thus increases liquidity in the derivatives business. In short, derivatives trading and arbitrage have become important elements of understanding risk management through a more dynamic cycle management approach toward the strategic positioning. So-called margining would be the posting of collateral with the clearinghouse, from the day of the trade until expiry of the contract.

There are, however, a few clear disadvantages of trading on the IMAREX market, particularly when a shipping firm is caught with the wrong position – short in a rising market or long in a declining market. In these circumstances, the shipping firm will have to inject additional funds, which means that considerable liquid reserves are required to stay with the clearinghouse until the money losing position is back to zero.

These trading-related risks must now be managed. The approach to follow is "good must always be done better." A critical part of this managerial competence needs to come from a company's own finance department. FFA trading is becoming an important financial tool for leading shipping companies. They must be able to undertake many types of forward trading and hedging, i.e., manage the risks related not only to FFA trading, but to a hedging function too, particularly interest rate developments and currency rate swap developments.

Let me give an example of a firm that is heavily involved in FFA trading as part of its shipping strategy. TMT Corporation is head-quartered in Taipei, Taiwan and headed by Nobu Su. The company is privately held and owns a fleet of approximately sixty directly owned ships, including large bulk carriers, ro-ro ships and LNG carriers. It also has around ninety ships on order. In addition, TMT constantly charters in a variety of ships.

TMT started FFA trading in the fall of 2004. According to the *Financial Times*, TMT accounts for up to 30 percent of all global FFA trading (Wright, 2008d, p. 19). Many observers think that there might have been a relationship between TMT's physical fleet of ships and the firm's activities buying and selling financial products based on future shipping costs. Since the early part of 2008, TMT's paper trading activities have dropped significantly and are reported to be virtually zero as of the end of 2008.

Nobu Su confirmed that there is a link between TMT's shipping activities and its position in the paper market. He claims, however, that the key to TMT's success is his superior understanding of the shipping markets. He feels his close link with major customers for ship transportation services is key.

Nobu Su's strategy for FFA trading is simple – when the market is on the up, invest before others and, conversely, when it is on a downward trend, sell before others. The *Financial Times* reports:

> For much of 2007 TMT was betting on increases in freight rates for dry bulk ships – a position that was justified by the markets reaching almost unprecedented rates of about $120,000 a day to charter Capesize ships, the largest kind. However, towards the end of the year, TMT, based on Mr Su's conviction that iron ore consumption was falling and ships were in oversupply, started betting on a downturn. Capesize rates then went still higher to reach record peaks just short of $190,000 a day. Many observers believe the wrong bet cost TMT hundreds of millions of dollars, but Mr Su says he broke even for the second part of 2007. He was betting – correctly – on rates for oil tankers to rise at the same time as betting on falling bulk rates. Just before Christmas rates for very large crude carriers – the largest kind – reached a record level of about $270,000 a day. The dry bulk market seems to have continued to run against him this year. He profited from a sharp fall in dry bulk markets early this year, but markets have since rebounded to new record levels. Average Capesize rates set a new record yesterday of $231,593 a day. Mr Su nevertheless insists there is a fundamental oversupply of dry bulk ships. He also insists the likely phasing out of single hull crude oil tankers will drive rates for oil tankers up – even though rates for very large crude carriers have weakened in recent weeks to about $150,000 a day. 'We are still short on dry and long on tankers,' Mr Su says in summarizing TMT's position (Wright, 2008d).

Let us now briefly review the use of FFAs at T. Klaveness, done within the Klaveness Commercial Management division (KCM).

FFAs are used in two main ways within KCM:

- in two spot pools, mainly used for hedging activities on behalf of different ship owners – Bulkhandling-Handymax AS and Baumarine AS (Panamax);
- in trading and portfolio management activities (responsible for Klaveness proprietary trading within the standardized bulk segments Supramax, Panamax, and Capesize).

The KCM portfolio consists of vessels taken in and relet on time charter, contracts of affreightment (CoAs) and FFAs, including FFA options. Most of Klaveness' vessels and cargoes are entered into the two pools, which are structured to give a spot return exchange index. Klaveness is able to handle the portfolio as a financial portfolio consisting of CoAs, time charters and FFAs. In this way, Klaveness is in a position to use the different products and instruments to offset unwanted risk, take exposure in the market it considers best value, and use the different instruments and markets available in order to structure transactions for the pool of customers and for the company itself. This toolbox is used to tailor risk/revenue profiles in line with each individual shipowner's needs. If Klaveness is going to be able to deliver attractive risk management products to the market and manage its own risks, FFAs are critical for its daily activities. Furthermore, with the high volatility in the FFA markets, Klaveness is able to take short-term market positions according to well-defined and monitored risk mandates, allowing it to generate a healthy return on capital. Most trading parties typically set maximum self-imposed limits. These typically would be determined internally by credit – and market – risk analysts.

As discussed, a lot of new liquidity has come into the shipping industry. The advent of freight forward trading has become a driving force for attracting new capital and new players. The freight derivatives markets represent a new asset class that has low correlations with other commodities and financial assets. This is particularly important when it comes to the development of more robust corporate portfolio strategies.

While derivatives trading has gained a lot of ground over the past few years – above all in the dry bulk trades, but also in wet tanker cargos – according to Aury and Steen (2005, p. 28), interest is also developing in a container derivatives market. A number of principals and brokers are in the process of developing an index for these products, both for freight and asset values. The area of most interest is creating a tradable container-based product, analogous to FFA bulk products. The main problem, however, seems to be that there is relatively little spot activity in the container ship sector. Most of the ships are on long-term charters to container operators. In today's relatively robust market, there may be relatively little short-term trading.

Freight derivatives (FFA) trading in shipping depends on two main factors:

- that there are a number of actors on both sides – if too few, the paper trading will not work;
- that there is a commonly accepted, fair, and equitable freight index.

If these two factors are present, freight derivatives trading activities will not only flourish but also generate liquidity.

Pairs of actors – each on their own side of the paper trading – can only trade with each other up to a given maximum limit. Once this is exceeded the trades will have to be cleared. The liquidity benefits will be less when clearing. Still, FFA trading is far less capital intensive than owning ships.

Trading in the dry bulk derivatives market is now more or less like any other type of commodity trading. Typical commodities include grain, aluminum, coal, minerals, and even steel. Iron ore, however, is not yet a basis for freight derivatives trading. We are talking about a few large producers/shippers (BHP Billiton, Rio Tinto, Vale) and one critical importing country, China. These players prefer long-term contracts between themselves to derivatives trading. While steel futures are not common (as of the end of 2008), they do exist on a limited scale. And BHP Billiton is reported (end 2008) to supply iron ore to certain Chinese steel mills on an index-linked pricing basis. While still small, both steel and iron ore futures are foreseen to grow in use in the future.

Why has freight derivatives trading not become central to management in container shipping? Container ships are chartered to liner operators, and each container is part of the liner operator's working assets. It would cost more per container to send one single container than to send 1,000. There is no standard product, nor standard freight forward index to rely on.

Is it thus realistic to create a market for FFA trading in container shipping? There are three competing options:

1 Time charters. These tend to be long in container shipping, and it would be difficult to have them as a base for trading.
2 Synthetic indexes for freights (e.g., a daily time charter rate for model vessels). But how can such an index be developed realistically, particularly when there is an almost total absence of short-term trades for container ships?
3 Real TEU freight costs (i.e., basing trading on the real cost of shipping a TEU on a particular standardized route). Again, the real costs of each operator may vary – large mega-carriers set very low-cost standards. Would this be acceptable to all?

Perhaps one can conclude that FFA trading may simply not lend itself to the container business. But, despite the number of issues and difficulties ahead, there nevertheless seems to be a clear move toward developing a container-based derivatives market similar to the FFA markets for dry and wet cargos. However, there are many different types of container ships and it may be difficult to know which type of standard vessel to select as a base for indexes for developing an FFA-type product for the container industry. Strategic positioning, as part of more dynamic management of the freight rate cycle, can provide increased operating flexibility, in as much as one might take advantage of hedging opportunities to improve performance. Hedging instruments are an important part of a professional management approach in shipping companies.

Let us now look at the strategy for Clarkson Shipping Hedge Fund. This fund emphasizes trading in FFAs as well as in stock equities, based on its management's fundamental view of the long-term opportunities in the global shipping markets. Clarkson Hedge Fund is not the only freight fund. Others would be Castalia, Tufton, and GMI. Each of these freight funds employs their own strategy, as combinations of all or parts of physical chartering, owning shipping equities, and FFA paper trading swaps and/or options.

The fund invests in the tanker and dry bulk markets, through freight derivatives and equities. It aims to take advantage of the high volatility, cyclicality, and relative lack of sophistication in the growing freight derivatives market. The fund presently has a mix of FFAs that focuses 80 percent on the dry bulk market and 20 percent on the tanker market. It also invests in stocks of a select number of listed shipping-related firms. The current mix of FFAs and equities is roughly 50/50.

This balanced mix of shares and derivatives expands the fund's pool of liquidity, increases the diversification, and augments the fund's opportunities for short selling. It also gives Clarkson the potential to exploit any mispricing between shipping derivatives and equity markets (Clarkson Shipping Hedge Fund, 2007).

UBS BLUE SEA INDEX

UBS launched its UBS Blue Sea Index, a tradable investment index built on FFAs, to exploit the growing interest in shipping futures. The FFA market has grown to about US$125 billion (February 2008), compared to US$50 billion in 2007. Banks and hedge funds account for 40 percent of this. "Banks and hedge funds have helped drive this market as they now make up a large slice of the volumes. Interest in the field has thus grown as the credit risk has, in effect, closed other markets, such as asset-backed securities, forcing banks and funds to look for other ways to make profits" (Oakley, 2008). Banks that are active in FFAs include Citigroup, Merrill Lynch, Macquarie Bank, Goldman Sachs, Credit Suisse, Lehman Brothers, Morgan Stanley, and UBS. Large hedge funds that are active in FFAs include GMI and

Akuila Okeanos (Davies, 2008, p. 29). "UBS believes that the index will attract investors who seek some refuge from the volatility in financial and equity markets, but who retain an appetite for the exposure to the further expansion of China's economy. Underpinning this new interest in shipping is evidence of the explosive growth in freight derivatives. In 2007, the freight derivatives market more than doubled to US$117 billion from US$55 billion a year earlier, and it is forecast to climb by another 20 percent this year, as more banks and hedge funds get into the market" (Bray 2008).

Problems with derivatives

As noted, the FFA market is relatively new – according to Aury and Steen (2005), the first such arrangement was made in 1992 for dry cargo, in 1995 for tankers, and in 2001 for the first cleared trade. There are several potential problems with derivatives like FFAs, including:

- **Lack of significant steel manufacturing sector participation**. According to Aury and Steen (2005), there is still relatively little involvement in the FFA markets from the steel manufacturing sector. While many of these companies are used to trading/hedging when it comes to raw materials, they seem reluctant to get into FFAs when it comes to shipping their raw materials and their finished products. An analogous argument can be made for most of the world's shipbuilding sector – a reluctance to get into FFAs relating to steel.
- **Lack of credits and clearing capacity**. While this is still a problem for FFAs, more capital is now coming into this market segment and clearing capacity is being developed more effectively. Adequate free liquidity is a prerequisite for any realistic market mechanism to work and all participants involved must be able to live up to their obligations.
- **Perception**. Many actors in the shipping markets may still not see FFAs as entirely natural or legitimate. There is still a lot of skepticism associated with these types of trading activities. This is understandable, given that a shipowner will have a wide array of other instruments that

can be made use of – time charters, bare-boat charters, contracts of affreightment, equity positions in other firms, and so on. For each of these instruments, the actor can now also decide to trade, i.e., go short versus long or vice versa. In other words, there are already a lot of trading possibilities, so they may well ask, "Why do we need FFAs?" One answer is that FFAs open the door to trade in smaller units rather than in entire ships (I am omitting trading in stocks). Another reason is that they may offer more flexibility for attracting new capital to the industry and for bringing in new players.

Other trading instruments are also being developed (Aury and Steen, 2005). These include:

- **Sell Purchase Forward Agreements for ships (SPFAs)**. This option is becoming more and more popular, as shipowners want to lock in specific future values for their ships, particularly in rising markets. Residual value considerations can represent significant uncertainty for many shipping projects. SPFAs might ameliorate this.
- **Demolition Forward Agreements (DFA)**. These follow the same type of reasoning, where a shipowner can lock in the price for demolition x years in the future.

Freight forward derivatives markets are definitely here to stay. But the quality of these new market mechanisms must be adequate. Aury and Steen (2005) identify some key requirements for a successful derivatives market:

- There must be a realistic amount of liquidity underlying the market. The influx of new capital will play a positive role here.
- There has to be a set of clear yardstick trades to which all players in these markets can relate. This must be straightforward and standard so that panels of reputable shipbroker firms can set daily rates for these standard trades in an unambiguous way. The freight index must be reliable, realistic, and reasonable, indicating objective prices. The Baltic Exchange has succeeded in this, issuing a daily authoritative index relating to the FFA markets.

- There must be interest in a particular type of trade from a wide set of market participants. Interest in SPFAs and DFAs now seems to be sufficiently broad.
- The settlement price must be clear and unambiguous. It helps if players can rely on one particular index, like the one provided by the Baltic Exchange. It may be more difficult to reach a meaningful settlement price in the wet market, where "world scale" implies putting an ideal value for the dollar as the base for calculation at a given point in time. It can be difficult to find a true settlement price until quite a long time after settlement has been made, because of lack of clarity as to what the dollar price was at the point of trade.
- Large, sudden price fluctuations, evaporating liquidity, and irrational behavior from some participants can make the FFA market frustrating to operate in.

For one or more of these reasons it is difficult to develop derivatives trading instruments within areas like:

- **The container market.** There have been attempts to develop instruments for TEU trading and there is reason to be optimistic about coming up with realistic FFAs here. However, the potentiality of trading and arbitrage has largely failed for container liner shipping so far. There is no index that tracks container box rates. However, companies like Intra, a spin-off from A.P. Moller-Maersk, may be able to spearhead a movement in this direction. Intra is presently engaged in putting cargos together, for various shippers to fill containers more efficiently. Intra's services are paid for by container shipping operators.
- **The offshore supply market.** The main problem here is the inability to identify standard trades. Offshore supply ships operate all over the world on specific projects relating to the development and exploration of offshore oil and gas fields. It would be hard to come up with a few standard trades that might be commonly agreed upon.
- **The LNG market.** The main problem in this market is the relative lack of shorter term market activities, as most of these ships will be tied up on long-term charters – as part of full-fledged supply chains.

TRADING TERMS

I'd like to delineate further a few trading terms involving FFAs or stocks/shares.

Options vs. swaps

A premium is paid for options, whereas there is no premium for swaps. One would tend to enter into an option agreement when there is an uncertain environment and a swap when the environment is more certain. Options are typically used in more uncertain environments, as the most one can lose on one's hedge is the premium one will have paid for it. Of course, one will benefit when favorable market movements occur.

Puts vs. calls

Momentum is critical in markets: when they go up, they will continue to go up in the same way, at least in the short term – and vice versa, when they go down. Turning points are relatively rare – but when they happen they are of critical importance. In rising markets, call options will be underpriced and relatively cheap. However, you must be careful about buying call options in falling markets – as well as put options in rising markets. You buy put options when the market is expected to continue going down. A charterer or operator, who may be short in a freight position, can hedge by buying a call option. In contrast, a ship-owner or operator who may be long in a freight position can hedge by buying a put option. Similarly, a hedge fund can buy options to take a view of the market with much smaller downsides than through an FFA. Turning points do happen, though, and spell disappointment and losses for actors with put/call strategies. Koekebakker *et al.* (2006) have analyzed the pricing of freight put/call options for FFAs with their forward/put–call options with reference to the pricing of so-called "Asian style freight derivatives." Their model gives very accurate expected price estimates, especially from this type of forward trading freight option. This provides a relevant tool for pricing options generally.

Clarkson Shipping Hedge Fund has lost on some of its put options, but gained a lot on most of its call options. If the market does not change, Clarkson Shipping Hedge Fund loses money, but if the markets go up or down it gains. Market volatility is good for forward traders, just as it is for most shipowners.

Stocks and shares

Now let's move on to trading in stocks and shares, of which J. Lauritzen provides a good example. The company is not heavily engaged in FFA-type trading: it buys and sells shipping company shares instead, distinguishing between two types of company share trade positions.

- **Trade.** This involves buying and selling for profits, based purely on an understanding of the underlying freight market and the company's ship values.
- **Target.** These are long-term holdings, perhaps with a view to taking over a given company at some point in the future. These shipping firms would fit into Lauritzen's portfolio strategy – to add growth in dry bulk, product tankers, and/or small gas carriers.

Rate forecasts in each specific business segment (dry/wet/gas) are also essential for understanding the movements of stocks/shares for both trading as well as owning ships. It is important for J. Lauritzen to be consistent when it comes to the market outlook/rate forecasts for both trading activities and shipowning activities within each market segment (dry/wet/gas), as they are done by the same groups of executives.

So trading is perceived as being part of shipping. Because of this, trading results (from shares and a few FFAs) are part of this particular shipping segment's profit and loss statements (for the dry, wet, or gas segments respectively). Although J. Lauritzen is a steel-owning firm – it owns a large fleet of ships – it is still characterized as a market-focused specialist, particularly in its activities within the dry bulk and product tanker segments. The small gas carrier segment, on the other hand, is more of a long-term industrial shipping activity. Both types of specialization are going on under the same shipping roof, i.e., bulk-carriers and product tankers versus small gas carriers. Trading, however, only takes place within the more mature, established dry bulk and tanker segments.

Though trading in shares/stocks is seen as part of shipping, it has not always developed as expected, judging from movement in the freight markets. This is partly because relatively few shipping companies can be classified as strictly in one particular market segment. Finding a "pure" shipping company to relate to specific freight market movements for the relevant underlying trades may be difficult.

There can also be special circumstances. Jinhui, the Hong Kong-based bulk carrier shipowning company, is an example. Jinhui is controlled by two Chinese families residing in Hong Kong. The stock price was expected to fall during the spring/summer of 2007, but Greek owners then bought a 10 percent stake in the company, leading to a higher stock price. This sort of development can lead to unexpected price changes for shares/stocks that could not have been foreseen by strictly following freight market forecasts.

TIME CHARTERS

Time charter activities, bare-boat charters, and CoAs open up another way of trading. Here, a user of steel might take ships in on charter at a fixed price when the market is expected to rise in subsequent periods in time. The ships would then be relet, i.e., chartered out again, if the freight market was expected to drop in the future.

Frontline

Frontline is listed on the NYSE and has been controlled by John Fredriksen since 1996. Frontline has exclusive charter agreements with both Shell and BP for the use of very large crude carriers (VLCCs). Frontline's single-hull tankers are being modified to oil production ships, in time for the 2010 deadline for double-hull tankers.

Golden Ocean

Golden Ocean, previously a Canadian company that owned both large tankers and bulk carriers, is listed on the Oslo stock exchange. John Fredriksen bought the majority of its shares in 2000. The tankers were taken over by Frontline and the company was converted into a publicly listed bulk shipping company. In late 2007, the company had an impressive fleet of large bulk carriers on order: twelve Panamaxes, eight Kamsarmaxes, and eleven Capesize bulk carriers. A major source of revenue was to sell some of the ships on order before they were delivered – a lucrative move in an increasingly expensive newbuilding market.

The company has since split into a shipowning part and a steel-using operating and trading part, analogous to what Fredriksen's steel-using company, Frontline, did with its affiliated shipowning company, Ship Finance.

Golden Ocean has developed an impressive approach to trading on newbuilding orders. Newbuilding contracts have been entered into at relatively low prices and the company has subsequently sold several of those contracts at a considerable gain.

Western Bulk

Western Bulk is a successful company that focuses exclusively on trading within the dry bulk segment. It has chartered in more than sixty bulk carriers, primarily in the Handymax segment, but also in Panamax and Handysize tonnage. The company has six offices worldwide, and its trading is broken into seven teams with total profit and loss responsibility. Cargo contracts are entered into for different durations, and combined with various trading patterns to fill the ships, minimize empty back-loss and achieve synergy.

Managing risk is a critical success factor for a firm that follows an exclusive trading-only business model. Western Bulk has built up a four-dimensional approach to risk management:

1 The board and top management define maximum risk limits.
2 An independent risk management department assesses all transactions and reports directly to the CEO.

3 The company uses a model for quantifying risk for every CoA and FFA entered into.

4 There are clear counterparty risk approval procedures for FFAs.

After several difficult years and net losses in 2006, the company made a remarkable turnaround in 2007. Its top management attributes its success to the strong bulk shipping markets and the organization's disciplined involvement in a pure trading-oriented business (Western Bulk Annual Report, 2007, p. 8, 12).

PURCHASE OPTIONS

It is becoming more and more important to have purchase options that might be executed at the end of a charter – *assuming that the owner is willing to grant them*. J. Lauritzen reports that a three-year time charter for a Panamax bulk carrier, entered into three years ago with a US$21 million purchase option at the end of the charter, can be resold today for US$65 million. A purchase option would allow charterers to have much more active participation in any upward movement in the underlying asset value. Needless to say, the owner of the asset gives up a vehicle for value creation and will not necessarily be willing to do so. However, negotiation power comes into effect here – the owner may have had to do this to secure the charter in the first place.

In general, one should try to buy ships when the market is expected to go up. It is difficult to get out of long-term time charters and cut one's losses when the market is falling. On the other hand, owners always have the option to sell ships, even if they have to do so at a loss, i.e., an effective stop-loss policy. This underlines the dilemma of time charters: they are certainly more risky than owning, but they prove that you can make good money without owning steel.

THE ROLE OF AGENTS

Shipbrokers are a prominent category of customer relations specialist firms and can be an important type of agent. But can they always be fully trusted? Would shipowners want to deal directly with the customers and/or the market?

Certain shipowning firms, such as Seaspan, working with only one type of customer – container line operators – will want to deal directly with customers. Seaspan's CEO, Gerry Wang, aims to deal directly with the top management of all its customers, which include around seven of the largest container liner firms.

While commission will be saved, a more important reason for dealing directly with the customer is that it may be counterproductive to have a broker in the middle. This raises the questions of who the broker works for and what the broker's priorities really are.

For many other infrastructure firms in the basic bulk or tanker business, it would be almost impossible to go directly to the customers. Shipbrokers are necessary, but a potential problem with using them is that they may be transaction oriented, rather than relations oriented. Because their fees result from transactions, they may be motivated to arrange as many chartering transactions as possible, as opposed to better and longer-term charters to the benefit of the shipowners. Since there is a real incentive to enter into a charter, at almost any price, the infrastructure owner could end up being short changed by terms that favor the customer. Because of this, many shipowning firms have their own chartering activities to safeguard against potential opportunism from independent chartering companies/ship brokers/customer relations specialized firms.

Shipbrokers are prone to more potential conflicts of interest than those operating in other commodity businesses, such as oil, gas, etc., which have more direct trading activities. The perceived lack of neutrality of some shipbrokers may be an impediment to trading in shipping. On the other hand, a good broker can provide effective facilitation, by bringing relevant parties together. While some companies, like Seaspan, make little use of brokers, others, like General Maritime, use them extensively for developing their business focus. Both companies are leaders within the shipping business – but their reliance on brokers differs.

CARGILL: A CUSTOMER RELATIONS
SPECIALIST – USER OF STEEL

Cargill, the world's largest privately held firm, has major worldwide activities in agribusiness and is also one of the world's largest ocean shipping trading companies. This part of Cargill's business has seven offices worldwide with a total of 190 employees. It chartered in a physical volume of 150 million tonnes in 2006 and traded about 100 million tonnes of freight derivatives. The time charters, in terms of vessels chartered in, went up from 45 vessels in 1995 to 250 vessels in 2006. The FFA volume grew from 15 million metric tonnes in FFA contracts in 1999 to 140 million metric tonnes in FFA contracts in 2006. The physical volumes handled grew from 58 million metric tonnes in 1998 – of which only 10 million were external – to 150 million metric tonnes in 2005, more than half of which were external.

Until 2000, when it sold all of its ships, Cargill was in chartering, trading, and shipowning businesses. After that, it became a pure customer relations specialist firm in chartering and trading. Cargill has redefined itself to deal with different types of risks vis-à-vis the customer, rather than seeing itself as a conventional chartering and trading firm. Its risk-handling capabilities include bunker costs, foreign exchange rates, credit risks, charter party risks, contract risks, operational risks, and so on.

In summary, Cargill has gone from a pure trading and chartering company to one that works with various types of risks, on behalf of the customer, to come up with the best possible deal via various types of trading. Cargill relies not only on FFAs, but also on the chartering in and out of ships, currency swapping, and the active use of other instruments. All of this is done to serve the customer, with a strong residual profit for Cargill.

BARRIERS TO ENTRY

Companies involved in customer relations shipping activities tend to be smaller and the competitive advantage or barrier to entry comes from the people employed – their skills, their relational abilities with suppliers and customers, and their understanding of the market dynamics. Scope – not size – dictates barriers to entry in this category. Brands are also important, because customers associate brands with trust, quality, and the best people.

DFDS

DFDS, based in Copenhagen, operates a total of sixty four ships and is active in five business segments:

● ro-ro shipping
● container shipping
● passenger shipping
● terminal services
● trailer services

The company also attempts to deliver integrated freight sales solutions to major customers, integrating several or all five business areas. While all five business entities are independent, there is clear coordination vis-à-vis major customers. Computer-based support is critical for achieving this (Figure 7.3).

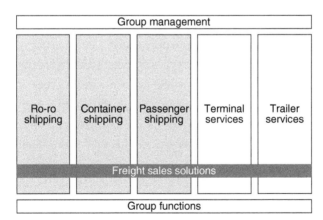

FIGURE 7.3 DFDS overall strategy
Source: DFDS Annual Report 2007, Copenhagen, p. 7.

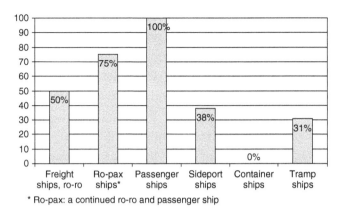

FIGURE 7.4 DFDS ownership share per ship type (%)
Source: DFDS Annual Report 2007, Copenhagen, p. 10.

The ownership share per ship type varies in relation to the ship's specialization. All else being equal, a low ownership share represents a better opportunity to run an effective operation. Figure 7.4 gives the ownership rates for each ship type. We can see from this that DFDS sees itself primarily as an operator of ship services – a liner organization – rather than an owner of steel.

CRITICAL SUCCESS FACTORS FOR USING STEEL

When trading in freight derivatives such as FFAs and FFA options, the shipping company will have to look for "mispricing" relative to prevailing charter rates in various markets. FFAs require a thorough understanding of which way the markets are going.

Basic stock market position-taking opportunities, based on anticipated patterns of movements for stocks/equities in shipping companies, are important sources for trading. This also includes obligations/warrants and the in-between convertibles, with stocks at the other end of the scale. In addition to understanding the movements in the freight markets, and the corresponding links to the stock market, traders must also understand the fundamentals of the specific companies in which they plan to invest. Fleet composition, chartering policies (including the portion of the fleet to be chartered out long versus the portion that is open), as well as the financial position – above all the free cash flow (after servicing debt) and cost breakevens – are critical.

The less liquid, over-the-counter (OTC) market is particularly important when it comes to trading in derivatives. It is advantageous to know which counterparties one is dealing with to avoid liquidity risks. More exclusive information, which comes from being close to specific deals in the market, will also be important. A realistic assessment of a counterparty's liquidity position, to assess whether he can realistically fulfill a trade put, is key.

It goes without saying that any sort of insider trading is unethical and unacceptable. Nevertheless, the freight derivatives futures OTC markets are not as tightly regulated as the stock markets are. Because of this, it is important to have a general understanding of "who is who" – and certainly not illegal to do so. It is useful to distinguish between general market intelligence, which is legal, and insider intelligence, which is not. Acting on general information available in the marketplace is fine; acting on unique specific insights only available to one party is breaking the law.

Every shipping company has its own operating costs and financial structures. It is particularly important to understand this when it comes to focusing on stocks and shares, since the firms with the lowest breakeven points are better able to withstand extended periods of depressed shipping rates and better equipped to implement new projects, particularly when the markets are down. This also applies to FFAs associated with specific firms. Free cash flow, based on low breakeven points, is critical.

Understanding the markets is crucial for timing, i.e., knowing when to commit to shorter-term or longer-term charters and CoAs, longer-term or shorter-term positions in stocks/shares, and time horizons for FFAs. This also applies to put/call options.

Shipbrokers and other market forecast-based specialized firms must have a strong organizational capability if they are going to handle trading-related, finance-focused, operational engineering and related activities. They must understand the markets, i.e., the mentality of traders and be able to execute in this context. They must be able to manage a diverse set of strategic knowledge types, all relevant for these tasks – in other words, to connect brains. Different disciplines must work together effectively within a trading-focused, specialized firm.

CONCLUSION

This chapter has focused on viewing trading in ship-related derivatives and chartering as vehicles that provide a means of developing a shipping strategy. With the growth of the freight derivatives markets – both dry and wet – there is no longer a need physically to own ships. Companies can take trading positions instead. Trading in FFAs has grown and several trading platforms are available, of which IMAREX is the most developed.

The growth of derivatives trading is another indication of the high degree of professionalization within the shipping industry, related to a prominent focus on financial understanding. Companies that are successfully making use of derivatives trading include Frontline, Golden Ocean, Western Bulk, and Cargill.

Despite the growth in FFA trading, it has a number of limitations, of which the most important is the sheer volatility and risk associated with it. The parties involved must be solid, and have sufficient liquidity to settle on deals into which they have entered. Some areas within shipping, notably container shipping, are too heterogeneous to allow for the development of an FFA trading market.

Chartering remains a major feature of shipping. By chartering in tonnage, companies can operate significant fleets without outright ownership. Western Bulk and Frontline are good examples of this. A good understanding of the market – in/out, short/long – and turning points is critical for a successful chartering strategy.

Finally, there is trading on newbuilding contracts – ordering newbuildings and calculating on a subsequent rise in newbuilding prices. Golden Ocean is a good example of a firm that has extensively followed this strategy. Recently, Golden Ocean has, however, not been able to follow this strategic path due to lack of potential buyers in the market.

8   Operating steel

An important complement to the shipowning segment is the operation of ships. Integrated ship management services are comprised of
crewing, ship management, vessel inspection, and crew training.
Companies that operate ships must deliver quality services in a cost
effective, transparent, and consistent way. Compliance is increasingly part of this. Leading operations providers within this area
of shipping are OSM, V. Group, Thome, Schulte Dynacom Tankers
Management, Univis, International Tanker Management (ITM), and
Wallem. Much of the driving force behind these companies comes
from Southeast Asia, but with know-how links to more traditional
shipping areas such as Europe and the US.

Critical success factors in this segment are safety, regularity,
and efficient operations, particularly when it comes to crewing,
inspections, routines, dry-docking, etc. Many shipowning firms have
subcontracted their operations to specialized ship-operating companies, or run the operations side of their business through separate
business units, often located in East Asia, Southeast Asia (including
Sri Lanka), the Philippines, Singapore, etc. Eastern European countries,
Ukraine, and countries of the former Soviet Union are also sources of
good quality, reasonably inexpensive crews. Some shipping companies
have developed specialized schools to train their crews to perform
better in the context of modern ship technology. Companies rely on
the major providers listed earlier for crewing and day-to-day operations. For example, the operations of the Fredriksen-controlled Ship
Finance fleet are managed by V. Group, ITM, Wallem, and Thome.
This mode of operating normally works well. However, when a major
accident (or near accident) occurs, the picture can be a little bit
more blurred.

Cost efficiency is critical, which is one of the reasons why technical management and crewing have geographically moved to Asia, where this manpower-intensive activity can often be undertaken by operating companies exploiting lower salaries in the region. Outsourcing implies a variable cost for ship owners, in contrast to the fixed costs they would have if they ran the ships themselves. A problem with this approach is being able to hire highly qualified crews. There is a shortage of good crews, even in Southeast Asia. Reputable ship operating companies, such as V. Group, Thome, and Wallem might be key in this respect, and they may be raising the bar for standards in these low-cost regions.

The authoritative British chartered accountants, Moore Stephens, undertake an annual benchmarking study of operating costs for twenty three types of vessels. Figures 8.1 and 8.2 give their summary of operating costs for bulk carriers and tankers respectively – broken down in terms of crew costs, stores (supplies, spare parts on board) repairs/maintenance, insurance, and administration. For both of these major ship categories, the largest operating cost factor by far is the crew. Repairs/maintenance

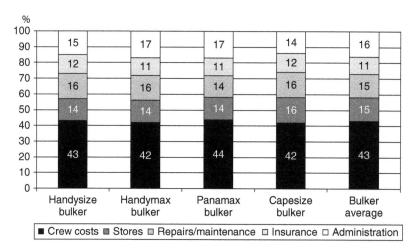

FIGURE 8.1 Proportional distribution of operating costs for bulk carriers
Source: Moore Stephens, Chartered Accountants, *OpCost* 2007, London, 2007.

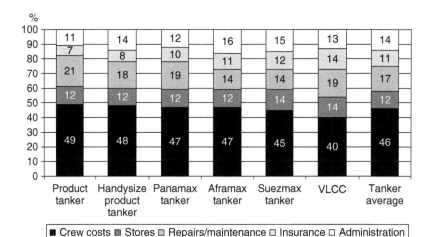

FIGURE 8.2 Proportional distribution of operating costs for tankers
Source: Moore Stephens, Chartered Accountants, *OpCost 2007*, London, 2007.

represents the second largest cost category. These two categories are precisely those under the control of ship management companies. Efficient ship operation is critical, whether it is done in-house or outsourced.

OSM

Let us take OSM as an example. This company, headquartered in Kristiansand, Norway, is an independent provider of marine services for all types of ships (OSM, 2008). It employs more than 6,500 people around the world, and is active in three business areas:

- ship management services, independent of shipowning interests, never competing with its customers;
- crew management services, claiming that it can mobilize the most competent crew for each ship it manages;
- engineering and offshore services, in which it has a strong track record and experience.

OSM's independence from shipowning, trading, or innovation companies is essential. This operating strategy once more underscores the trend toward focused independent initiatives within this field.

COMPETITIVE FOCUS: MUST-WIN BATTLES

There are two critical success factors in operating steel: low costs and delivery to an acceptable quality level.

- **Low-cost crewing**. As we have seen, low-cost crews are recruited in Southeast Asia, India, and countries from Eastern Europe like Russia, Ukraine, and Croatia. Developing effective training is part of this – to secure both new crews and adequate quality of service. Crewing requires organization through recruitment, assignment, competence management and training, payroll and cadet management, and development. The lack of well-trained, low-cost crews is a growing problem. Crew shortages, especially at officer level, are well documented. Competition for crews is leading to significantly higher wages and inevitably higher operating costs.
- **Maintenance**. Good systems and rigorous planning for maintenance and docking are critical, and central to this is co-operation with the certifying agencies. The lack of maintenance facilities and docking capacity can seriously complicate the cost efficiency of ship operations.

CUSTOMERS

Ship operating firms' customers are shipowning companies. While cost-efficient crewing is important to shipowners, crew quality and ship maintenance are equal concerns: deterioration of the ship structure can cause expensive repairs and/or loss of life. Some ports require crews to be of a certain quality level, for safety reasons. Mobilizing a high-quality crew is a key factor for success for crewing operations firms.

CONCLUSION

A critical consideration for operating steel, i.e., running a ship fleet, is crew costs, by far the most significant cost component in ship operations. While low crew costs are important, it is also essential to ensure that operations are carried out satisfactorily – in other words, you need well-trained crews. These operations are increasingly carried out by specialized firms that recruit crews from low-cost countries. These firms have their own training approaches, as well as systems and processes for efficient maintenance. In general, our prediction of more specialized shipping activities is confirmed by this.

9 Innovating around steel

Innovation comes in many forms. Technical innovation includes the design of a ship's hull, propellers, gears, axles, unloading cranes, coating the hull to reduce friction, and so on. Shipyards, ship design consultants, and ship classification organizations are all involved in innovation. Commercial innovations include ship freight rate forecasting breakthroughs, future trading innovations, novel ship financing, new management processes within shipping firms, etc. When it comes to companies that specialize in innovating around steel, it is important to distinguish between those product innovators that are focused primarily on technical innovations for specialized ship niches, ship design, and shipbuilding, and the diverse array of innovative organizations that focus on commercial innovations, such as Marsoft, Clarkson Shipping Hedge Fund, AMA Capital Partners, or Tufton Oceanic.

COMPETITIVE FOCUS: MUST-WIN BATTLES

An innovation edge is of course the key to competitive success for firms that innovate around steel. However, the innovation must be perceived as relevant by the customer. If the customer fails to see the relevance of an innovation, it will have little or no value. So an active link with relevant stakeholder groups – shipowners, brokers, and traders – is essential. To be successful, product innovators must have:

- Truly innovative approaches. This implies unique creativity not only in ship design, but also in areas such as market forecasting. Eclecticism is key here – and the ability to draw on teams that can contribute different and complementary ideas – but innovations must also be cost-effective. Low reduction is a central part of the innovator's challenge.

- Aggressive marketing. Markets have to be developed to "reserve space" for innovative solutions. The shipping industry is naturally conservative – things must be seen to work, so no risks should be taken on untried approaches. This makes it particularly important for innovation companies to have an effective marketing team and a strong customer focus. A lead customer can make all the difference here.
- Innovative forecasting. In a commodity market, innovators are consulting research firms like Marsoft, which forecasts ocean market freight trade developments for bulk, wet cargos, containers, and second-hand tonnage. The customers are primarily shipowners who need a better understanding of when to go in or out, when to go long or short, etc. Ship financing banks are another important customer segment. Marsoft is strongest at forecasting broader scenarios for movements in the markets, while customer relations-oriented firms are needed for day-to-day movements in the markets. Consequently, one would assume that Marsoft's forecasts would need to be complemented by individual data gathering by each type of specialized firm, particularly for issues such as port congestions/delays, etc. Shipbrokers may also provide forecasting services for shipowning firms concerned with the timing of new ship acquisitions and negotiating the best possible freight deals – and/or with their customer relations-focused counterparts. Shipbrokers' customers are shipowners and the companies that need the owners' tonnage for transportation – oil companies or ore providers. For brokers, customer relations are always a balancing act.

SPECIALIZED SHIP NICHES

For specialized ship niches, innovation focuses around product innovation companies, like ship design consultants. Skipsteknisk, for example, specializes in innovative ship design for offshore seismic search and supply ships. Carl Bro, in Copenhagen, specializes in chemical carriers, gas tankers, and refrigeration plants for gas carriers. These specialized companies can command a considerable value when traded. For example, the Norwegian ship design company, Wik and Sandvik, was recently sold to Wartsilä of Finland for NOK1,250 million.

The customers for these companies are primarily infrastructure-focused, shipowning firms. It is nevertheless important for innovator organizations to have relationships with relevant customer relations-focused companies, to confirm the quality of the ships or solutions that they are providing to shipowners. Product innovators in this niche use shipbrokers to verify that a particular ship is up to specifications; and they must verify that they are providing potential users of the ship with what they want.

Skipsteknisk designed the large offshore platform supply ship, Active Swan, with an effective deck capacity of $1,020\,\mathrm{m}^2$, for the offshore platform supply ship company S. Ugelstad. The ship was later chartered by R. S. Platou Offshore on a three-year time charter to Eidesvik. The technical specifications of the ship were of great importance, and led to close dialogue between Skipsteknisk and R. S. Platou. Even though S. Ugelstad was the customer, there was a strong relationship between Skipsteknisk, R. S. Platou, and Eidesvik. In the end, the ship was chartered to Conoco-Phillips, which also needed to be satisfied with the ship's specifications.

CUSTOMERS

For innovators, like shipbuilders, keeping the customer satisfied means a high degree of innovation in their newly designed ships that markedly improves performance. For firms like Marsoft, it means developing new ways of improving their forecasting capabilities.

A more fundamental understanding of emerging customer needs can lead to a redefinition of one's very business rationale. Consider this example from Maersk Line – the container liner operation of A. P. Moller-Maersk.

An online solution offering easier shipping for small to medium-sized shippers was launched by Maersk Line in early 2008, called yourship.com. This is a new concept – intended to be the "Ryanair of shipping." It reduces the shipping complexity and time for the shipper-cum-customer to a few clicks of the mouse. It guarantees space, around-the-clock opening hours, and transparent prices.

Paperwork is dramatically reduced. This service is currently in place out of a few hubs such as Hong Kong, Rotterdam, and Antwerp (*Maersk Post*, 2008).

THE ROLE OF TECHNOLOGY IN SHIP DESIGN

Technology plays an important part in ship design, where there are several interesting developments. As we know, double-hull ships are becoming standard for very large crude carrier (VLCC) tankers and increasingly for bulk carriers. In addition to this, there are significant improvements to the aqua-dynamic quality of the hull shape, leading to relatively less use of fuel, and allowing higher ship speed. Onboard technical equipment is also allowing for more automation, notably in the engine room and on the bridge, with less need for expensive crews, easier maintenance, less need for frequent dry docking, ship reclassification off-hires, etc. There has even been innovation in ship paint – epoxy paint offers significantly less friction in the water, allowing for fewer dry dockings. Advances in loading and unloading equipment make ships more versatile in using various ports, avoiding congestion, and speeding up the time for loading/unloading.

ENVIRONMENTAL INNOVATIONS

A fundamental source of innovation is demonstrated in the way environmental protection has influenced vessel specification. Based on international conventions, national legislation, and classification bureau requirements, Seaspan reckons that the following are mandatory requirements for their ships:

- fuel tank protection
- ballast treatment
- sewage treatment
- emission compliance (NOX, SOX, CO_2)
- antifouling paints

Innovations around pollution control are now critical. Wilhelm Wilhelmsen, like Seaspan, is committed to reducing the emission of

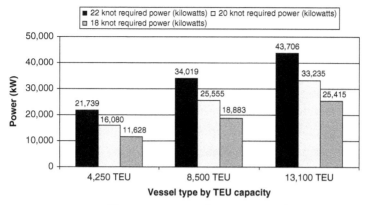

FIGURE 9.1 Slow steaming: vessel power vs. speed
Source: Seaspan (2008).

undesired gases from its ships. It has taken a multidimensional approach to fuel reduction:

- Reducing speed. Let us take a large container carrier of 13,000 TEU as an example: if the speed is reduced from twenty two knots to, say, twenty knots, the fuel consumption would go down about 25 percent. If the speed is reduced another two knots, to eighteen knots, the fuel consumption goes down another 30 percent. See Figure 9.1 for an illustration of this for several types of container ships. This is doable for Wilhelmsen, which has the bulk of its ships in liner service, focusing on car transportation. Slow steaming means that the cars reach the customers a little later, but this does not usually have significant negative consequences. In most cases, the cars or containers would be put in storage for a few days on arrival anyway. What matters is the weekly liner services schedule – there is some slack for marginally slower steaming.
- Weather routing systems.
- Steady steaming. Significant fuel savings can be made by maintaining speed during a journey. This requires working with ships' officers and crews to influence their attitude toward fuel consumption.
- Improved hull design. The rudder system has been improved with the addition of fins, and the propeller system and anti-fouling hull have been improved with friction reduction paints.

- Propulsion systems. Electronic fuel injection into diesel engines can create significant fuel savings. A research project is being carried out with Shell and Det norske Veritas (DnV) to develop a more viable, sustainable propulsion system.
- Low sulfur fuels. Wilhelmsen is now focusing on emissions like sulfur and CO_2. Its ships are all burning low sulfur fuel, which typically has 1.5 percent sulfur content, as opposed to the norm of 4.5 percent. The difference results in an annual sulfur emission saving similar to that of a city the size of London. The big remaining question, however, is how to deal with CO_2 emissions. To obtain a perspective on the CO_2 emission challenge, it might be useful to compare emissions from various means of transportation (Figure 9.2). Ships are relatively more CO_2 emission efficient than other means of transportation.
- Reducing NOX emissions. Wilhelmsen has entered into a joint venture with Jara – the Norwegian fertilizer company – for reducing the emission of NOX (nitrogen oxide). The fees for NOX emissions are currently light, but this is expected to change. Catalytic converters are being developed with urea products (from Jara) being used as chemical catalysts. NOX is being transformed into nitrogen (air) and water. Wilhelmsen has also entered into a second joint venture with BP with the aim of making use of seawater to clean sulfur from bunker fuel – "snubbing" technology.

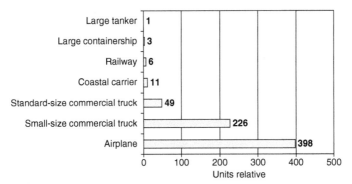

FIGURE 9.2 CO_2 emissions per unit load for various types of transportation (comparison by transport mode)
Source: Seaspan (2008).

Overall, Wilhelmsen estimates that it has reduced its emissions significantly – bunker fuels have been reduced by 40 percent. A question it faces is whether these innovations are leading to better contracts for the car-carrier business, its major business and a typical business-to-business market segment. This seems to be the case with some customers, for example, some of the German car manufacturing companies. The position is less clear with other shippers, such as major Japanese customers. After all, low costs are key.

A ship's trim can also prove critically important in reducing fuel consumption at an optimal speed. A modern ship's bow is constructed to be positioned for a particular water depth. If too low or too high in the water, speed will be reduced and energy consumption increased. Similarly, if the ship's stern is too high or too low, it can have a serious negative effect on water drag.

The Finnish software company, Eniram, has developed a pioneering approach to this problem – the Dynamic Trimming Assistant (DTA). The DTA consists of two trim tanks in the bow and stern areas and a software-assisted system for calculating the best trim (Eniram Ltd, 2008).

STIMULATING INNOVATION

It is increasingly recognized that companies need to look outside their own boundaries to stimulate innovation – looking for what Seely Brown and Hagel (2006) describe as "creation nets" and "open innovation." For most shipping firms this means working outside their niche – even outside their industry. Seaspan, for instance, is working closely with key stakeholders such as the major container liners-cum-charterers, and four or five major Korean and Chinese shipyards. Innovations come about through focused interaction with key stakeholders.

An important element of innovation has been Seaspan's ability to achieve standardization across the fleet. Examples of this are:

- **The main engine**. Seaspan has standardized primarily on Burmeister & Wain engines. The only difference between its longer and smaller ships is the number of cylinders – otherwise, the engines are identical. This means that a large set of spares can be used by all ships in their fleet. A shift from mechanical fuel injection to electronic is now being implemented for the newbuildings, however.

- **Air compressors**. Common air compressors are used across the entire fleet, with significant savings on spares, crew training, etc.
- **Alfa oil lubricators**. Using alfa oil lubricators has resulted in less consumption (about half previous levels) of lubricant, and significant cost savings.

Seaspan has decided to add slightly thicker steel plates at various places in the design of its ships. It has also specified that all reefer containers should be kept on deck, and not in the hold, to save energy on ventilation. In general, Seaspan's technical specifications are solid, but not excessive.

Innovation can provide clear cost benefits. The key is to seek solutions that work and that are fair to all in terms of costs relative to impact. Shipowning companies must stay ahead of the innovation game and make sure that charterers perceive their ships to be more modern and effective than their competitors'. But they must not be so avant-garde that they use unproven key technologies, which might lead to too many off-hires. Proven efficiency of the ship's engine system, hull shape, and outside paint coating will affect bunker consumption. When a ship is on hire or bare-boat charter, bunkers are paid for by the charterer, not the shipowner. Charterers will therefore put more value on fuel-saving innovations in the ships.

BARRIERS TO ENTRY

When it comes to product innovation, barriers to entry are all to do with people: who has the best cadre of innovators, the best engineering team, the most creative group, and the ability to attract and keep them? People management dictates barriers to entry in this category. Closeness to leading academic centers like MIT, which has a strong technical tradition, is also important for both technical and economic innovation. This is one reason why Marsoft, and others, are headquartered in Boston.

CONCLUSION

The shipping industry has always had important innovations – witness the shifts from sail to steam to diesel, or the emergence of container ships and large natural gas carriers (LNGs) – and it remains a critical driver in the industry. There are four main areas where innovation takes place:

1 Ship design, including types and sizes of ships, for example, the ultra-large 15,000 TEU container ships. Hull and propeller designs are constantly being modified. The innovative use of modern anti-fouling coatings has also led to significant increases in efficiency.
2 Environmental innovations, especially those dealing with the emission of gases, waste, etc. These are closely related to innovations in ship design, for example, lower friction (anti-fouling coatings) means lower fuel consumption, which means in turn reduced emissions. Filtering technology is also being advanced, with particular effects on reducing SOX and NOX emissions. Massive innovative efforts are being mobilized to battle the CO_2 emission challenge as economically as possible.
3 Advanced methods and processes. These include improved forecasting capabilities for a better understanding of shipping markets, and innovations in risk management.
4 The form of the shipping firm. More focused, specialized firms are needed in all areas of owning, using, operating, and innovating around steel. New types of corporate vehicles are also emerging, like the Clarkson Shipping Hedge Fund.

Continued innovation will remain at the core of the shipping industry for many years to come.

Part III   The firm's portfolio strategy

10 Portfolio management   *page* 187
11 Risk and revenue management   215

10 Portfolio management

I have argued in this book that it makes sense to consider shipping as a set of four specialized archetypes rather than one generalist firm – owning steel, using steel, operating steel, and innovating around steel. The advent of information technology (IT) based approaches, which have lowered transaction costs, is one driver of this change. But another more important one is a clear management focus on critical success factors. Interestingly, the trend toward specialization is occurring in many industries, including the airline business, the hotel business, automotive corporations, newspapers, credit card businesses, and pharmaceutical companies. From a legal point of view, these specialized entities can all reside within one common corporate firm.

Risk management considerations have also contributed to the trend of splitting a company into specialized business activities. Splitting makes sense from the investors' points of view because they are able to develop portfolios of investments with risk profiles they prefer. But when it comes to shipping, portfolio management means more than finding an appropriate balance between the four specialist archetypes. Risk can be managed by building on different portfolio instruments and result in a set of compromises rather than preferences. In the end, it is up to each management team to decide, based on how much complexity they can cope with.

Several of the disasters involving Scandinavian shipping companies in the early 1980s can be traced back to confusion about their risk exposure. These companies often owned one, two, or even more types of ships that were highly correlated in terms of market exposure. In addition, they tended to be heavily involved in chartering/brokerage activities for each of these businesses, and had their own crewing activities. As well as this, they had strong technical departments to deal with the innovation of their fleet. Needless to say, this all became overcomplicated, and risk exposure grew.

Diana Shipping, Genco, Eagle, Aegean Marine, and Genmar have all gained favorable valuations as they have focused on a particular sector, albeit on more than one size within the sector. Examples of mixed fleet companies that have had relatively lower valuations include International Shipholding, OSG, and Seacor – all engaged in diverse shipping activities.

Peter Georgiopoulos is the chairman of three New York Stock Exchange (NYSE) registered shipping companies:

- General Maritime Corporation (GM), which owns large crude oil tankers, was listed on the NYSE in 2001 and has a current capitalization of around US$870 million. Peter Georgiopoulos owns 13.7 percent of this company. During 2005–6 Georgiopoulos sold about thirty single-hull tankers. He has refrained from ordering new tonnage because of heavy newbuilding prices and a strong backlog of newbuilding orders.
- Genco Shipping and Trading is the dry bulk segment and has a current capitalization of about US$2 billion. Genco was listed on the NYSE in 2005, and Peter Georgiopoulos owns about 13 percent of the company. Relative to GM, Genco has benefited from the relative strength of the dry bulk market compared to the market for tankers.
- Aegean Marine Petroleum Network operates special purpose tankers that carry bunker fuel to other ships. The company's present capitalization is around US$1.8 billion, of which Peter Georgiopoulos owns 10 percent. This company was incorporated on the NYSE in 2006. Aegean Marine operates in a highly specialized shipping segment, with less exposure to commodity-based shipping than its two sister companies. Figure 10.1 gives the evolution in share price of the three companies for 2007 and for the first six months of 2008. Share prices for the tanker company, GM, remained flat, while the price for Genco, the dry bulk company, went up, with peaks and valleys. Agean Marine, the specialized shipping company, had a steady growth in share price.

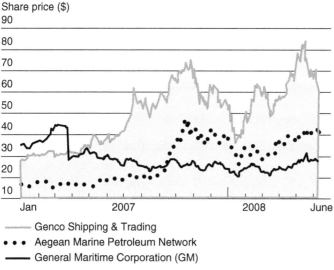

Share price ($)

— Genco Shipping & Trading
• • • Aegean Marine Petroleum Network
— General Maritime Corporation (GM)

FIGURE 10.1 Peter Georgiopoulos' sphere of shipping companies
Source: Thomson Datastream, June 2008.

Conventional wisdom in investment theory states that investors rather than firms should diversify, allowing investors to build a portfolio that matches their propensity for risk. It follows that publicly traded shipping companies should try to be relatively focused, with clear risk profiles. And investors should be able to pick the shipping stocks with the risk profiles they prefer – whether they are owners, users, operators, or innovators around steel. It is up to investors to hedge their risks, not the shipping companies. Shipping companies are to be efficient in their particular niches and have clear risk profiles. In practice, such pure-bred firms are rare. A typical shipping company is involved in activities that span two or more specialized archetypes. But, ideally, the internal organization respects the specialized nature of each activity.

In an article published more than thirty years ago in January 1979, Leif T. Loeddesoel, former president and chairman of the ship-owning firm Wilhelm Wilhelmsen, talked about why some shipping companies do well and others less well. He stressed the importance of clear chartering policies, each within a strategic plan, and also of making an early exit – stop-loss – when markets are going down. An exit possibility, perhaps enabled by owning a large enough portfolio of ships and by extension a larger ability or willingness to pay cancellation fees, seems critical. Loeddesoel implied that a clear portfolio strategy was important, both in terms of trying to develop non-correlated businesses and non-correlations on the financial side – liquidity, currencies, and costs. Many of the elements of a good portfolio strategy seem the same now as they were then.

Examining the chart for the development of vessel earnings – (see Figure 3.4) – we again see that a significant change set in around 2002. Before then, the vessel earnings for bulk carriers, tankers, and container ships developed at a more or less similar rate. After that point, they developed differently with bulk carrier rates shooting up dramatically. Tanker rates also rose to a lesser extent, as did container rates. But the co-variation between the three types of shipping markets clearly became lower than it was before the three became different markets. This may be important for portfolio strategy about diversity.

But will these differences remain, even after a downturn? The experience from the downturn in 1982–3 suggests that they won't – the three main markets may become similar again, with less diversification in portfolio strategy. Only time will tell.

PORTFOLIO STRATEGY

There are new realities when it comes to portfolio planning for shipping companies. In the past, there were often a number of discrete investments in various types of ships, which usually turned out to be highly correlated in terms of freight market exposure. Consequently, it was difficult to apply the principles of diversification. Today, however, with the emergence of freight derivative markets, stock picking, and chartering-based market options, it is easier to develop a diversified portfolio by incorporating forward freight agreements (FFAs) and/or ship-related stock components. The result can be more meaningful portfolios.

How might we go about developing a concrete portfolio strategy for a shipping company? If investors can diversify cheaply, there may be no reason for corporations to do so – a convincing concept of classic finance. Nonetheless, in some cases diversification makes sense. For example, diversification can allow for higher leverage with the same risks, such as when a corporation is able to create extra tax shields, valuable to investors, without increasing its cost of debt financing. This will work particularly well when diversification does not create negative managerial transaction cost value. For example, if managerial expertise is similar in the areas of diversification considered, negative synergies would be created. In shipping, there are many examples of this kind of diversification to take advantage of tax shelters.

The predictability of cash flows creates value for shareholders and investors in general. Publicly traded companies must aim for predictable cash flows and dividends, an argument for some diversification. Financial analysts prefer predictable cash flows. However, they are not shareholders and do not necessarily represent the thinking of sophisticated investors. When predictable, cash flows can help create value, for example, with regard to the management of tax shields through time, as well as through a higher and more stable dividend payout ratio. But there are situations where management might prefer predictable cash flows, while shareholders might prefer more risky cash flows – where the risk is clear.

Those with portfolio responsibility should undertake a regular systematic revision of the portfolio, in the light of the company's overall objectives. Because of the well-developed second-hand markets, a portfolio can be changed quickly. However, the portfolio can be adjusted just as easily through a leverage decision rather than through a ship sales decision. A chartering decision can also open the way to rapid adjustments – if desired. This would certainly be the case when employing FFAs and stock picking. Due to the imposition of the risk-aversion requirement, the search for the best portfolio can, in practice, be limited to a search for *efficient* portfolios. The number of alternatives to be considered then drops significantly.

The portfolio planning scheme offers a way to "put it all together" (Lorange and Norman, 1973). The original portfolio selection problem comes from investments in corporate finance, and these have been extensively researched over the past forty five years (Mossin, 1973). There are similarities and differences between portfolio management in classic stock markets and portfolio management in shipping markets. In stock markets there are two general approaches: the stock picking approach toward portfolio management and the index-based portfolio approach. These have analogies in shipping.

ASSET CHOICES

Figure 10.2 gives a general approach to finding the "best portfolio" based on risk/return considerations in a shipping context. It is important to look at all the ship assets in a commodity-based portfolio, in the sense that they are all exposed to market-driven risk/returns. Bulk carriers, tankers, and container ships are likely to be part of the portfolio. Examining the scattering among the six types of ship assets in Figure 10.2 and 10.3, we see first of all that the risk/return differences become more profound in the post-2002 period than before. A portfolio strategy approach increasingly makes sense. Second, observing the scattering among the various business types, one might ask to what extent this might be due to limited liquidity or other factors, given that

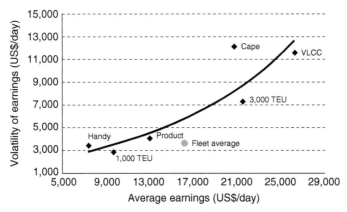

FIGURE 10.2 Risk/return tradeoffs in shipping (based on time charter rates for the period 1980–2002)
Source: Marsoft (2008a, b, c).

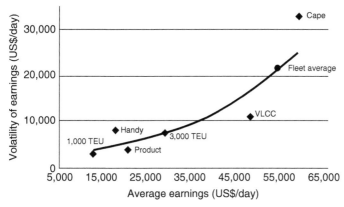

FIGURE 10.3 Risk/return tradeoffs in shipping (based on time charter rates for the period 2003–2007)

arbitrage is very feasible. According to the Black–Scholes model, the efficiency of the capital markets should explain all spatial differences.

In contrast, there are now indices for many different sectors of the stock market (small caps, large caps, hi-tech, etc.). Of course, many investors see indices as an optimal way to trade in the markets because they offer a well-diversified approach to investing, they are not easy to manipulate by managers, and they minimize the transaction costs that make many active management styles underperform for investors. This is what we call "passive investing" and it might be preferred for transaction cost reasons. The question then is whether passive investment should have a bearing on an index and, if so, which index. This relates to where value is created by investment management.

In stock market portfolio management, we can differentiate between risk selection, asset selection, and market timing. This is analogous to shipping portfolio's leverage decision (risk), asset mix selection, and chartering/trading strategy (timing). Risk selection (which comes not only from asset selection but also from leverage) defines the return one should expect if one performs normally. Asset selection consists of picking stocks that have positive alphas, meaning stocks that overperform. Many professionals spend most of their time doing this, but increasingly doubt the practical merits of such asset selection. In fact, it is unproven academically, hence the trend for passive investing. Finally, market timing refers to the major impact on portfolio performance of being in the right market at the right time, i.e., in small caps vs. large caps, or in bonds vs. equities. This can affect performance strongly.

As pointed out, these considerations from stock portfolio management are interesting if one thinks of specific ships as entities in one's portfolio. However, an individual ship can represent too large a finite entity to represent a meaningful unit in a portfolio. The advent of trading, for example with FFAs, opens up smaller units for consideration.

One implication of this is that to implement a portfolio management approach, one must establish clear performance criteria, with explicit and consistent articulation of the acceptable levels of risk. Companies must apply this approach consistently across decision-makers. Also, the company must set clear stop-loss criteria for *exiting*. The problem here, however, is that in practice ships are less liquid than stocks, and it might be hard to exit when you wish, bearing in mind that even commodity-based shipping markets may be difficult bases for executing asset transactions when the markets are down. Again, the emergence of FFAs might – at least in part – ameliorate this.

Asset play in shipping, associated with shipping portfolio strategies, must be seen in conjunction with an operating strategy, in effect when one is holding the ship. In general, the financial costs for older ships are lower than for new ships, generating higher operating income during the holding period, at least for ships that are in reasonably good shape and not excessively old, with moderate running and maintenance costs. New ships tend to have heavy financial holding costs, even though the strict cost of running and maintaining them might be relatively lower than the same costs for older ships. However, the "amplitude" of the selling prices is much larger for younger ships than for older ones. Thus, one can develop successful portfolio strategies, for both older and younger ships, as long as one goes for consistency and applies a portfolio strategy that is sustainable from an economic risk/return point of view.

The problem with cross-sectional portfolio diversification is that most shipping segments in the past tended to peak – as well as go down – more or less simultaneously. Diversification across shipping segments could still be seen as meaningful. But a somewhat different paradigm may be more predominant since 2002. Let's look again at Figures 10.2 and 10.3. During the pre-2002 period, we can clearly see – from Figure 10.2 – the comparison between six different shipping business segments for average earnings vs. the volatility of the earnings (i.e., risk). There are lower returns – and lower risk – for Handysize bulkers, feeder container ships, and product tankers than for Capesize bulkers, very large crude carriers (VLCCs) and large container ships. The latter group enjoyed higher returns, but also higher risks. Portfolio diversification would make sense in this case. Figure 10.2 also indicates the "fleet" earnings relative to the risk level, which is in this case calculated for a portfolio of six parts of equal size – falling between the two clusters, and with higher earnings than the bottom three, but with virtually the same risk level – i.e., a clear portfolio strategy benefit.

Figure 10.3 provides a similar analysis for the period 2002–7. Contrary to what we might have expected, there are no clear benefits from a portfolio diversification strategy. Indeed, ex-post, the winners were those who invested in bulk carriers – especially Capesize. So, rather than considering a diversified portfolio strategy, a pick-the-winner strategy seems to have predominated. With an exceptionally strong, and fast-rising market, this may be more critical than focusing on portfolio diversification.

Portfolio diversification into various ship types seems to make less sense – overall earnings might go down, without significant lessons learned about the accompanying risk.

Time-correlated diversification, however, can also be meaningful. We have discussed the merits of operating ships in the spot market, while others may be on long-term charters. Consider also the following data, provided by Marsoft: second-hand values have traditionally been driven by a combination of one to three-year time charter, freight levels, and newbuilding prices. But, over the last four years, second-hand values have been dominated by newbuilding prices alone. Even though the freight rates have fallen, notably in the tanker segment, second-hand values have stayed up. But will this continue? Perhaps only a long-term charter can pursue good second-hand values when the market is strong. A falling second-hand value will, of course, imply an immediate rise in the cost of capital.

A PORTFOLIO MODEL

Let me illustrate this using Seaspan as an example of a shipowning firm that might develop a portfolio approach.[12] Figure 10.4 illustrates the portfolio strategy setting issues. A first step is to determine the financial structure – equity vs. debt financing, interest rates encountered, including forward fixing of these, and dividend payouts. A meaningful

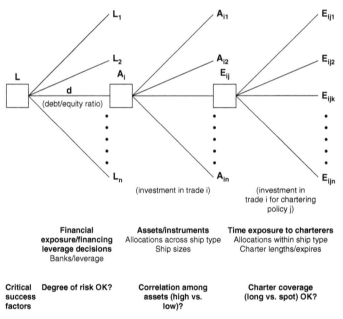

FIGURE 10.4 Portfolio, owning ships/infrastructure firms – Seaspan example

---

[12] This way of conceptualizing a portfolio strategy was first introduced by Lorange and Norman (1973).

portfolio of financial institutions will also have to be involved. Needless to say, these considerations are readdressed more or less continuously. Issuing of new equity, for example, tends to be done whenever the market seems favorable, perhaps even on a yearly basis.

As a second step, the choice of (container) ship types must be considered, for example, a class of 2,500 TEU ships, time-charted to China Shipping (eight) and K. Line (two), a class of 35,000 TEU ships, time-chartered to COSCO, a class of ca. 4,500 TEU ships, a class of ca. 8,500 TEU ships, and a class of 13,100 TEU mega container ships, etc. As a third step, the length of charters would be considered, such as a ten-year time charter (t/c) at a given set of rates for the 4,500 TEU class of ships to COSCO, an eight-year t/c at a given set of rates for the 8,500 TEU class of ships to Hapag-Lloyd and a ten-year t/c to COSCO for the 13,100 TEU ships, etc. The cumulative effect of all of these decisions will be a portfolio strategy that will reflect the firm's desired risk propensity. In this case, the risk level implied by this portfolio is rather conservative.

Seaspan's portfolio strategy builds a balance between five different types of stakeholders to satisfy the long-term interest of all (see Figure 10.5). Seaspan's top management puts a lot of emphasis on developing direct relationships with senior executives within each of the key stakeholders – and not working via brokers or agents. Achieving balanced deals is a priority for Seaspan's management. Developing such a stakeholder-based balanced portfolio requires a strong focus, and financial and operational strength. The business model is all long-term.

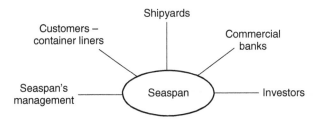

FIGURE 10.5 Seaspan's stakeholder-based portfolio strategy

Why is Seaspan so successful? There are five main factors behind the company's strong performance, and these seem to have general validity when it comes to portfolio strategies.

- A strong, dedicated top management and CEO. Gerry Wang knows his industry, and is a hard-charging, charismatic leader.
- Occupying space prominently in a growth niche. China has been a major source of growth in the world economy over the last decade, above all in manufacturing. Seaspan's container ship business has been largely focused on the growing trade flows from and to China.
- A consistent, focused portfolio strategy that emphasizes modern and standardized ship assets, a long-term and close relationship with a relatively small group of customers cum container liners, and a competent financial management function – about a dozen banks to provide the debt financing and a favorable investor image.
- Seaspan's management pays close attention to the capital structure of the company. The explicit, proactive management of the financial structure requires a particular discipline.
- Seaspan has kept its promises to its key stakeholders. Notably, it signaled a certain level of fleet growth and bottom line performance. So far, the company has largely delivered on these. This is of major importance for building trust with the equity market, banks, charterers, and shipyards.

Figure 10.6 shows an example of what a portfolio strategy might look like for a shipping firm that uses steel – a trading/broker firm such as the Clarkson Shipping Hedge Fund.

- The first issue is to determine the level of capitalization that is required and desired. Realism is critical here – as we have noted, several marketing/trading-related firms have had to liquidate due to insufficient funding.
- The second issue would be to decide on the amount (and types) of stock equities to go for vs. the amount of FFAs (dry, wet, etc.).
- The third issue would be to decide on time horizons – long-short, options, hedging, etc.

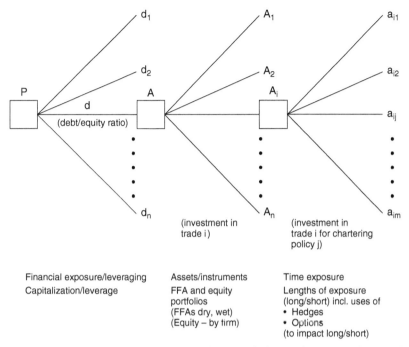

FIGURE 10.6 Portfolio – using ships – Clarkson Shipping Hedge Fund example

Another aspect of a realistic portfolio strategy is the emphasis on growth (in stock value appreciation) vs. yield (stock dividend). Peter Shaerf has made the following analysis for public firms traded in New York (Figure 10.7). The main difference between a yield-based and a growth-based portfolio strategy is the former's relatively heavy focus on predictable, stable cash flows through long-term charters and long-term financing. A growth-driven portfolio strategy, on the other hand, would focus on the spot market, perhaps with more opportunistic financing.

Determining a portfolio strategy for a steel-using firm, such as Clarkson Shipping Hedge Fund, might be much more transaction based. Trading is key – and the portfolio strategy is likely to change more frequently than might be the case for a steel-owning firm, such as Seaspan.

	Dry	Wet	Container
Growth	DryShips Navios Maritime Holdings TBS International Excel Maritime American Commercial Lines FreeSeas International Shipholding	OSG, Stealth Gas Tsakos Energy Navigation Torm, B&H Kirby, Golar Top Ships Aegean, Teekay Teekay LNG Teekay Tankers	Trailer Bridge Horizon Lines
Yield	Diana Shipping Genco Eagle Bulk Ocean Freight Paragon, Euroseas Navios MPLP	Ship Finance, US Shipping Nordic American, K-Sea Double Hull Tankers Arlington Tankers Knightbridge, Genmar Omega, Frontline Aries, CPLP, OSG America	Seaspan Corp. Danaos Marathon Acquisition

FIGURE 10.7 Growth vs. yield in the public market since 2002
Source: Shaerf, AMA Capital Partner (2008, p.12).

Finally, let us consider the delineation of a portfolio strategy in a typical product innovation-type firm, using Marsoft as an example (see Figure 10.8).

- Again, the first issue is to secure a proper level of capitalization, including the extent to which specific customers might actually provide capital.
- The next step is to decide what types of services to offer, for example, the bulk decision support system (BDSS) model that is provided by Marsoft, and to what customers – specific banks, specific shipping companies, etc.
- Next is to determine which of these relationships can be developed into long-term associations, which will have to be marketed day to day.

When it comes to setting a portfolio strategy for a firm that innovates around steel, much of the focus will be on the types of service the firm can develop and how it will gain credibility with desirable customers. For each of these services/customer groups, the question will be whether there is sufficient ongoing innovation/renewal momentum to retain the relationships.

As I have argued, it may be hard to combine portfolio elements across different archetypes. The challenges of understanding what risk

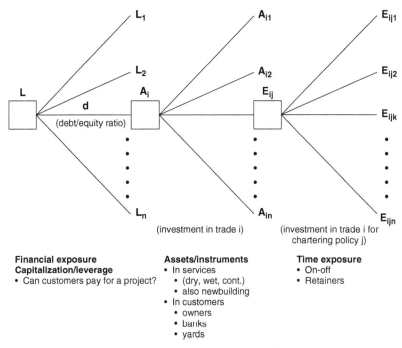

FIGURE 10.8 Portfolio – innovating around steel – Marsoft example

really means in such complex portfolio strategies – where all four business archetypes are represented – can be formidable. Figure 10.9 attempts to summarize such a portfolio.

Understanding risk exposure in a portfolio that involves several business archetypes could become excessively complex, raising cognitive managerial challenges. So why would some firms still want to do this? It is worthwhile to ask – in this connection – whether the overall portfolio might be seen as too narrow. A narrow portfolio may imply too high a risk and too little freedom to develop the firm further, via takeovers, for example. A portfolio that is too broad, on the other hand, may be too complex, and too flexible to mean much when it comes to balancing risks (strategy means choice). Further, it may be difficult to channel the resources to the best opportunities, if "anything goes." The challenge, therefore, is to come up with an

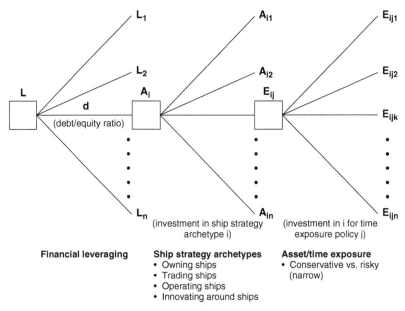

FIGURE 10.9 Portfolio shipping firm – owning, using, operating, innovating

appropriately balanced portfolio, with neither too much nor too little diversity. Diversity can be achieved within each archetype, without adding the excessive complexity that comes from combining archetypes. A portfolio for a specific archetype – with proper diversification – may be the answer.

Let us look at J. Lauritzen in Copenhagen. It is heavily involved in the Panamax bulker segment, with more than a hundred ships in its fleet. Some of these are wholly owned, while others are taken in on time charter – some on longer term, others on shorter term. This is a dynamic sub-portfolio, where things can change very fast. The dry bulk markets are constantly in flux, with new opportunities arising all the time. While J. Lauritzen is a significant owner in this segment today, some years ago it did not own any of its bulk carriers – all were taken in on time charters.

Lauritzen's tanker business segment is now focused on product tankers. The company has chartered in ten product tankers, and has six on order. Strong relationships with the small number of shippers of wet products, including the oil companies, are critical. Lauritzen's tanker sub-portfolio segment is slightly less liquid than the bulker sub-portfolio segment. This is because the fleet of Lauritzen's product tankers is specialized, in contrast to the company's bulk carriers.

Lauritzen is also active in the niche gas (liquefied propane gas, LPG) segment, which, in contrast to the heavy market focus that sets the tone for its bulk carrier and Handysize tanker businesses, is built on long-term relationships with a few shippers. To secure a realistic portfolio strategy in this segment, Lauritzen elected to go for organic growth. Presently, the company has thirty ships in this segment. It is getting out of the smaller ships (coasters), and building a series of ten larger LPG ships. This sub-portfolio is much more stable and longer-term focused than dry bulk and product tankers.

J. Lauritzen is now out of reefers, a niche segment that seems to have relatively little liquidity and relatively little opportunity for growth. The company had a long tradition in this segment; however, in order to improve its performance, it merged with Cool Carriers in Stockholm (S. Salén), which then became NYK/Lauritzen/Cool. Later on, NYK bought out Lauritzen's reefer business – ships and software. A general lesson on how to cope with less attractive portfolio segments – perhaps with a view to eventual exit – would be to seek restructuring by merging with others. After restructuring, the business may look more attractive as part of another firm's portfolio than it did in its original one.

For each of the segments that Lauritzen is involved in, it is critical to understand the market and the appropriate mix of owning and time charters. With this market-driven focus and by checking the appropriate mix between owning and chartering, one should be better able to control the risks – and that includes exiting at the right time.

Nevertheless, some prominent firms seem to pursue mixed portfolio strategies, but not necessarily as a mix of the four shipping related business archetypes we have discussed. Their portfolios might involve both shipping and some other (tradable) entity. For instance, ship chartering/trading and energy might be seen as elements in an overall portfolio by some companies, for example:

- Tufton Oceanic holds shares and is active in derivatives – both in shipping and in energy;
- Sector Maritime in Norway deals with both FFAs and shares (similar to the Clarkson Shipping Hedge Fund, but more broadly focused on both shipping and energy).

Morgan Stanley is becoming more and more active in the shipping and energy mixed portfolio market. It recently bought Heidmar (and subsequently sold 50 percent to Economos) and is now embracing a strategy similar to Enron's, trading around two types of physical assets – ships and power plants.

Shipping firms must have clear rules for each of these strategic elements. They must be able to separate them from each other within the portfolio, i.e., to develop a ship sub-portfolio on one hand and an energy sub-portfolio on the other. The risk of excessive exposure in these mixed portfolios is high. Strict discipline is needed when it comes to trading limits and maximum sizes of positions.

Strict discipline is also needed when setting conditions for making major diversification moves, such as acquisitions. If one or more of these conditions is not in place, then it would be better to wait for a later time, when market conditions are more favorable. Key factors would be:

- cost – the price for the asset to be acquired must be realistic;
- rate – this must be satisfactory to yield a reasonable return;
- operating costs;
- interest rates – and availability of debt capital;
- share price – when one pays with stock, there should be no heavy dilution effect.

Let us now look at an example of a company with a highly diversified portfolio.

A.P. MOLLER-MAERSK — A HIGHLY DIVERSIFIED PORTFOLIO

A.P. Moller-Maersk is one of the largest shipping companies in the world. The group is active in a number of non-shipping activities, such as oil and gas, industrial activities, distribution (supermarkets), etc. I shall not discuss all these activities here. I will concentrate on the group's six major shipping-related categories. Before going into a more detailed discussion of each of these, a word on managing complexity by striving for simplicity is called for.

A.P. Moller-Maersk has increasingly attempted to delineate its businesses into freestanding entities. And, in each case, it attempts to have more direct interactions with its customers.

Maersk Line, for instance, is now totally separate from the logistics business – the latter focusing on supply chain logistics, while the liner business is working toward the elimination of outside entities, such as classical freight forwarders, between them and the customer. Closeness to the customer is a key strategy, especially as a typical large freight forwarder can represent as many as fifty different lines.

For a few major customers, it will be important to coordinate activities across several business divisions. One example is Wal-Mart, which has a special internal coordinator at Maersk Line. However, there is no reason why the organization as a whole should have to become excessively complicated because of a relatively small number of major customers. The new president and CEO of A.P. Moller-Maersk – Nils S. Andersen – has made focus and simplicity a priority. He states, "Simplicity is a hard core business strategy," (*Maersk Post*, 2008, p. 7). He claims that acquisitions and growth in themselves can lead to more and more complex internal organizations, with ad hoc new process moves added on here and there to deal with the various growth challenges as they arise. After a while, too much complexity becomes burdensome, too many employees focused internally rather than on the customers. The customers might find that the company becomes hard to deal with, bureaucratic, and slow. Accordingly, at

Maersk Line, a new process excellence department has been set up to help streamline processes, keeping the customer's perspective in mind (Maersk Post, 2008, p. 8)

The container liner business

A.P. Moller-Maersk is an integrated shipping company whose success in the container liner business has overshadowed the rest of its shipping business. The capital- and resource-intensive container liner business is run on a freestanding basis in line with the trend towards specialization. In Figure 6.11 we gave an outline of the top twenty container liner companies in the world, ranked by total capacity in TEUs. It also indicates the number of ships owned, with its affiliated-owned TEU capacity, as well as the number of ships chartered in, with chartered-in TEU capacity. Finally, it indicates the percentage of TEU capacity that is chartered in. More than 50 percent of the capacity of the top container ship liner operating companies is chartered in. Most of them have gone a long way toward using other shipowners' financial capacity for owning the steel, while they concentrate on using steel and running the line. The drive toward more specialization is evident. One company has gone further than the others: CSAV, out of Santiago, Chile, charters in more than 90 percent of its container ship capacity. Among the least aggressive, in terms of chartering in, are Yang Ming Line, PIL Line, and Evergreen Line.

It is interesting to see that A.P. Moller-Maersk, by far the largest container shipping company in the world when it comes to container ship operations, has chartered in more than 50 percent of its overall fleet. It currently owns less than 50 percent of the steel it uses.

Service and closeness to the customers are critical. So too is a focus on costs, to ensure that A.P. Moller-Maersk can take full advantage of its larger size. Robert Wright's recent series of articles in the *Financial Times* (Wright, 2007, 2008a–d) seems to indicate that the company does not consider itself sufficiently cost efficient, and that efforts are underway to streamline the liner organization.

There is the potential for tension between the shipowning side of the business, with its cost focus similar to Seaspan, and the container liner operations activities, with its focus on business to business (B2B) customer service. Perhaps the liner business within A.P. Moller-Maersk Group might be split into a container shipowning group and a container line operating group – the former focusing on the infrastructure business and the latter on customer relations. The customer relations business would then be free to charter in ships from both its in-house shipowning counterpart and outside vendors, such as Seaspan (A.P. Moller-Maersk has already chartered in four ships from Seaspan). In contrast, the shipowning entity would be free to strive for the acquisition of cost-effective ships – both in terms of newbuilding price and cost-of-capital. Again, referring to the recent articles in the *Financial Times*, the company is splitting its liner business into maritime, terminals/ports (already autonomous), storage, trucking, and IT. The aim is to become more efficient – and profitable – through specialization.

Today, the company's large container ships are built at A.P. Moller-Maersk's Lindø yard, including a series of six huge ships with more than 15,000 TEU capacity each – the world's largest (the Emma Maersk class). This is cost efficient and provides the company with cutting-edge innovation. Finally, Maersk Line benefits from early delivery.

The tramp ship and logistics business

The focus in these segments is on providing cost-competitive tonnage to the prevailing market conditions. Timing and costs are the drivers of these standardized ships, operating in tanker markets. A.P. Moller-Maersk elected to exit the dry bulk carrier market in 2002, selling its fleet of bulk carriers to Thorvald Klaveness. At the time, this business segment was not seen as particularly attractive – which in retrospect turned out not to be the case – perhaps one of the company's most expensive mistakes. Perhaps, too, the company's management felt that the bulk carrier business would require a more container-driven specialized focus, i.e., potentially detracting from the cost focus. Thorvald Klaveness has solved this dilemma by splitting the bulk-carrying business into a customer-focused maritime logistics business and a cost-focused commercial management group.

Offshore supply ships

Similar factors apply to offshore supply ships – cost competitive standard anchor-handling and platform supply ships and customer satisfaction when it comes to, say, underwater construction ships. Some of the offshore supply ships are more specialized, with different types of customer relationships, than most of the fleet, where cost competitiveness vis-à-vis major oil field operations is a sine qua non. The offshore supply ship business is partly commodity-based, partly niche-based. A.P. Moller-Maersk is a major player in this business segment, and its supply ships are among the largest, most specialized, and most capital intensive.

Gas carriers

Gas carriers are a niche business, based on a strong relationship with individual customers and shippers. It is similar to a pipeline business for gas – but the gas is transported by ship instead. These activities are long term and part of an integrated value chain, with other companies investing in terminals at the production, loading, termination, and unloading sites. The investment in the value chain is much larger than for each separate ship. This, almost by necessity, is an integrated activity, with shipowning customer relations interrelated and inseparable. Customer service is a key part of the entire value chain. A.P. Moller-Maersk has made significant investments in this sector.

Interestingly, a number of large gas carriers have been built on speculation. A short-term charter market is developing. Some specialized gas carrier shipowners are breaking away from the integrated gas value chain. This implies that the terminals receiving the gas may become more independent from the producers in the future. Ships may also be independently owned and chartered out to specialized customer relations firms that are built around the operators of the receiving terminals.

Car carriers

As announced on January 30, 2008, Höegh Autoliners acquired eighteen car carriers from the A.P. Moller-Maersk Group, and A.P. Moller-Maersk simultaneously became a shareholder in Höegh Autoliners, formerly HUAL, the fourth largest car carrier liner in the world, with a 37.5 percent ownership. This purchase of a significant stock position is, of course, another way to diversify A.P. Moller-Maersk's portfolio.

Container terminals

Container terminals are similar to real estate. A.P. Moller Terminals, which owns and operates more than twenty three terminals around the world, is likely to develop new container terminal projects, where it will reserve 100 percent initial ownership. It would purchase the land, obtain the permits to build, arrange for the contractors to do the construction, and so on. This would be a relatively high risk, high return, even opportunistic activity. In three to five years' time, A.P. Moller Terminals might sell itself down to around a 60–80 percent ownership share, but would still be in control. This is analogous to a real-estate model, where the developer reduces his ownership share after the project has been developed. The cash flow will be predictable and stable in the long term, again analogous to a real-estate project. Figure 10.10 illustrates this model, with risk falling over time and revenue increasing and stabilizing. A.P. Moller Terminals' ownership share would be going down from the high-risk start-up phase to the lower risk ongoing business phase. Return on capital would be optimized for A.P. Moller Terminals. New owners come in later in the project, asking for a lower return as the risk is now lower too. A.P. Moller Terminals can charge higher management fees, both for its role in the financial engineering of the project and for operating the terminals.

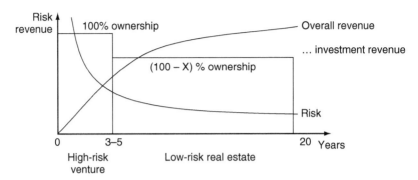

FIGURE 10.10 Container terminals business model
Source: Adapted from notes by Professor Tom Malnight.

Terminals, warehousing, and access to rail and truck are increasingly important. A.P. Moller-Maersk handles the outsourcing of logistics for other companies. Putting together all the relevant aspects for a customer – without creating too much complexity – is a key challenge. Customer service is paramount – a value proposition that can be understood.

Container terminals are the fastest moving emerging segment for A.P. Moller-Maersk, which is investing in moving the container from the quayside.

A.P. Moller-Maersk Terminals gives Maersk Line certain advantages, principally preferential terminal access. But this unit serves about fifty different liners and so must keep its sister division at arm's length.

Some formerly more integrated container liner business companies – most notably Hapag-Lloyd – have sold off their terminals. Many in the industry consider this a strategic mistake. Businesses have to be focused, stand-alone entities, but this does not preclude companies from coordinating across their portfolio of businesses to take advantage of opportunities. While liner and terminal businesses should be seen as independent, they are still related in terms of portfolio coordination.

Many container terminal operators are owned by container liner companies, but others are independent. The most prominent is ICTSI, the dominant container terminal operator in the Philippines, which ranks among the twenty largest port operators worldwide. ICTSI now operates twelve terminals on four continents. So there is certainly room for independent container terminal operators – in line with what we might expect, and in line with the major thesis of this book. The largest container ports in the world are:

- Singapore
- Shanghai
- Hong Kong
- Shenzhen
- Busan
- Rotterdam

Several of the large container lines have terminals in these harbors (Port of Rotterdam Port Statistics, 2008).

Commodity vs. niche

For all of these shipping activities, with their unique business models, there is a built-in commodity element (with a heavy cost focus) versus a niche element (with a strong service focus).

The commodity element assumes that there is a relevant market, and that the shipowner and/or customer relations specialist firm will adapt to it. This could be the freight market for dry cargo, wet cargo, second-hand ships, and/or newbuilding. These business segments are relatively mature and have a low-cost focus. There are three areas of consideration for success in commodity businesses:

1 When to get in and out, i.e., an understanding of how to play the scenarios for shipping market movements.
2 When to go long and when to go short, including committing to time charters, going on spot, including committing to FFA contracts, etc. Again, a good understanding of the shipping markets is critical.
3 Understanding the turning points for the shipping markets, crucial for the in/out and long/short decisions.

It cannot be overemphasized that underlying all this is the need for a strong cost discipline. Under any circumstances, the ship or cargo arrangement with the best cost/benefit properties will win the business, everything else being equal. The price "dictated" by the general ship market will prevail. While factors relating to overall safety, such as double hulls, will become important, the lowest cost provider will still "win" in the end, and all shippers, including major oil companies and ore producers, will follow this dictum.

In contrast, the niche shipping elements consist of developing specialized ships, often with the help of product innovator specialist firms. Shipowners often work directly with the final customers. Here, the key parameter for success is customer satisfaction, based on tailoring ships to meet the needs of the customer. Relationships with these customers will be long term, and the rate is only one element of what keeps customers satisfied. Good logistical solutions, performance, and service are all equally important. For example, Gearbulk's strong market position within the South American pulp business is based on close relationships with major producers, such as Aracruz, Votorantim, and Suzano.

Where portfolio risk management is concerned, it is important not to confuse the various types of business model and to maintain a clear view of the critical success factors for each. This concerns types of shipping, as well as whether specific types are commodity or niche players, with different activities and unique links to the customer.

The activities in a mixed portfolio for a given shipping firm need to be individually developed to achieve the unique stance required to succeed competitively in each of these activities. However, the situation is often dynamic. Niche businesses are likely to be found in newer markets, while activities are almost always commodity-focused in more mature markets. This evolutionary pattern is illustrated in Figure 10.11. A specialist business might start out as a customer-focused, niche business. Over time, there will be learning and accumulation of experience – both on the part of the customer, who will now expect to cash in on some of the cost benefits yielded from accumulated experience, and on the part of the shipowner, who can do

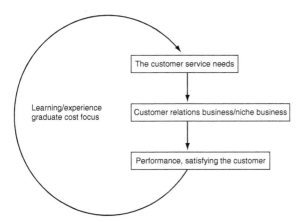

FIGURE 10.11 From customer relations niche specialist to infrastructure low-cost specialist

the job at lower cost over time, again due to accumulated experience. This learning curve effect will gradually lead to a shift in focus, from niche to commodity, from customer relations to infrastructure – from service to cost focus.

A common dilemma is that tailor-made specialist ship solutions are easily copied. Shipyards are good at this, supported by innovative engineering firms that might want to sell their novel solutions several times over. Again, it may be difficult to make a long-term distinction between a specialized customer relations business and a shipowning commodity business. It may start out being the former – with a clear customer focus – and evolve over time into the latter, now with a clear cost focus. These evolutionary moves, with many shipping projects finding themselves hybrids between the two business models, can create difficult challenges for shipping companies. How often will a business model concept have to be changed? And how much proactive support will a shipowning company need to give this evolution? There have been many examples of shipping companies that have clung on to a niche shipping concept for too long, only to lose the business.

An important implication for strategic process design stems from comparing Figures 5.2 and 5.3 (see chapter 5) – delineating the four archetypes of shipping business – with Figure 10.5, which delineates key portfolio strategy decision-making issues. The top-down vs. bottom-up balance regarding the strategic process differs. Archetypes one and three (owning and operating steel) lend themselves to a relatively straight top-down focus, while the opposite is the case for archetypes two and four (using and innovating around steel). The corporation as a whole should be sensitive to the assembly of top-down vs. bottom-up balance when comparing the way archetypes one and three interact with top management, in contrast to archetypes two and four.

CONCLUSION

Portfolio strategy can add important additional value to the shipping firm. The covariance in earnings between one or more different shipping strategies may be less than perfect, leading to additional overall robustness in earnings for the shipping firm.

A first portfolio diversification issue is where to focus – owning and/or using and/or operating and/or innovating. As always, the trade-off question is, "Would the potential gain in earnings from a more broadly diversified portfolio be justified in light of the added managerial complexity?"

A second area of consideration for portfolio diversification is whether or not to focus on more than one type of ship asset. Different asset types may be less than fully correlated when it comes to earnings expectations. Hence, a diversified ship portfolio may make sense. A variation of this consideration is to have various sizes of ships within the same category, for example, different sizes of container ships (Seaspan) or different types of tankers – Aframax and Suezmax (General Maritime).

A third area of portfolio diversification is length of charters and having some ships in the spot market.

A fourth area to consider is different financing arrangements – different banks, different instruments, occasional use of tax leases, etc.

I have proposed a model for developing an efficient portfolio strategy, but in the end the tradeoff will always be the extent to which the firm's added complexity can be justified – can the organization handle this meaningfully?

11 Risk and revenue management

Mezrich (2002) describes a group of MIT students who won significant amounts of money at blackjack in Las Vegas by card counting – memorizing the cards that had been played so that they could bet on those that remained. While shipping is certainly not blackjack, the message is clear: risk-taking is not a matter of random luck – it can be managed, through active involvement. Prior information – such as forecasts provided by Marsoft – may help the proactive shipping executive understand better the risks at hand. And, as events unfold, rapid – even proactive – adjustments in strategy can definitely pay off.

A key message of this book is: risk must be managed, through fast, proactive, flexible moves. This is true for each of the four shipping business archetypes I have identified, as well as for portfolio strategy. Managing risk in shipping is certainly not a matter of placing "passive" bets.

Shipping is exposed to many more exogenous factors than most other fields of business, so exposure management is key. Sources of risk for the shipping industry include: changes in demand and freight rates caused by global economic cycles and supply/demand imbalances; uncertainty over newbuilding and/or second-hand prices; currency and interest rate fluctuations; and technical breakthroughs that lead to premature obsolescence of ship assets. And there are others. The demand for shipping generally tracks global economic cycles, so shipping companies could aim to match supply with demand. But if you get the timing wrong, you could take delivery of new capacity just as demand drops. Freight rates can swing unpredictably for reasons like overheating in a local economy, or difficulties in local supply (including port delay).

The financial side – particularly when it comes to changes in currency and interest rates and the sheer availability of financing – offers its own demanding challenges. For example, the recent turmoil in the financial markets due to the sub-prime crisis in the US has led to significantly higher costs for debt capital, dramatically tighter credit facilities and an increasingly turbulent equities market, with an accompanying higher cost of equity. Virtually overnight, it became critical for shipping companies to have a close relationship with their bankers and other relevant financial institutions. In the face of new, more restrictive environmental legislation, the issue of the continued usefulness of a ship makes the estimation of residual shipping values more difficult. The Exxon Valdez incident, which led to double-hull legislation for tankers, was an unfortunate event in the sense that it was difficult to predict. And it meant that a close relationship with politicians, lobbyists, and shipyards became mandatory. Stakeholder influences have grown. The shipping industry has had to expand its focus on a broader set of consultations. The tanker business, in particular, has become almost a slave to strong global regulatory forces.

INFLUX OF NEW CAPITAL AND SOURCES OF FUNDING
Shipping is a capital-intensive industry with significant funding needs for fleet expansion and replacement purposes. However, many sources of financing became much less available – or even dried up – after the summer of 2007. The ripples from the sub-prime housing mortgage collapse had significant effects on ship financing.

Until then, there had been something of a sea change in the way executives looked at the shipping business. Capital used to come from traditional shipping banks and "friends of friends." More recently, however, capital increasingly has been coming from new sources, including private equity, investment funds, professional investors, etc. The influx of new capital changed the shipping industry significantly. As a result, financial performance, based on conventional shipping industry criteria, is no longer as relevant. Instead, performance expectations are increasingly dictated by the professional investment community, as they are in most other industries. While many of these sources of financing have dried up since the credit crunch, the emphasis on more rigid investment criteria remains.

GLOBAL COMPETITION FOR CAPITAL

Shipping projects now have to compete for capital with non-shipping projects. Private equity investors do not necessarily understand global demand requirements from a shipping perspective. However, they may be comfortable with assessing investment opportunities in general, irrespective of what industry they come from. Shipping investments must be financially competitive to be attractive – and this is all happening at a time when there is much less new capital available.

RISK MANAGEMENT

The highly volatile (risky) business environment in which companies in the shipping industry operate, makes it imperative for them to identify the sources of risk they face and know how to deal with them effectively. Implementing risk management strategies in the increasingly sophisticated and competitive environment in which companies operate nowadays, can often make the difference between being able to stay in business or not. It can give these companies a comparative advantage over the intense competition that they face in the sector. Knowledge of derivatives and risk management in shipping is required.

It will always be true that the amount of risk that a particular leader and his or her management team are willing to take will depend on the type of business in which they operate. This is different for each of our four shipping firm archetypes – owners, users, operators, or innovators. We know that individual decision-makers have different preferences when it comes to risk (Lorange and Norman, 1973). Acceptable risk depends on the risk-taking propensities of the decision-makers, so it is important that there is consistency within the management team when it comes to risk taking; otherwise, if the attitude toward risk differs widely among key individuals, it could be dysfunctional.

There are clear procedures for assessing the risk-taking propensity of individuals within a particular firm (see Lorange and Norman, 1973). It makes sense to attempt to formalize this for a given organizational entity, by comparing and discussing the risk propensity profiles of each top manager. Initial differences can be ironed out, so that a more or less consistent overall attitude toward risk can be arrived at for the firm. This would eliminate the danger of unintended risk-taking over time, depending on who was driving a particular decision within the top management team – some members might be more conservative than others. What matters is that there should be an explicit understanding of these people's differences, so that the resulting risk profile of the team is accurate and stable.

One critical aspect of managing risk is to avoid bankruptcy. In shipping, having enough free liquidity to enter into new shipping deals is key. Capacity has to be managed accordingly, bearing in mind that liquidity equals flexibility, preparedness, and financial stamina.

A focus on avoiding bankruptcy implies an asymmetric propensity to risk – it is more important to avoid huge downside outcomes than to go for larger upsides.

HOW RISK AND REVENUE MANAGEMENT CAN HELP

Once shipping companies have identified and measured their risks, they are able to make informed decisions about whether to reduce their exposure or alter their risk profile based on their risk preferences – hedging is one course of action. However, risk management is not synonymous with hedging, which is just one alternative for active risk management. Moreover, risk management does not necessarily imply risk reduction. In fact, the objective of risk management is not to eliminate risk, but to quantify and control it, to alter the risk profile according to the prevailing market conditions, risk preferences, and potential regulatory or contractual requirements. Risks are embedded in any business activity. For a shipowner, the decision to invest in a vessel signifies a belief that freight rates will go up, earning a return on investment that is higher than the "risk-free" interest rate. However, there is no free lunch in the economy; the decision to invest creates a natural exposure to freight rates – accepting the risk that freight rates may, in fact, have downturns. Risks are unavoidable in any profit-making activity.

Given the risks inherent in the industry, what risk and revenue management techniques will help alleviate them? And how should they be applied? Because the shipping industry is a capital intensive and volatile industry, it is critical to evaluate the various financial methods under risky and uncertain situations.

Before shipping companies attempt to make any decisions on risk considerations, they must identify the underlying risk factors (e.g., market downturns, exchange rate fluctuations, etc.) and understand their behavior. Next, they must estimate the probability of these events occurring. In doing so, macro-economic information such as historical price movements and price forecasts will be applied under different scenarios to all contracts booked, and subtract from each contract's book value the amount that is, on average, at risk. After identifying the underlying risk factors, they must determine their significance and quantify their influence on portfolio value and financial results.

Revenue management enables companies to understand the fit between their capacity and future demand and to price and allocate capacity for different customer segments in a way that maximizes revenues. Risk and revenue management can improve the performance of freight transportation.

HOW FORECASTING SCENARIOS CAN HELP WITH
RISK AND REVENUE MANAGEMENT – MARSOFT

It is important to understand the possible downside of scenarios when communicating with the financial markets and banks. On the other hand, if you want to raise equity capital from investors, you should convince them of the potential upsides. Objective analysis of the sort provided by Marsoft can help.

Marsoft's inputs can be useful for scenario planning within the process of budgeting and financial planning. Financial organizations will want to know that a shipping company can survive fluctuations in the market and will look for the answer in the company's liquidity pattern. Another important use of scenarios is to try to get the timing of ship purchase and sale decisions right, given that ship value depreciates and appreciates with the market, making the timing of market turning points crucial. The key questions are: what do you believe in? Could you survive a downside? What is the upside? How do you plan to handle the risk, including chartering actions?

During project financing, scenarios can help the shipowner understand a project better, particularly its timing in the cycle. And in corporate fleet financing, scenarios could help the firm to understand the robustness of the fleet's position, especially during a downturn. Scenarios must be part of the judgment of the individual decision-maker; they are not mechanical. They should be used to help the firm meet the hard targets concerning a ship, for example, that the cash situation is robust, and that the firm can pay its dividends based on contributions from the deal, etc.

Scenarios might ultimately lead to the construction of probability distributions, with a high case, base case, and low case. However, the decision-maker must not make the fundamental "mistake" of treating the base case as the equivalent of a certainty. A scenario should be stress tested. How can the firm make the probability distribution "real," so that it is easy to communicate, easy for decision-makers to understand, and easy to distribute internally and externally?

When all is said and done, the key parameters to consider when making a particular shipping decision are: owned or chartered? Newbuilding or second-hand? Predominantly equity or predominantly debt financed? Marsoft's approach is to develop computer-based forecasting scenarios, in the form of decision support systems, for explicit, systematically developed market and risk policy statistical inputs; specific decision rules for determining the overall strategy, tactical moves and implementation steps; and systematic benchmarking regarding one's performance and assessment of one's performance relative to internal budgets, as well as relative to external targets, including competitors. To "deliver," Marsoft offers several quarterly reports, for example on the dry bulk, tanker, and container markets.

The first is its Timing and Risk Management System (TRMS), a data platform that has been under continuous development and incrementally improved since 1985. It is for use by banks to upgrade their assessments of loan risks to shipping projects and to help ensure compliance with the Basel II Accord. TRMS provides a common market view as part of a clear strategy for the specific cycle-position in a particular shipping market. The focus is on understanding turning points or breakpoints. Marsoft focuses on the interaction between workstations and the more conventional data and management processes within the shipping firm, an attempt to build on internal market expertise and maximize its potential. There is an often-impressive wealth of internal know-how and expertise on shipping markets and cargo runs that can be accessed to help achieve even better forecasts. Marsoft tries to develop more transparency in the interplay between the data provided by the firm and the know-how within the shipping organization itself.

The Marsoft approach also allows risk levels to be set by specifying specific risk parameters, both for a single transaction and for the portfolio of ships/transactions. The benchmarking and performance measurement should lead to improved learning in the organization. The speedy reporting of results should highlight deviations and track performance, setting the stage for triggering ameliorating decisions, as needed.

Marsoft has two other complementary database packages, which have applications for specific ship decisions. The first is the Marsoft Decision Support System (MDSS), which provides specific freight market monitoring, helping the decision-maker to time chartering and purchasing/sales decisions. MDSS focuses on the timing of the freight rate cycle, i.e., trying to identify turning points or breakpoints. It also allows the shipowner to undertake specific strategy analysis, running simulations of the effects of various types of chartering or newbuilding decisions ("what if" analysis). The second forecasting package, Shipping

Risk Management (SRM), helps the decision-maker manage risk more actively. It takes the "what if" analysis even further, and gives the decision-maker a better feel for the potential payoffs of various risk exposures. This is supported by insistence on a standardized financial reporting system, so that disciplined risk-taking can be maintained easily – a key challenge when more than one decision-maker is involved in a given transaction.

VALUE-AT-RISK

Handling financial risk is more critical today than ever. Value-at-Risk (VaR), or the maximum likely loss over the next trading day, is becoming the standard way of looking at investment portfolios for asset management companies. VaR is widely used in almost every market-sensitive industry, and is recognized by regulatory authorities. The Basel II convention for the management of risk in financial lending institutions is gradually being phased in. VaR estimates the maximum percentage of value likely to be gained or lost as the result of normal price movements, over one day. For example, if VaR were US$1 million at a one-day 99 percent confidence level, there is only one chance in 100, under normal conditions, of a loss greater than US$1 million occurring.

The Danish shipping company, Norden, has developed a VaR approach that assesses risks relative to expected returns for a given deal or, conversely, the expected return acceptable for a specific deal, given a certain level of risk. It has also developed probability distributions for the returns expected at various risk levels. Several shipping companies follow similar approaches. This has been inspired by best practices in invest-ment banks, several of which use VaR to measure market risk. As Henry Paulson, then CEO of Goldman Sachs, stated, "No one likes trading losses, but they are a feature of our business. In fact, it is our willingness to tolerate such occasional, sizeable losses that enables us to earn attrac-tive returns over time" (Goldman Sachs, Annual Report, 2003).

As a predictor of trading results, VaR has historically worked well in relatively stable markets, but less well in more volatile and non-liquid markets. VaR also has several other limitations: it is based on historical data; it uses a one-day time horizon and so might miss the market risk of positions that cannot be liquidated or hedged in that timeframe; confidence levels have to be chosen that limit potential losses beyond that figure; because it is computed at the close of a business day, it may miss intra-day exposures (Pretzlik *et al.*, 2004).

MANAGERIAL OPTIONS FOR RESPONDING TO RISK

A shipping firm faces many types of risk. Some involve developments in the shipping markets, over which the firm has no control. Managerial response, however, can affect the risk exposure, which must be handled with competence and professionalism. The chartering policy, FFA trading, and hedging can effectively lower market risk exposure. In the end, it will be the risk exposure of the overall portfolio that matters.

Dealing with currency risks is often also of critical importance. For example, it is becoming more and more important to build currency term options into many transactions. Interest risks are also important – even critical – particularly in financing ships on long-term charters. Interest rates represent an important cost element for ship newbuilding projects, particularly when the projects are large. While interest rates have been dramatically low over the last few years – an important cost advantage that helped fleet expansion – today's much tighter market for ship financing has seen rising interest rates. Assuming a stable, low-level interest rate outlook has become a critical success factor for many shipping firms, but the realism of this assumption must increasingly be challenged. Interest rate swaps are increasingly being built into deals.

Managing currency and interest risks underscore the importance of having a strong financial management group within a shipping company. Higher interest rates may not be passed on to the shipper/charterer through higher freight rates and the shipowner will carry all the risks of fluctuation in currency and interest rates.

One key area for financial professionals to deal with is credit risk – the possibility of loss occurring due to financial failure by one's counterparty to meet one's contractual obligations. The assessment of the charterer's financial situation is especially critical where time charter or bare-boat charter agreements are concerned. This includes assessing the probability of default, as well as the size of the losses that would be incurred through default. If the charter party agreement turns out to be insufficient to support the debt burden involved, there is a credit risk. It is important to establish that the parent company of the counterparty carries the exposure, not a distant subsidiary that the counterparty might walk away from. Another type of serious risk exposure occurs when a ship on the spot market generates insufficient income to cover the financial obligations.

Other credit-related issues that need to be managed include the perception of credit worthiness of shipping companies, Basel II, anti-money laundering laws, the "war on terror," and so on. All these risks should be part of a risk management approach and need to be followed up systematically by the company. This is the "discipline for living with the possibility that future events may have nasty effects; or risk management is the ongoing process of identifying, quantifying, planning for, tracking and controlling risks" (Bischofberger and Rybak, 2003).

Although we have already discussed market risks, it should be added that decision-makers can now deal with them in entirely new ways, with freight volume hedging (FFAs), bunker hedging, freight rate hedging through long-term versus short-term time charter exposures, credit risk hedging when it comes to payment from major freighters, etc. But most of these hedges come at a cost.

There are several trends that might lead to less commoditization and atomism in various segments of the shipping industry. Most of these are admittedly weak but let's review the exogenous factors here. First, the shipping firms' own managerial actions might lead to more niche-oriented strategies. Second, more-or-less free access to capital has had the effect of keeping the main bulk shipping markets highly competitive and highly atomistic. So it is good to see some recent trends toward more *restrictions* on the capital inflow to the shipping industry. Many banks have been more restrictive regarding the financing of shipping projects. It has become harder for banks to resyndicate out such loans, with the result that they end up with the loans on their own balance sheets and less capacity to provide new shipping loans than before.

BASEL II ACCORD

Risk capital has become more costly and harder to get, particularly for smaller firms. At one time the existing capital accord agreement (Basel I) harmonized capital regulation very successfully. However, this regulation is no longer in tune with current banking practice. The deficiencies of Basel I included the comparative crudity of the framework and risk ratings and the omission of developments in risk management. The new regulation, Basel II, seeks to regulate complex banking business using generally accepted rules in a banking world that is neither simple nor homogeneous. The aim, once again, is to reinforce the stability of the financial system. A bank is now required to make use of systematic project risk assessments for each new deal to finance a ship. Innovation research companies, such as Marsoft, have tackled this by building shipping market risk scenarios into their packages. Additionally, each bank is only allowed to allocate so much of its lending capacity to shipping projects – if it allocates more than a reasonable fraction to shipping, there will be less capacity available for other types of projects that might be potentially more lucrative for the bank. So the bank has to apply an overall portfolio approach to its lending. Ship project financing cannot be seen in isolation.

The Basel II convention requires all banks systematically to assess the decision to give ship credits, in accordance with rigorous predetermined criteria. Their dealings with shipowners will become much more standardized as a result. This regulation implicates all banks, which must set aside a certain reserve (de facto "dead" capital) for every amount it commits to a particular project as a loan. Top management in a bank will allocate quotas to each business sector, and make sure that each sector then optimizes its sub-portfolio of projects, in order to pursue the best return for the bank. There will be competition between sectors within the bank and the most lucrative projects will be favored. In future, if shipping projects are to compete successfully for capital, most banks will require them to yield relatively high returns and relatively low risk. The net result of this is that the cost of capital for shipowners will rise. There is even a question mark over whether there will be enough financing available. Some smaller shipowners may be severely restricted or even squeezed out of bank financing altogether. This could lead to a smaller increase in overall new ship capacity. So far, however, we have not seen a lessening of newbuilding activities due to the tighter financing climate. Newbuilding contracts are often entered into during "good" times, with delivery projected several years in the future and without secure financing. What will happen to these projects now?

Basel II was intended to lead to more realistic loan pricing and to the banks setting aside more realistic reserves, taking the risk exposure of the lending banks into account. But some authorities claim this is not happening (Benink and Kaufmann, 2008). Leading banks are allowed to make use of their own models when calculating risks and reserve requirements. It is claimed that several of these banks may have underestimated their risk exposures, in effect increasing their capacity to issue loans. Basel II may be facilitating exactly the opposite of what it intended – riskier loans and fewer reserves.

Insisting that all banks use the Basel II model may be a way to establish consistency in ship financing.

KEY REQUIREMENTS FOR TAKING ON RISK

Taking on risk involves much more than explicitness about the risk of ship projects and individual decision-makers' propensity for risk. The corporate entity itself will have a structure, which implies that risk can be taken – or withstood – to varying degrees. There are three important and interrelated requirements that should prevent a firm from taking on a larger degree of risk than necessary:

1 **An appropriate capital base**. Too often companies get started with inappropriate capitalization, "hoping for the best," and take larger than acceptable risks.

2 **The skills of the team in charge**. It is important to have the entire relevant skill base in place. This will be different for each of the four shipping archetypes but, for all, it is critical for the team to understand shipping markets. For most of the archetypes, financial skills are a must. Operating skills are also important, certainly for the customer-related shipping archetype and for operations/crewing.

3 **Appropriate support systems**. This is dependent on the type of firm one is dealing with. There could be systems for:

- customer relations (use of steel), for each (major) customer, trade, port, etc.
- shipowning essentials
- understanding of fixed vs. variable costs and breakeven points
- liquidity measures
- levels of exposure to FFAs, equities, swaps, etc.
- product innovation statistics
- delivering complex projects on time, with realistic cost–benefit assessments.

ADDITIONAL RISK EXPOSURES

Let me elaborate on some of the major risks and risk exposures that each of the four types of shipping activities faces.

- Market risks, leading to inadequate returns, such as the demand/supply cyclicality risks typical in the shipping industry (freight rates, second-hand rates, newbuilding rates, scrapping rates).
- Weather-dependent risks, such as storms, etc., which can lead to unexpected delays and even off-hires.
- Risks of supply problems (say, for crude oil), harbor congestion, etc.
- Risks from unexpected moves by competition, such as price wars, new technology, etc.

- External, one-of-a-kind risks, such as those associated with regulatory shifts relating to health, safety, pollution, etc., as well as changes in accounting or fiscal standards. Risks such as strikes also fall into this category.
- Supply chain risks, such as defaults by certain suppliers, non-compliance with time-charter and/or bare-boat charter payments, problems with accounts receivable, etc. (A. P. Moller-Maersk had a problem claiming many of the accounts receivable it took over when it acquired a former competitor, P&O-Nedlloyd Container Lines, in 2005.)
- Internal risks, such as management errors, trading errors, etc. This is critical when it comes to trading in FFAs, put/call options, etc., and financial swaps or hedging relating to the coverage of interests and/or currencies. Clear stop-loss procedures must be in place to handle this.
- Financial risks, such as foreign exchange risk, interest rate risk, default risk in case of unsatisfactory value of collaterals, etc.
- Management mess-ups, e.g., poor implementation of organizational restructuring, unexpected delays on key projects, inability to achieve efficiency improvements, etc.

RISKS SURROUNDING THE RESIDUAL VALUE OF A SHIP
Understanding the residual value of a ship – what its second-hand value will be at the end of a long-term or bare-boat charter – is also critical. Newbuilding prices have risen but what if they come down? Residual value considerations (replacement costs and vessel valuation) are a growing issue. This will have an impact on the financing side – large falls in residual value may trigger loan defaults.

Residual value is volatile, and it is critical to understand the degree to which the shipowner is exposed. Many shipping companies may assume that second-hand prices will continue to go up, and calculate their risk exposure accordingly. But one cannot assume that this will be the case – second-hand prices have fallen many times in the past. Similarly, some companies may wrongly assume that the linear depreciation of their ships' values is sufficient. Shipping companies must simulate the effect on their portfolios of the outcomes of differing residual values. They cannot assume that the strong economic conditions will continue (Wolf, 2008). The following factors have a strong influence on residual value:

- The demand side at the time when the long-term or bare-boat charter expires. Where is the shipping market at that time? It is next to impossible to forecast exactly where on the market cycle one will be years into the future but some assessment is necessary. Marsoft can help here.
- Regulatory shocks, such as the double-hull legislation that followed the Exxon Valdez incident. We can expect more of this type of regulation about controlling CO_2 emissions.
- Technological breakthroughs, such as cost-efficient technology to handle CO_2 emissions from ships.

MANAGEMENT'S RESPONSIBILITY TOWARD RISK

For each business type, consistency about various types of risk exposure over time is important and should be in line with the overall risk propensity of the firm. If there is discomfort over risk exposure, management should consider risk insurance, or securitization, through pledging certain assets against coverage for other types of risks. Securitization is normal for bank financing, but can also be used to minimize other types of risks.

Senior management:

- Should ensure that there is a consistent view toward risk taking within each of the relevant business teams, in line with the intended risk propensity for the particular business, whether it is owning, using, operating, or innovating around steel.
- Must make sure that the overall portfolio risk for the whole firm makes sense, taking into account the subjective weighted aggregate of the risk of each of the various businesses.
- Must make sure that appropriate steps are taken to reduce all risks as far as possible – there is no need to take more risk than required. In situations that call for it, management should undertake risk insurance.

A critical question around risk taking involves stop-loss management. More research is needed into how to formulate stop-loss criteria and approaches for liquid and volatile markets. Why do we have stop-losses at all? Perhaps a new framework is needed, based on accepting the key risk exposures associated with the business in which one has chosen to operate.

RISK MANAGEMENT IN PRACTICE

Aker Kvaerner is a large engineering firm with particularly heavy exposure to offshore oil businesses. While the company is not in shipping as such, there are useful lessons to be learned from the way it handles risk. Its management sees risk management focusing on four factors:

1 A good understanding of the various elements of a business, to enhance one's understanding of the risk exposure of each. This involves calculation of the "correct" risk level for the key underlying factors for each part of the business.

2 Appropriate risk pricing within each of the major categories identified. The customer should be charged for a given level of risk. Aker Kvaerner's strategy differs from that of most shipping companies in this aspect, in that it has a unique technology and so can specify prices, whereas in shipping the price is set by the market. In shipping, the key question is whether to undertake a particular deal or not, based on one's understanding of the underlying risks. There may be many competitors for a deal – a company's decision to take the deal will be a function of how it assesses the value of the risks it faces.

3 A strong balance sheet and financial base, to be able to withstand adverse situations if risks work against the company. In shipping, scale is important. A large company with a broader portfolio of activities can undertake a more flexible set of risk-taking opportunities, and absorb adverse developments. Seaspan's management, for example, believes that the minimum container ship fleet size is 100, to allow for more opportunistic risk taking. This complements the company's current

focus – new ships are contracted at set prices, only after long-term charters have been secured and the financing has been put in place. This means that Seaspan's major risk is assessing the residual value for its ships. Similarly, the head of Clarkson Shipping Hedge Fund, Pierre Aury, specified that his fund would have to be a minimum size, before it could realistically start trading – size is, above all, a factor that allows one to be seen as a serious, plausible trading player by others.

4 A general focus on learning in risk management. Mistakes will be made – the important thing is to learn from them. Learning means a better understanding of each of the key underlying factors and what appropriate risk exposure really means – taking no risks at all would be sub-optimal, and taking unnecessarily high risks equally so.

RISK MANAGEMENT INNOVATIONS

Risk has always been a prominent factor in shipping. What is different today is that we are now in a better position to deconstruct the various factors that involve risk, and aim for a better understanding of each of them through forecasting, scenarios and the accumulation of experiential insight. Most of these factors can be securitized. One result of this is that cost of capital might come down. The specialized focus adopted by many shipping companies leads to a greater ability to deconstruct shipping into fundamental archetypes, allowing for a better understanding of the underlying risk factors through forecasting. This leads to more deliberate management of risk exposure and a fall in the cost of capital.

Moreover, risk and revenue management reinforces their value to freight companies. The greater understanding of forward prices and VaR that a company gains from risk management feeds into the company's decisions about allocating capacity on particular routes in order to maximize revenue. In many ways, the freight industry resembles the airline and power industries, in which both concepts have succeeded.

CONCLUSION

Minimizing risk is becoming more and more critical in shipping. The large influx of new capital into the industry, until recently, might have tempted many to pursue projects that would otherwise have been judged too risky. The current rate of newbuilding orders may be a reflection of this. The Basel II convention, while intended to facilitate a more prudent approach to risk taking, might in practice have led to the approval of projects that were inherently too risky. Many banks may have seen it as being in their best interest to go for such deals, increasing their business volume.

The residual value risk is potentially large when newbuilding prices are high. If a ship comes off charter when the market is down, the fall in value for the ship asset may be considerable. Understanding one's exposure to trading risk, for example, when active in FFA derivatives trading, is critical.

Above all, as I have stressed throughout this book, good market understanding and rate forecasting support remain key factors in improved risk management. And senior management must be consistent in their attitude toward risk over time. Having consistent procedures, such as a focus on VaR, is essential. It is equally important to have in place independent executives who can assess the risk exposure dimension associated with any project in a detached way.

Part IV   In conclusion

12 Two unique issues in shipping – family and governance   *page* 235
13 In the end … a question of management capabilities   248

12 Two unique issues in shipping – family and governance

While shipping is in many ways analogous to other major types of business – and not so uniquely different as some traditional shipping executives have claimed at times – there are at least two aspects of the shipping industry that require special focus, namely the unique role played by family entrepreneurs, and the need for speed and immediate reactions when it comes to board work and governance.

THE FAMILY BUSINESS DIMENSION

As we can see from Figure 12.1, most shipowning companies are still largely privately held: 64 percent of the fleet of very large crude carriers (VLCCs) is privately owned, as is more than 80 percent of Panamax and Handymax bulk carriers.

Empirical evidence, documented in research by two IMD professors, Dan Denison and John Ward, shows that well-managed, family-dominated firms tend to outperform well-managed, publicly traded firms (Denison *et al.* 2004). Why is this the case? Does it mean that family-dominated firms benefit from a longer-term time perspective? Does more stable and perhaps more committed ownership support performance? Would a not-for-sale philosophy lead to more performance focus and stability? These issues have been analyzed by Professor Joachim Schwass and others (Schwass, 2005), and have led him to make four distinctions between family-owned businesses and public corporations:

1 Family firms have more congruence between ownership and management interests. In contrast, in public corporations, management will often play the role of an agent for the stockholders – to strive for maximizing shorter-term stockholder value. There will also be higher

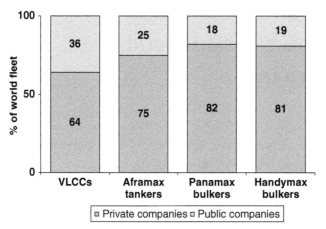

FIGURE 12.1 Public vs. private company ownership
Source: AMA Capital Partners (2007).

governance costs. There is often a lack of congruence between management and owners, even though there are certainly publicly held companies where this conflict is only latent or non-existent.

2 Family firms tend to take a more long-term point of view, with management/owners' interest focused on the next generation. This is particularly important in shipowning companies, where it is crucial to take a long-term point of view and consider the entire cycle. In contrast, public corporations often have a shorter-term focus, perhaps only as long as the duration of the CEO's contract. This type of ownership is well suited to shipping companies that use steel. As a result, family-owned brokerage firms, for example, are rare. Brokers/traders tend to own brokerage/trading firms, or at least significant parts of them.

3 The family firm may often have a better understanding of the underlying critical success factors for the business. The history of the business can be similar to the history of the owning family. In contrast, in public corporations, diverse stakeholders are always coming and going and financial analysis is more predominant here. With the advent of more liquidity and more professional management, one can expect to see more of this type of focus in shipping companies than before – rivaling the family-based management philosophy.

FAMILY	BUSINESS
Inclusive	Selective
Birthright	Competence
Memories	Future
Love	Money

FIGURE 12.2 Family business vs. publicly traded firms – two different systems
Source: Schwass (2005).

4 Finally, the value orientation in family businesses is "we, we, we" as opposed to the "me, me, me" management focus in many public corporations. Schwass summarizes the dichotomy between the two types of firms in Figure 12.2.

Schwass (2005, p. 108–11) cites a quote from Hermès, the France-based luxury goods family firm: "We do not inherit the family business from our parents. We borrow it from our children."

Many family oriented shipping companies have done very well. There is an additional, and fundamental, reason why family firms dominate the shipping industry – decision-making speed. It is often critically important to make decisions fast in shipping. Public companies, dictated by governance regulations, have extensive decision-making committees. Their processes can be too slow for shipping companies, which can be faced with having to make almost instant choices between strategic options, rather than pursuing the more compromise-oriented decision-making so often found in public firms. Speed and decision-making power go hand in hand. However, these are general observations. Seaspan, for instance, a publicly traded company on the New York Stock Exchange, has a CEO – Gerry Wang – who has the mandate (and the inclination) to move fast and to be highly focused. There are committees, yes, but few delays. Perhaps the key here is that Seaspan has an entrepreneurial CEO. Other public companies with entrepreneurial CEOs, like General Maritime and Frontline, are also very dynamic, but some family owned/controlled shipping firms are notoriously slow. Perhaps there, the entrepreneurial spirit is lacking.

Despite what has been said about well-managed, family dominated firms, there are also many examples of family oriented shipping firms that have degenerated. Some of the issues that contribute to this include:

- Questions about the next generation's management competence. If the next generation of family members is incompetent, the result is a degenerating situation. There has certainly been a lot of this in shipping. Many of the *Gründers* were seafarers themselves – often captains – with hands-on drive and understanding. The next generation often falls short, however.
- Sibling rivalry can be an issue, especially if one sibling is more competent at running the business than the other(s). This can lead to performance being stifled, something that is frequently found in some family dominated shipping companies – leadership is by family committee, and the decision-making clarity so essential in shipping is weakened.
- A sense of unfairness among various shareholders. This can be aggravated when some family members earn large salaries, while others only receive the normal dividends. In countries with heavy taxation regimes – such as Norway – this is a particular issue. While the asset value of a shipping company can be substantial, the dividends paid may be too low to cover wealth taxes and even dividend taxes. So while passive family owners may be wealthy on paper, in fact their cash flow can be strained. Understandably, this is a difficult base for the future management of family business firms.
- Static strategy and stagnated culture. Obviously, issues of business renewal, internal entrepreneurship, and growth can end up suffering when family members of average caliber put their stamp on the company, generation after generation – over time, mediocrity pervades the organization. It is not uncommon for a brilliant, insightful owner to be succeeded by mediocre next generation members and, when this happens, the performance of shipping companies fades. For a more detailed discussion of these issues, see Schwass (2005), who recommends a clear shareholder agreement for family firms.

Examples of shareholder agreements
To safeguard the proper evolution of the family-based company, Torvald Klaveness had a shareholder agreement that regulated management succession.

> What he [Klaveness, founder] feared the most was having children who would waste everything that he had built up. You can read that clearly in the shareholders' agreement. In his time, shipowners were "Mr. Big," but he saw the families [of many of them] disintegrate. He saw the values disintegrate. And that he did not want. He had a clear identity for his company."   *(Ward and Lief, 2002, p. 4).*

Among other things, Klaveness' shareholder agreement stipulated that the aim was to preserve decision-making in the company, to promote the individual professional growth of those active in the firm, and to protect the accumulation of assets and wealth in the firm as a going concern. Family members who held ownership also had to work actively in the company and only one family member from each of the two owning branches could be active in the firm. This meant that other family members from each branch would have to be bought out. In this way, the agreement addressed the issue of "watering down" and/or fragmenting the family ownership side, maintaining concentration of ownership in the hands of the active members of the family.

At Leif Höegh & Co. family ownership is also in a few hands – initially those of the founder, and until recently two cousins, one grandson from each side. All other members of the family have been bought out. The owners had to borrow funds to do this – a clear sign of commitment. The pruning of the family tree has had the effect of concentrating the focus and commitment of the remaining owners. At Leif Höegh, the owners are not active in running the firm – a professional management team does this – but they exercise their influence through active presence on the board.

At Tschudi & Eitzen, founded in 1883, there has been one partner from each family side since the start, and the fifth generation worked together until 2005. A decision was then made to split the ownership between the two sides – perhaps to allow each side of the family to follow its own strategy. One side, headed by Felix Tschudi, remains strictly private. It has been proactively broadening its shipping company focus, with relatively heavy emphasis on non-traditional shipping business activities, such as an integrated logistics service in the Baltic, and extended iron ore mining and harbor terminal activities in the far north of Norway (Kirkenes).

The other part, headed by Axel Eitzen, has become the embryo for several publicly traded shipowning companies – one for large bulk carriers and another for chemical tankers. Both firms have expanded aggressively via newbuilding programs as well as acquisitions. The Eitzen risk profile is less conservative than the Tschudi side.

For all of these companies – and I could have cited many more – family succession and the successful evolution of the firm go hand in hand. Other shipping companies go under because of bad succession planning. The next generation of the family may simply not have the talent needed to run a complex, modern shipping company. But those with talent should be allowed to participate in the company. The question is how to allow family talent to maintain a role in the family firm, while still pursuing and maintaining professionalism. A good way is to create a mechanism that ensures active managerial participation and restricting family ownership to those active in the company.

In family oriented companies, such as Leif Höegh – as well as A.P. Moller-Maersk, Farstad and others – non-family members have taken over as president/CEO. The family takes roles on the board of directors, often with a family member serving as chair. The firm compensates the owners through dividends rather than salaries. This is an alternative strategy to pruning the family tree: the family is no longer active in the day-to-day running of the business, and allows professional management to step in.

So, there are two main options. The first is for the firm to invite family members to play a more passive role, via the board, and bring in professional management to run the business. This implies the development of a long-term dividend payment strategy and in turn, the development of a shipping strategy that allows for the generation of enough free cash flow to meet dividend payments. An example of a company in this category is the A.P. Moller-Maersk Group, which is not only the world's largest container liner shipping company but is also engaged in a number of other shipping and non-shipping areas, such as oil, shipbuilding, and industrial activities. The company's diversified base allows it to pay a steady dividend stream. The interests of the various shareholder owners should therefore be covered, even though none of the next generation is actively involved in the management of the group, except on the board.

An alternative strategy is for those family members who remain active in the company to buy out the others – pruning the family tree. To do this, the residual owners will need access to substantial funds – a burden that may put the firm in jeopardy.

So succession in family firms works best when it is based on one or two principles. The ownership side can be closely held, and combined with active management so that non-active family members in the firm are bought out by those who remain active in the firm. Alternatively, all family members can withdraw from active participation in the management of the company, and instead rely on an active dividend policy and exercise their ownership role as members of the board. Examples of the former are Klaveness, Leif Höegh & Co., and Oldendorff (Henning Oldendorff). Other family members were bought out, and it is stipulated that only active managers/owners should participate from the main family. Examples of the latter are A.P. Moller-Maersk and Farstad.

GOVERNANCE

In the past, the CEO of the traditional shipping firm was also the majority owner and would often have all the say in the organization. Many classical shipping companies were built up around strong owner-CEOs, who ran their organizations more or less dictatorially (Höegh,

1970). Today, the CEO needs to be catalytic, less directive. It is important that he or she is able to unleash the creative thrust of the entire organization in a top-down/bottom-up dialogue. What are the key inputs from the CEO in such a balanced dialogue?

First, the CEO needs to stimulate visionary global thinking. This means being able to demonstrate a strong feel for the shipping business, but also an open mind, true curiosity and an ability to get excited. The CEO must take the time to be with the organization, above all to participate in potential new business projects. The CEO needs to "walk the talk," to demonstrate a readiness (and ability) to contribute – to sit down and think together with the organization's management. In this way, the CEO builds the credibility of his abilities and adds to decision-making resolve in the firm.

Second, the CEO needs to drive the key people in the organization to more speedy action. A good way to do this is to allocate additional resources to specific strategic initiatives. In this way, the CEO acts as a "pumping station," making sure that critical talents and funds are available. The CEO needs to keep a keen eye on the timeline associated with the planned rollout of a strategic project, and to ask, can these milestones be passed even faster? Can I allocate more resources to this project to speed it up and increase its chances of success? It should be pointed out that this can conflict with typical budget-based resource allocation – when the CEO asks his organization to do more with less. But it is important to recognize that strategic innovations need a lot of resources.

Let us now turn to the chair and the board of directors of the shipping company. It is important for the board in a shipping company to provide broad guidelines for the risks the company should take. These guidelines should be based on a thorough discussion of the business platforms in which the shipping company operates. The board must determine the overall rudiments of the company's portfolio strategy. Peter Shaerf has proposed the IGLOO concept of governance – the board must provide Insight, Guidance, and Lots Of Oversight (Peter Shaerf, private communication).

In a shipping company, strategy – from the board's perspective – is prepared by mapping out the general direction that it is desirable to follow. At the same time, it is important that the board does not delay specific decisions. A shipping company can only thrive if decision-making is fast. The board must give management enough leverage to act aggressively and independently within the overall guidelines that the board has set, including which areas to be active in, which niche platforms to pursue, and the risk levels to take when it comes to financing, leveraging, chartering, etc. The CEO and the top management can then appropriately push for decisions within this overall mandate.

Good governance is ensured through a balance between the board of directors and the CEO and top management. The climate of the company should be such that good, balanced governance can take place. This will show in the unique strategy of the shipping firm, its implementation focus and the accompanying risk profile. As we have seen, speed and focus are essential. Therefore, the decision-making role of the CEO is often more accentuated in shipping firms than in other types of corporations. Clearly, this gives rise to unique governance challenges. How can balanced, effective governance be achieved without degenerating into dictatorship? The following examples might illustrate this:

- Too much power for the CEO. In this company, a large, closely traded family corporation, the CEO had a very strong command of the business, understanding many of the details better than the board members. Both the CEO and the board members came from the family. Over time, the CEO came to dominate the board meetings with long presentations and monologues that asserted that things were going in the right direction and determined how the momentum could continue. Because of his dominance, there was little dialogue among the board members. Consequently, the board was not sensitized to potentially negative developments that could hurt the company, and which would not necessarily have been picked up on the CEO's radar.

- Too much dominance by the board and its chair. In this family-controlled company, primarily in the container feeder shipping business, the chair allowed himself to be dragged into many details of the business. He became too associated with the specific business activities of the firm. The CEO, also a family member, was relatively weak, and the chair felt that he had to step in to make sure that "proper" decisions were executed. He came to associate himself more and more with the CEO. As a result, the chair became increasingly tainted by many of the poor decisions made by the CEO. Again, there was not a good balance between the board and the CEO.

There are a number of truisms regarding how the company functions, which might have overriding effects on governance. It will be the role of the board, together with top management, through participative, balanced interactions, to make sure that the firm's governance culture remains healthy. I have identified several issues concerned:

1 Good governance is associated with an **open attitude**, as opposed to an "I know best" attitude. Shipping companies (and other companies for that matter) can be plagued by silo thinking. I have already pointed out the risks of too much dominance at the top. Specialized functions, such as finance, may also see themselves as silos, as can chartering, technical, etc. This sort of specialization should be avoided. Multitasking is important, not just to save costs, but even more importantly to enhance creativity and renewal. Eclecticism is essential – each function will learn from the others. The CEO can gain the most by being open to multiple inputs – rather than adopting an imperial attitude.

2 An **action orientation** must be preserved in shipping companies, and good governance must be built around it. It is important to experiment and to work fast. Too many governance-dictated committees, at times generating demands for excessive analysis, testing, and plans – at the expense of execution – can be bad for a company; shipping markets move fast, and good opportunities can be lost just as quickly. Decision-making speed also has its perils, however, so it is important not to stigmatize those managers who are behind what turn out to be poor decisions. Over

time, however, a manager must be able to show a reasonably consistent track record of good decisions – and this will only become apparent through action: to fail early is to succeed sooner. Good governance must be action-oriented.

3 It is important for the organization to be **a meeting place between opportunities, problems, challenges, and solutions**. Key strategic issues should be openly discussed in the organization. Eclectic teams often see solutions that individual members of the organization, working in silos, do not consider. Creativity, not specialized silos, is critical.

4. The **customer's view is vital**. Companies have to understand what creates value for the customer. As I pointed out before, the power in many shipping companies seems to be shifting away from the shipowner/supplier and into the hands of the customer and the final link in the value chain: we could say that the critical focus in the shipping supply chain has shifted downstream. Successful shipping companies come up with new ways to create value for the customer. This is true for all four archetypes. What are the critical success factors to create significant value for the customer – *now*? Good governance should stimulate a focus on this.

5 **Management processes**. Cumbersome management processes should be avoided. Shipping organizations are often asset intensive but not necessarily large. It is possible to keep management processes simple, to-the-point and non-bureaucratic. Governance should assess management processes, to ensure this. There are two central types of process.

- **Human resource management processes**. How can one attract, keep and develop the best human talent? How can one create job rotations, so that key people keep developing and do not get stuck with functional "tunnel vision"? Management bonuses can be important factors here. Big money is generated in shipping. It is essential to have a fair process, so that those who contribute to the bottom line are adequately compensated.

- **Planning and control processes**. The annual planning/budgeting process so often found in industrial firms may not capture opportunities that come up fast and unexpectedly. It is important for top management to be able to react fast and reach a conclusion in time. Plans should be laid – but they should be seen as bases for subsequent revisions, not as a process that might stifle opportunism. This should also be the case for budgets.

6 Always have some **available liquidity** in the bank and/or assets that can be easily liquidated. Arrange loan facilities that can be drawn on to tap unused debt capacity. Liquidity is vital – not only to take advantage of developing business opportunities, but also to safeguard against the risk of bankruptcy, which would rule out active participation in the ownership of the business.

7 **Ability to go to the market to raise more equity**. This is particularly important when the stock value of the corporation, judged by its market value, is *less* than the asset value of the firm. This is often the case for US-based shipping companies, giving them access to reasonably priced equity capital.

8 It is important to have **internal entrepreneurs** in the shipping firm, to identify and bring new business initiatives up to speed. They must:

- see business opportunities before they are obvious to everyone else – this involves a good understanding of the relevant shipping markets, as well as the key customers;
- be good at mobilizing the necessary resources, developed by the firm itself, and other outside organizational entities, rapidly, to scale up and implement new entrepreneurial ideas.

9 An ability to **lead by inspiration** and attract other outstanding managers to be part of the internal entrepreneurial initiatives.

10 It will be a key requirement for good governance that the board assesses the availability of **internal entrepreneurship capacity** – in shipping, it is essential to be able to strike good deals.

Seaspan is a great example of this. Gerry Wang, Seaspan's CEO, is an outstanding internal entrepreneur. He is able to spot business opportunities early and to work with yards and container shipping operating entities to turn business visions into reality. He inspires a network of people, working on aspects of the various strategic initiatives, because of his integrity and impeccable reputation. He is also experienced in raising capital. His vision is to propel Seaspan to becoming the world's largest container-owning shipping company by 2010.

With all governance considerations, the key is to keep it simple. Too much complexity, too much time spent on lengthy analysis, too many central staff discussions and delays, etc., weaken the decision-making resolve of a shipping company. It is particularly important to keep things moving, and not overburden them with too much bureaucracy. Good governance should strive to ensure this. The need for speed and decision-making focus poses a unique governance challenge.

In shipping, good governance means being supportive of fast decision-making, understanding the essentials of the business, and avoiding becoming bogged down in bureaucracy and excessively for-malistic practices.

CONCLUSION

Shipping is distinct from many industries in at least two ways. First, most shipping companies are run by successful entrepreneurs. Either these firms are not public, or, if publicly traded, the individual entre-preneur is still firmly in charge, like Maersk Mc-Kinney Møller of A.P. Moller-Maersk, Gerry Wang of Seaspan, John Frederiksen of Frontline, and Peter Georgiopoulos of General Maritime. Family firms can provide a great platform for such entrepreneurship but equally there are examples of family firms with slow, unfocused, often fragmented, and conservative management.

There are unique governance challenges in shipping firms, where speed is critical. Boards will often not have time to deliberate each major prospective deal, in the way boards of other companies can. It is important for the board to support the general strategic direction of the firm. This will allow top management to develop deals swiftly and to move aggressively to bring such deals to closure. The board's involve-ment can be cursory, as long as the prospective project falls within the agreed strategy.

13 In the end ... a question of management capabilities

I have indicated that in the past many shipping companies were dominated by a generalist approach, with the integrated shipping firm as
the model. These integrated shipping firms were involved in many
aspects of shipping under one organizational umbrella. For example,
shipowning, chartering, and ownership of an innovative shipyard were
combined at A. P. Moller-Maersk; shipowning and substantive freestanding chartering activities at Björge and Fearnley and Eger; shipowning and
freestanding ship management and crewing at A. O. Sorensen, and so on.
Shipowning was often the core of this tradition, built around some
particular decision-making heuristics:

- the enlightened vision of the shipowner to buy ships cheaply and then
  sell them at the high end of the market;
- the power of owners who were tough negotiators;
- a strong sense of control;
- an acceptable element of arrogance, given the perceived superior power
  of shipowning organizations.

In this book, I have argued for a different point of view. Specialized
shipping organizations have become dominant, each requiring a separate type of focus when it comes to owning steel, using steel, operating
steel, and innovating around steel. Different critical success factors are
at play, which means that a different organizational approach is also
required – not only when contrasting today's firms with the integrated
shipping firms of the past, but also when comparing these four different
shipping archetypes.

- **Owning steel**. The key success factor for shipowning firms is to develop
  economies of scale. This requires a clear commodity point of view and

an understanding of the specifics of the dry, wet, and container markets. A simple, strong, cost efficient, no-nonsense, motivated organization must be established for each shipping market, with clear responsibility for running the particular type of ship on a cost-efficient basis. Performance assessment and incentives might be based on cost efficiency in one's markets.

- **Using steel**. In order to make money out of steel, users focus heavily on marketing and the customer. They will have a strong understanding of negotiations, based on flexibility and the realization that the negotiation power rests with the customers, not the shipping entity per se. Critical success factors are scope (relationships with key customers); understanding the day-to-day shifts and movements of the markets to spot opportunities before they are obvious to everyone else; and developing relationships with specialized shippers.

- **Operating steel**. For operations-focused firms – crewing – the focus is on cost-efficiency but with a constant eye on quality. This involves training crew members, including officers and maintenance while the ship is in operation.

- **Innovating around steel**. For product innovators, the focus is on speed and the ability to attract outstanding talent. Innovating organizations are not very large, and are more employee-centered, attracting exceptional world-class talent for understanding the shipping markets and cutting-edge ship technology.

Companies that have separate operating units focusing on a different aspect within a specialized archetype have a portfolio strategy, built around one or more of the operating units. These units might be focused around a particular archetype – this is the case for market-driven brokerage firms. R.S. Platou, for instance, has special units to deal with the offshore supply sector, the tanker sector, the dry bulk sector, and the purchase and sales sectors. Alternatively, the portfolio could be focused on one or more specialties within, for example, "product innovation." Skipsteknisk has special units for the design of offshore supply ships, fishing vessels, and seismic supply ships.

Shipowning organizations could be focused around various ship types. J. Lauritzen has special units for the ownership of dry bulk ships, product tankers, and small gas carriers.

The portfolio, and the corresponding organizational structure, can range from simple to complicated, particularly if there are business activities within two or more of the archetypes. Nevertheless, it is important to have a specialized, strong and focused organization to support each of these business activities. At corporate level, the organization must deal with setting the overriding portfolio strategy, which focuses on achieving an overall risk profile according to the wishes of the owners (the investors).

There must thus be a clear focus, based on market realities – a clear understanding of the relevant details of the markets for a given shipping archetype. Each distinctive business would work toward clear targets to take advantage of unique market opportunities within their particular business context. Action targets would be a function of the benefiting business.

This type of shipping organization consists of professionals within their specialized segments, rather than generalists. Experience is, of course, critical.

Peter Georgiopoulos, chairman of General Maritime and Genco Shipping and Trading, has a disciplined approach to acquisitions that has stood him in good stead with investors. At General Maritime, his publicly listed tanker company, he made a splash with the 2004 acquisition of Metrostar's fleet of Aframaxes and Suezmaxes, but after that made only one further acquisition – the Soponata fleet. Instead of increasing capacity, the company has refinanced its corporate debt, issued a US$450 million special dividend, and bought back a significant volume of the outstanding stock. The shareholders have continued to support management and the company has continued to perform in the top tier of public shipping companies.

Genco, the dry cargo company, has similarly made a large fleet acquisition and has continued to increase its dividend, focusing on maximizing shareholder return. These moves demanded a significant amount of patience from Georgiopoulos over a period of three years. Shareholders buy into the promise and the delivery of the promise. Genmar and Seaspan are other prime examples of this thesis.

Until recently, there has generally been a lot of capital available, "looking" for deals in the shipping markets – entering and exiting at the right times. The power of those who intellectually understand the markets for both shipping and financial investment is on the rise. The two markets should be viewed together more frequently, to enhance the ability of deals made. Organizationally, specialization implies that teams with both sets of competencies will be at work.

The shipping company, in whichever archetype, needs to be truly global – to see itself as a network of activities that can draw on talent from all over the globe. And in spirit it also needs to be virtual – not confined to a dominant group of people in a particular headquarters location, or associated with a particular country of ownership. The host country should dominate less in human resource management, and instead welcome all types of talent, irrespective of where they come from, as long as they can do the best possible job within the specialized business context.

In this sense, we can talk about the emergence of the focused, specialist-driven, stateless corporation. The consequence is, of course, that human resource policies are adapting to global specialized competence. Performance within an area of competence, rather than generalist shipping cultural or geographical experience, is increasingly sought (Evans *et al.*, 2002).

ORGANIZATIONAL ISSUES

As a premise for commercial success, shipping organizations must be built around the four specialized shipping archetypes. But it is interesting to observe how commercial success can still lead to organizational problems, which are manifested in several ways:

• An increasing emphasis on silos or kingdoms. Various departments can take on their own life, focusing on what is happening inside the silo, without enough cross-fertilization within other departments in the organization. This can compromise effective overall portfolio management, one result of which is inconsistent implementation of risk management. Ironically, success can lead to fragmentation and sub-optimization.

- Bureaucracy can increase, related to the silo phenomenon. Individual executive status may become more important than consideration of how to build business.
- Consistent with this, credit rises to the top, while the blame is directed to the lower echelons. This can create a risk-averse culture, where few are willing to take the kinds of risk that lead to extraordinary performance.
- Professionalism and new blood have become crucial to the shipping industry but, at the same time, the industry emphasizes experience. Many members of the old guard have invaluable inputs. The winning shipping organization employs a mix of experienced managerial talent and younger specialists.

STRONG LEADERSHIP

Leading these emerging, relatively flat, networked shipping corporations – less hierarchical, more project oriented – requires charisma and drive from the top. Today's shipping leaders need global appeal. They have to have impeccable stakeholder acceptance, a relevant shipping competence profile that creates broad bonding with various talent groups. The national generalist shipping leaders of the past may be less effective.

As always, this industry needs entrepreneurial, inspirational, and motivational leadership. The leader of any of these four archetypes must be able to spot new business opportunities and be capable of putting together relevant eclectic teams to pursue them. Gone are the days when a leader could do everything more or less by him or herself. And the days when he/she could rely on close friends as surrogates for a team have also disappeared.

Headquarters can now be expected to be small and highly professional. The shipping firm has been largely restructured along project initiatives, i.e., ad hoc temporary organizational units, so that it is both "large" and "small." Small autonomous entities are created to safeguard entrepreneurialism and drive within particular business segments, for example, various ship categories within bulk, which again are part of an archetype shipping company. They are, however, supported by "shared services," in order to take advantage of the size and scale advantages of larger firms, so that an overall portfolio strategy can be developed. The net effect of this is more flexibility and the ability to deal with change.

VOLATILITY IN VALUE CREATION

Huge fortunes are regularly created within shipping today, with remarkable speed. Similarly, established fortunes are being wiped out – also rather regularly. The so-called rich within shipping are often "newly minted," while the established, traditionally wealthy individuals and shipping families have become less important. The bottom line is a pattern of increased volatility – on the ownership side.

There has been a shift toward specialized professionalism in shipping. To succeed nowadays, a shipping company must also have the old entrepreneurial *Leitbild*. There is still an abundance of strong-willed – even flamboyant – individuals who are setting their imprimatur on the shipping business, perhaps more so than in any other industry. Decision-making power and ability is still firmly fixed at the top. This leadership style, however, must encompass a clear vision, clear creativity, and a clear ability to be consistent over time – all in line with a specialized business context as the base.

Let us now briefly summarize what shipping companies need to establish in order to deliver on their economic performance:

- A competent, specialized, focused organization that attracts, keeps, and develops the best possible team of executives within its field. The most difficult challenge in shipping companies is to find groups of top specialists for each particular specialized business.
- More emphasis on effective corporate governance, with complementary roles for the board of directors, top management, and staff. This does not

mean slow-down and added bureaucracy, but nor does it mean – at the other end of the spectrum – abdication of governance.

- Effective processes for consistently setting and managing the particular strategy of the shipping firm with its risk/return targets. Reaching a common view on a risk/return profile can be a real issue when several decision-makers are involved, say, in managing a fleet of up to several hundred vessels. Each shipping deal will have its own risk characteristics. The overall portfolio strategy, however, should be consistent with the intended risk profile.

- Consistent rules and policies, etc., are required, similar to those used by credit lending banks. These must be tailored to the particular shipping segment that the firm is in for chartering and forward freight agreement (FFA) trading, as well as currency and interest rate tracking or swings – for example, with respect to stop-loss guidelines.

THE KNOW-HOW BASE

Executives with a key understanding of shipping markets are critically important, as are highly specialized groups of executives from finance or technical areas. How can such specialized cultures work together, symbiotically and positively? How can an "either/or" culture, which puts too much weight on categories of professionals, be avoided? While cross-cultural organizational issues have been studied extensively, when it comes to differences between nationalities and their impact on organizational culture (DiStefano and Maznevski, 2003), there has been relatively little study of cultural differences based on differing professional backgrounds (DiStefano and Ekelund, 2002).

Five cultures need to come together in the successful shipping firm:

1 A shipping market culture – the expertise necessary for pursuing a classic, market-based shipping strategy. Crucial to this is a keen understanding of the relevant market(s), such as a particular segment of the bulk market or a particular segment of the tanker market, with a good feel for eventual turning points in the dynamics of the market(s).

2 A chartering and trading culture – the expertise necessary for pursuing various customer-focused strategies. Knowledge of brokerage and trading is needed here.

3 A technical innovation culture that pushes for better solutions. An innovation focus can be along less technical areas, too, for example in forecasting.

4 An operations culture – the ability to "make good even better." This means having the necessary know-how for operating and crewing a given ship, focused on delivering the best possible transportation service at the lowest possible cost.

5 A financial culture – the ability to manage financial flows and budgets, to deal with currency issues, interest rate developments and, increasingly, new instruments and derivatives as they relate to futures freight market trading. Financial engineering is becoming increasingly important.

These different managerial cultures stem from the four shipping arche-types we have looked at in this book. To a larger or lesser extent, they must all be present for each shipping business archetype – but with different weighting depending on which shipping archetype is con-cerned. Finance, however, will always be key.

In most segments of the shipping industry today, the critical underlying success factors are evolving very fast. To some extent, this evolution is a function of macro-economic turbulence; most segments are still volatile. But it is linked to the speed of evolution in the shipping company *customers'* views of their need for transportation support. The configurations of their supply chains are constantly changing. Technological factors contribute to this, as do trends toward outsourc-ing and supply chain management. Additionally, the drive to seek out new non-commodity niches never ends. A shipping organization must be fast, dynamic, and non-bureaucratic. It must prove its ability to create value every day, in rapidly changing contexts. Shipping organizations are engaged in a never-ending process of organizational change.

Networked organizations are one answer to the need for dyna-mism and change. In traditional shipping companies, it was important to run ships to keep the operating organization intact and maintain a stable of officers and sailors. This emphasis on stability, based on a set operating model, often led to strategies that made less sense from a more opportunistic view of commercial shipping.

Excessive complexity is now a problem. In the past, many shipping companies employed a diverse variety of ships, without necessarily having the requisite competence to serve the dynamic growth platforms of each of these trades effectively and realistically. Today, focusing on one or a few growth platforms and breaking up the organization into smaller, more focused organizational entities is the key to success.

Shipping companies must also keep their costs down. A shipping firm cannot expect to be sustainable if it has a higher long-term cost level than the competition. Crew costs are a very important component of this, linked to country of origin. Norway, for instance, has high seafarer wages and employee benefit costs, even compared to neighboring countries such as Sweden and Denmark. Many of the most reasonably priced crews now come from former Yugoslavia, Russia, the former Eastern European countries, India, and the Philippines. The response from many traditional shipping countries is to give their seafarers tax relief, and in some countries (the Netherlands, Sweden, and Denmark) even total freedom from taxes.

The classic hierarchical shipping organization – based on functions and integrated ship trade involvements – is disappearing, as firms now pursue relatively simple and clearly focused shipping strategies. The new network organizations are based on a core of "brains and talent" that meet the value-creating needs of company strategy. The rest can be outsourced.

For example, Frontline, the world's largest tanker fleet operator, with twenty seven Suezmax tankers and thirty nine very large crude carriers (VLCCs) under its management, has no operating organization. This is all outsourced. Frontline is small and networked, focusing on timing – through chartering, financing, and asset play. Outsourcing operations keeps costs low and, more importantly, flexibility and speed of execution very high.

Middlemen – shipbrokers, project brokers, financial brokers, insurance brokers, etc. – have always been used in shipping. Experts now expect a trend away from the use of middlemen toward direct contact between shipowners, shippers, and other principal actors. There are many reasons for this.

- "The broker is often wrong, but never in doubt." So why are some brokers successful and others not? A strong broker relationship can be very important, such as the relationship between R.S. Platou and S. Ugelstad, in the development and execution of the company's strategy. In its relationship with brokers, a shipping firm should avoid transaction volume biases, i.e., residual values might be systematically overvalued by the broker, so that a project may look "too" good. Also, back haul rates tend to be overestimated, again making the project look better than it is. All of this is done to make the calculations for a particular project work well, paving the way for a transaction that, in the end, might be unrealistic. Brokers can "sin" here but it is ultimately up to management not to fall into their trap.

- "Middlemen can be expensive, too, levying heavy commissions – funds that owners could benefit from themselves." The cost benefits of using brokers must always be carefully assessed. Although humorous, the following limerick, by Peter Shaerf, Managing Partner of AMA Capital Partners, depicts the difficult position that brokers cum middlemen often find themselves in:

> The broker to get his commission
> Solicited the Owner's permission
> To deduct it at source
> For the Owner of course
> Was not known for his timely remission.
>
> *Source:* TradeWinds, *Volume 19, Number 11 (March 14, 2008).*

The limerick's sentiments indicate another argument for striving for fixing the lowest brokering costs. All unnecessary expenses have to be eliminated – winners in the industry pursue this with a passion.

- Owners, understandably, may want to build direct relationships with key market contacts to develop their own intelligence about their customers. They may hope to have a better dialogue with them, understand their needs better – in short, to be full-fledged partners with their customers. Extensive in-house brokerage organizations have been developed in companies like A. P. Moller-Maersk, Norden, the Torvald Klaveness Group, Leif Höegh, and Farstad. These organizations deal directly with their customers/shippers, not through brokers.

As we have seen, it is important to be able to differentiate oneself from one's competitors, i.e., to develop one's organization to focus effectively on the customer. This is positive differentiation. When working with brokers, the pressure for differentiation falls on the broker, so it is easier for them if shipowners are not particularly customer oriented. There is a potential built-in conflict between brokers and owners, in the sense that while the owners want to differentiate themselves, the brokers want to keep the owners' services as standard as possible. As Morits Skaugen states: "To have direct access to the market is key, and the brokers can only hamper this."

Another dilemma is that brokers work for several companies. It can be difficult to establish "Chinese walls" around companies' confidential and exclusive data. When brokers are given interesting commercial opportunities, they often face a dilemma about which shipping company on their client list they should offer the deal to. In theory, all new deals should be offered to all the shipbroker's clients; in practice, this rarely happens. A shipbroker, therefore, becomes a "deal router." The problem of exclusivity can be particularly difficult with unique niche deals, where the very nature of the information around the commercial aspects of the deal requires one-on-one handling, not a broad sharing of information. In these situations, the traditional broker function easily becomes compromised. Many of the benefits from the middleman function – creating a more perfect market – are lost.

So why this interest in world shipping? Does this sector deserve special attention? Is there something unique – even fascinating – about world shipping? The answer is yes – I believe so – for three major reasons.

First, we are experiencing a revolution in world manufacturing and trade. China has become the manufacturer for the world and India and Southeast Asia are not far behind. The result has been a shift in world trade. Raw materials are increasingly being channeled to these countries. Finished goods are being shipped from them to the major consuming regions, especially Europe and North America. Ocean shipping has been central to making these shifts feasible. Thus, shipping is more than ever a central element of economic growth and prosperity. Without an effective shipping industry, it is hard to see how this new order of specialization in the world could have taken place.

Second, mankind continues to be fascinated with rapid shifts in wealth, creation, and destruction of new fortunes – and shipping continues to be the industry that stands for those compelling elements of volatility and rapid change. A number of charismatic individual entrepreneurs add to that unique magic. In short, public fascination with shipping is stronger today than ever.

Third, there are powerful new strategic approaches that work in shipping. A lot of these are to do with specialization – owning, using, operating, and innovating around steel. Each of these unique business niches requires its own competitive strategy. Others involve portfolio strategies and risk management.

Shipping is one of the oldest industries in existence but it is constantly evolving to meet new challenges and opportunities. Nowadays, it is a more exciting field than ever to work in and to study.

Epilogue

The shipping industry has gone through extraordinary negative changes during the latter part of 2008. The speed, as well as depth of fall in the markets, has been unprecedented. For instance, the freight markets have collapsed. Daily spot rates for a Capesize bulk carrier are now (November 2008) less than one twentieth of what they were in June 2008 – down from US$230,000 per day to around US$4,000 per day. And *all* shipping freight markets are affected.

All related markets are falling too. Second-hand values have gone down accordingly and newbuilding prices are also coming down. Shipping company stocks are trading at a significant discount, at lower levels than ever. Seaspan's shares, for instance, are priced at less than a quarter of what they were two months prior to the end of November 2008. Oil prices are well under US$50 per barrel, as of February 2009, down from the peak of US$147 per barrel in mid-2008. World trade is shrinking too, as country after country is falling into recession. Even China's growth is slowing down, including a significant drop in steel production.

And of particular significance for the capital-intensive shipping business, there is virtually no capital available for investment in new projects. The illiquidity in the banking sector, above all when it comes to ship financing, is almost complete.

All in all, the shipping industry is facing an unprecedented crisis, and there are indeed reasons to be pessimistic. Still, there should be some room for optimism! First, the shipping markets have always been – and always will be – cyclical. A contrarian view is, therefore, potentially beneficial. Now may be the time to make good purchases of second-hand ships, for instance. And now may be the time to take in ships on t/c and/or to purchase shipping company stocks, and so on.

For those who have cash and are in a highly liquid position, there might be good opportunities and attractive deals!

Second, one can hopefully expect a better understanding by the government sector of what drives the market forces, as well as a more coordinated effort by governments to counteract negative economic developments. There is room for some optimism, stemming from government intervention, even though we cannot expect miracles.

Third, the likely restructuring and consolidation of the shipping industry itself might, in all likelihood, have long-term positive effects on the industry's attractiveness. This might mean fewer and larger shipowners, more pooling of available ship capacity, fewer and more resource-endowed shipyards, and so on.

A highly focused and disciplined approach to doing business in the shipping industry is certainly called for. This is what this book is all about: more sharply defined shipping business strategies, with a better understanding of the underlying critical success factors, and more robust risk exposure assessment as part of better-developed portfolio strategies. So, the state of professionalism – the managerial skill levels – in the shipping industry should also be enhanced as a consequence of this crisis.

References

Achi, Z., Hausen, J., Nick, A., Pfeffer, J-L., and Verhaeghe, P. (1996) "Managing Capacity in Basic Materials," *McKinsey Quarterly*, No. 1, pp. 58–65.

Adland, R., Gia, H., and Strandenes, S.P. (2006) "Asset Bubbles in Shipping? An Empirical Analysis of Recent History in the Dry Bulk Market," *Marine Economics and Logistics*, Volume 8, pp. 223–33.

Adland, R. and Strandenes, S.P. (2007) "A Discreet Time Stochastic Partial Equilibrium Model of the Spot Freight Market," *Journal of Transportation Economics and Policy*, Volume 41, May, pp. 189–218.

Andersen, T. and Wijnolst, N. (2006) "Maintaining Europe's Maritime Superpower Status," in Wijnolst, N. (ed.), *Dynamic European Maritime Clusters*, Amsterdam: IOS Press BV, Maritime Forum-Norway and Dutch Maritime Forum, p. 8.

Aury, P. and Steen, P. (2005) "Derived Potential," *Lloyd's Shipping Economist*, February, pp. 26–9.

Benink, H. and Kaufman, G. (2008) "Turmoil Reveals the Inadequacy of Basel II," *Financial Times*, February 28, p. 8.

Bernstein, W. (2008) *A Splendid Exchange: How Trade Shaped the World*, London: Atlantic Books.

Bhagwati, J. (2004) *In Defense of Globalization*, Oxford: Oxford University Press.

Bischofberger, A. and Rybak, M. (2003) *Basel II: Implications for Banks and Banking Markets*, Zurich: Credit Suisse, Economy/Policy Consulting.

Bot, B.L., Girardin, P.A., and Goulmy, M.F. (2001) "First-class Returns from Transportation," *McKinsey Quarterly*, No. 3, pp. 108–19.

Bray, J. (2008) "Blue Sea Thinking," Lloyd's List blog, April 30, www.lloydslist.com/ ll/home/blog, accessed August 18, 2008.

Chakravarthy, B. and Lorange, P. (2007) *Profit or Growth? Why you Don't Have to Choose*, Philadelphia, PA: Wharton Press.

Clarkson Shipping Hedge Fund (2007) *Due Diligence Review Questionnaire*, London, May 16.

Courtney, H. (2001) *20/20 Foresight: Crafting Strategy in an Uncertain World*, Boston: Harvard Business School Press.

Darwin, C. (1859) *On the Origin of Species*, London: John Murray.

Davies, P.J. (2008) "UBS to Start Freight Futures Index," *Financial Times*, April 24, p. 29.

de Jong, D. (2000) *Damen Shipyards 75 Years*, Gorinchem: Damen Shipyards.

Denison, D.R. Lief, C., and Ward, J.L. (2004) "Culture in Family-owned Enterprises: Recognizing and Leveraging Unique Strengths," *Family Business Review*, pp. 61–70.

DiStefano, J.J. and Ekelund, B. (2002) *Managing Across Cultures: A Model for Bridging the Differences*, Shaftesbury: Donhead Publishing.

DiStefano, J.J. and Maznevski, M.L. (2003) "Culture in International Management: Mapping the Impact," *Perspectives for Managers*, Lausanne: IMD.

Eckbo, P.L. (1976) *The Future of World Oil*, Cambridge MA: Ballinger.

Eniram Ltd. (2008) *Company Brief*, Helsinki, Finland, May 7.

Evans, P., Pucik, V., and Barsoux, J.L. (2002) *The Global Challenge: Frameworks for International Human Resource Management*, Boston: McGraw-Hill.

Fischer, R. (2004) "World Needs to be Open to Globalization," *Financial Times*, May 31.

Garelli, S. (2006) *Top Class Competitors*, Chichester: John Wiley.

Goldman Sachs (2003) *Annual Report*.

Hagel, J. III and Singer, M. (1999) "Unbundling the Corporation," *Harvard Business Review*, March–April.

Hale, D. and Hale, L.H. (2003) "China Takes Off," *Foreign Affairs*, Volume 82, Issue 6.

Hause, O.H. and Stavrum, G. (2005) *Storeulv: En Uautorisert Biografi om John Fredriksen*, Oslo: Gyldendal.

Höegh, L. (1970) *I Skipsfortens Tjeneste*, Forlag, Oslo: Glydendel Norsk.

IMD (2008) *World Competitiveness Yearbook*, Lausanne.

Jakobsen, E.W. (2003) "European Maritime Benchmark," *Research Report*, Oslo: Norwegian School of Business (BI).

(2006) "The Norwegian Maritime Cluster," in Wijnolst, N. (ed.), *Dynamic European Maritime Clusters*, Amsterdam: IOS Press BV.

Janssens, H. (2006) "The Dutch Maritime Cluster," in Wijnolst, N. (ed.), *Dynamic European Maritime Clusters*, Amsterdam: IOS Press BV, p. 108.

Klaveness, T.E. (2003) *The Art of Business (Tom Erik's "Green Book" on Corporate Culture)*, Oslo: private publication, pp. 7–8.

Koekebakker, S., Sødal, S., and Adland, R. (2006) "Are spot freight rates stationary?" *Journal of Transportation and Economic Policy*, Volume 40, No. 3, pp. 449–72.

Kotler, P., Kumar, N., and Scheer, L. (2000) "From Market Drivers to Market Driving," *European Management Journal*, Volume 18, No. 2.

Loeddesoel, L.T. (1979) "Hvorfor Gjoer Noen Rederier det Godt og andre det Dårlig," *Internasjonal Politikk*, No. 1B, p. 167–74.

Lorange, P. (2005) *Shipping Company Strategies: Global Management under Turbulent Conditions*, Oxford: Elsevier.

(2007) "Leaders: Q(uestions) and A(nswers) with Gerry Wang, President, Seaspan," EBF, Volume 30, Fall, pp. 58–61.

Lorange, P. and Norman, V.D. (1973) *Shipping Management*, Bergen: Institute for Shipping Research.

Maersk Post (2008) Number 1, pp. 7, 17.

Marsoft (2008a) *Marsoft Dry Bulk Market Report*, Boston, July.

(2008b) *Marsoft Tanker Market Report*, Boston, July.

(2008c) *Marsoft Containership Market Report*, Boston, July.

Mezrich, B. (2002) *Bringing Down the House: The Inside Story of Six MIT Students who Took Vegas for Millions*, London: Arrow Books.

Mossin, J. (1973) *Theory of Financial Markets*, Eaglewood Cliffs, NJ: Prentice-Hall.

Murphy, H. and Tenold, S. (2008) "Strategies, Market Concentration and Hedge Money in Chemical Tanker Shipping, 1960–1985," *Business History*, Volume 50, No. 3, May, pp. 291–309.

Ng, E. (2008) "COSL Offers to Buy Norway's Awilco in Deal Worth US$3.6 b," *South China Morning Post*, July 8, p. 3.

Oakley, D. (2008) "Freight Futures Surge Ahead as Sanctuary from Credit Squeeze," *Financial Times*, February 25.

OSM (2008) '*It's All About People*,' Kritiansand, Norway.

Peeters, C. and Wijnolst, N. (1994) *De Toekomst van de Nederlandse Zeevaartsector*, Delft: Delft University Press.

Porter, M. (1998) *The Competitive Advantage of Nations: With a New Introduction*, Basingstoke: Macmillan Business.

Pretzlik, C., Wells, D., and Wighton, D. (2004) "The Balancing Act that is Value at Risk," *Financial Times*, March 25.

Schulz, T. (2007) "Schneller, Grösser, Meer," *Der Spiegel*, No. 8, pp. 80–3.

Schwass, J. (2005) *Wise Growth Strategies in Leading Family Businesses*, Basingstoke: Palgrave Macmillan, p. 91.

Seely Brown, J. and Hagel, J. III (2005) "The Next Frontier of Innovation," *McKinsey Quarterly*, No. 3, pp. 83–91.

(2006) "Creation Nets: Getting the Most from Open Innovation," *McKinsey Quarterly*, No. 2, pp. 41–51.

Shaerf, P.S., AMA Capital Partners (2008) "New York – The Capital for Shipping," presentation given at the Hong Kong Shipowners Association, April 28.

Shiller, Robert J. (2000) *Irrational Exuberance*, Princeton, NJ: Princeton University Press.

Stopford, M. (1997) *Maritime Economics*, London: Routledge.

Taleb, N.N. (2004) *Fooled by Randomness: The Hidden Role of Chance in Life and the Markets*, New York: Texere Publishing.

Tenold, S. (2006) *Research in Maritime History No. 32: Tankers in Trouble: Norwegian Shipping and the Crisis of the 1970s and 1980s*, St. John's, Newfoundland: International Maritime Economic History Association.

TradeWinds (2007) November 23, p. 50.

Ward, J.L. and Lief, C. (2002) *The Torvald Klaveness Group: From Old Tradition to Future Innovations*, Lausanne: IMD case (IMD-3–1123).

Western Bulk Annual Report (2007) Oslo, www.westernbulk.no.

Whittaker, G. (2003) "Owners Face Strong Winds," *Financial Times*, November 10.

Wijnolst, N. (ed.) (2006) *Dynamic European Maritime Clusters*, Amsterdam: IOS Press BV.

Wijnolst, N., Janssen, J.I., and Sødal, S. (eds.) (2003) *European Maritime Clusters*, Delft: DUP Satelite Press.

Wolf, M. (2004) *Why Globalization Works*, New Haven: Yale University Press.

  (2008) "Why the Financial Turmoil is an Elephant in a Dark Room," *Financial Times*, January 23, p. 9.

Worldyards (2007) *Worldyards Segment Definition*, Singapore.

Wright, R. (2007) "Maersk Line Chief Defends Restructuring," *Financial Times*, December 6, p. 18.

  (2008a) "Maersk to Cut Staff in Push for Profit," *Financial Times*, January 9, p. 19.

  (2008b) "Shipping Lines Rethink Strategy," *Financial Times*, March 25, p. 3.

  (2008c) "Maersk Overturns Key Strategies on Size and Vertical Integration," *Financial Times*, May 27, p. 1.

  (2008d) "Taiwan's Mr Controversy Runs a Tight and Very Private Ship at TMT," *Financial Times*, June 5, p. 17.

Zannetos, Z.S. (1966) *The Theory of Oil Tankering Rates*, Cambridge, MA: MIT Press.

  (1999) "Oil Tanker Markets: Continuity Amidst Change," in *Energy, Markets, and Regulations, Essays in Honor of M.A. Adelman*, Cambridge, MA: MIT Press.

Index

acquisitions, approach by Georgiopoulos, Peter 250
Aegean Marine Petroleum Network 188
agents *see* using, shipbrokers
archetypes 251
  critical success factors 86, 111
  four specialized 187, 215–32
asset bubble 42
asset class, derivatives as 152
asset ownership, split from operation 84
asset play strategy 52, 194
  selection defined 193
  timing 100
Awilco 97

Baltic Exchange 148
Basel I 225
Basel II Accord 56, 222, 225–6
  unintended outcome 226
benchmarking, and specialization 87
bias, hindsight 60
biases, in data 59
branding 104
  coherent strategy 105
  cruise lines 27
  customer focus 105
  shipbuilding segments 27
brokerage, in-house 258
brokers, cost-benefits 257
bulk carriers, safety 19
bureaucracy, increased 252
business order, and political forces 8
business views, juxtaposing varied 108
BW group, conversion program 19

Capesize, winning strategic choice 195
capital, abundance of 11–12
  and competitive advantage 12
  scarcity 11
capitalization, significance of distribution 72
Carnival 27

cartels 45
change, response to 14
China 22, 124
  container shipping 4
  demand growth 6, 47, 48, 259
  energy efficiency 22
  environmental issues 22
  iron ore 33
  shipbuilding growth 54, 124
Clarkson Shipping Hedge Fund 155, 198–9, 231
Clipper, diversification 92
clusters 62
  and human talent 67
  and national state entities 65–9, 84–5
  and specialization 84
  composition 69–70
  concept as paramount 63
  Danish 73
  Dutch 65, 68
  focus in 64
  global vs. national 65–9, 73–4
  logistical/port 62, 74
  maritime, financially oriented 62
  network, importance of 63, 70
  Norwegian 69
  policy 62, 73
  prime global shipping 62–3
  prominent companies not in 63
  shipping 62–75
    secondary 64
    success factors 64–5, 66, 139
CO_2 emissions, environmental challenge 10, 180
commodities
  demand growth 4–5
  freight rates 36
  supply shortages 4
commodity business, shipping as 36, 44–50
competition, in shipping industry 79
competitiveness 10, 138

competitors, differentiation from 258
complexity 256
consolidation 80
  horizontal 83
container-based shipping, demand
  growth 4
containerization, impact on industry 21
Contracts of Affreightment
  (CoA) 95
corporate culture 79
cost, capital, success factor 102
costs, need for control 256
credit crisis 7, 11, 80
  tighter financing due to 116
culture
  global vs. national 94
  headquarters 94
  risk-averse 252
  trading activities 94
cultures, five, in shipping firm 254
currency, speculative, risk 58
customer insight, key 109
customer relations firms 88
  strategies for 105–10
  trading as focus 142, 248
customer satisfaction, 104
customer value, critical success
  factors 245
customer view, importance of 245
customer-based network, importance of 91
customers, inspiring solutions
  108, 109
customs barriers 72
cycles, shipping, 118
  long-term view 118
  surviving 118

Damen shipyard 126
Danaos 13
  and IT services business 92
debt, higher prices for 116
decision making, speed 244
  shipowning built around 248
decomposition 82–5
derivatives market 99, 142, 152, 156
  and container-based 154
  and dry bulk 142, 153, 248
  key requirements for 157
  trading instruments, developing 158
  see also FFAs

DFA (Demolition Forward Agreements) 157
differentiation, positive 258
Diogenes Fund 100
double hull tankers 102
double hulls, requirement 18
Dynamic Trimming Assistant 181

economic performance 253–4
economic stability 6–8
employee development 108
entrepreneurs, internal 246
  Wang, Gerry 246
environmental concerns 9–10
equity, ability to raise 246
equity, need for sufficient 112
EUKOR 25, 29
exit strategies, options 42, 51
experimentation, need for 107
Exxon Valdez 9, 216

family business dimension 99, 235–41
  archetype 235–47
  congruence between ownership and
    management 235
  decline 238
  fragmentation 239
  Klaveness 239
  Leif Höegh & Co 239
  longer term view 236
  management competence 238
  orientation 237
  publicly traded firms 235
  shareholder perception 238
  sibling rivalry 238
  stagnation 238
  success factors 236
  succession 240, 241
  Tschudi & Eitzen 239
FFAs 99, 147–58, 167
  and new liquidity 152
  clearing platforms 149–50
  derivatives 147–58
  market, number of players in 148
  tradable investment index 155
finance, as key 255
financial crisis 12, 98
financial engineering, importance 35, 58, 255
financing, function, importance 92–3
firms, specialized, dominance 248
fiscal policy, as essential for shipowning 84

flag of convenience 62, 139
flexibility, importance of strategy for 42
forecasting consulting firms 101
   see also freight rates, forecasting; market
    forecasting; Marsoft
forward trading instruments *see* FFAs
Fredriksen, use of ship operating companies
   100
freight rates 31–61
  and commodities 36, 45
  and currency fluctuations 58
  and demand 33–5
  and financial markets 46
  and financially oriented entrants 57–8
  and finished goods, availability 36–7
  and new capacity 47, 48
  and newbuilding and scrapping 38–44
  and port congestion 37–8
  and ship type 55
  and timing 55
  and trade developments 35, 36, 45
  container, falling 37
  drivers for 31, 35–6, 44, 61
  forecasting 31, 51–7
   and shipbrokers 55
   changes in 47
   customers for 54
   cycles paradigm 43, 51, 52
   difficulties of 43
  freight markets 31–2
  locking in 57
  model for future VLCC spot rates 42
  ship utilization key to 34
Frontline 94, 102
fuel consumption, and trim 181

Gearbulk, closeness to customers key 106,
   107, 108, 109–10
Genco Shipping 188
General Maritime Corporation 88, 188
geopolitics 8
governance 235–47
  action orientation 244
  and dictatorship 243
  and simplicity 247
  balance between top team 243
  CEO 242
  chair and board, role of 242
  challenges 243
  healthy culture, issues 244

IGLOO concept 242
  open attitude 244
  risks, guidelines for 242
  speed and focus 243
  truisms 244
growth platforms, key to success 256
growth, and political stability 8
growth, and Western Europe 7

hedging 38, 149, 150, 154
Höegh Autoliners 25, 29
hull design 10, 18, 19, 129, 179
hull shape, aqua-dynamic 178
human resource policies, and global
   competence 251
human resources *see* governance

IMAREX 99, 149
  disadvantages 149, 150
industry conditions, taxation influence on 71
industry, shipping 3–14
  capital-intensive nature 11
  demographic shifts, impact on 5–6
  dispersed manufacturing 4
  economic growth, uneven 6–8
  globalization 3–4
  new entrants 12
  speed of change 3
  trading blocs 4
  value chain 3
information sharing, customer service 109
innovating, focus on speed and talent 249
innovation 101, 181–2
  and ship design 178–81
  clusters, importance for encouraging 74
  environmental 183
  focus on scope 103
  forecasting capabilities 183
  fuel-saving, charterers valuing 182
  in US economy 7
  J. Lauritzen 250
  research leading to 74
  Skipsteknisk 249
  see also steel, innovating
innovativeness, as cluster success factor 66
integrated company, revision 89
integrated shipping company, decline 82
investing in shipping 97–100
investment
  costs, increasing 10, 11

mode of 97
turnaround time 35
iron ore, demand for 19
irrational exuberance 42, 118, 136

J. Lauritzen 96, 202–3, 250
John Frederiksen 63, 96–7
Jotun 73

K Line 29
Kommanditgesellschaft investment funds
    (KGs) 101
Kyoto protocol 10

leadership 246, 252–3
    style, clarity in 253
learning, systematic, need for 107–8
Leif Höegh 83
liquidity availability 246
logistics, critical competence 13
luck, key to success 60

Maersk Line 132–5
    difficulty with integrating IT 26
management capabilities 248–59
management focus, driver for specialization
    93–4
maritime network, Dutch 65
market capitalization 72–3
market forces, microeconomic 7
market forecasting 51–61
    biases and uncertainty in data 59
    importance of accurate assumptions 56
    need for shipowners to supplement data 57
market, freight derivatives 95
markets, shipping 15–30
    bulk carrier 19–21
        bulk, utilization rates 20
        Capesize 19
        Handysize 19
        Panamax 19
        potential for growth 20
    car carriers 24–6
    chemical tankers 28–9
    commodity strategy 15
    container 21–4
        trend to larger ships 24
        worst case scenario 21
    cruise ships 26–7
    LNG/LPG carriers 28

niche markets 15
offshore ships 27–8
passenger ships 26–7
reefers 27
ro-ro 24–6, 29
    Norwegian focus on 24
    strategic advantage from IT 26
tanker 16–19
    Aframax 18
    conversion to bulk 19
    Handysize 18
    Panamax 18
    product tankers 18
    rates, and oil prices 17
    Suezmax 18
    VLCC 18
Marsoft 53, 56
    and independence 92
    and risk management 53
    Decision Support System 221
    dry bulk case 54
    factors taken in to account 56
    limitations 57, 60, 61
    Shipping Risk Management 221
    tanker freight model 43
    Timing and Risk Management System 221
middleman function 257, 258
    trend away from 257
    see also using steel, shipbrokers
Mitsui-O.S.K. Line 29
Moller-Maersk 83, 91, 101, 205–11
    container market, share 24
    see also Maersk Line
Moore Stephens 171
MTM, conversion program 19

New York, as powerful cluster 64
newbuilding and scrapping 38–44
    capacity 20, 35
    managing programs 136
    tankers, double hull requirement 18
    trading orders 144
    see also shipbuilding
not invented here syndrome 108, 109–10
NOX emissions, reducing 180
NYK 29

OBO see ore-bulk-oil
    multiple markets, ability to serve 20
OOCL, effective approach to IT 26

operating steel,100, 170–4
    annual benchmarking study 171
    competitive focus 173
    cost-efficiency 171, 249
    crew costs 173
    critical success factors 170, 172, 173
    customers 173
    key dilemmas 91
    outsourcing 171
    shorter term focus 89
options vs swaps 159
ore-bulk-oil 19
organizational change, constant 255
organizations, networked 255
OSM 172–3
outsourcing 83
    Frontline 256
owners, relationship with users 94–5
owning steel *see* shipowning
    and operating 95
    and trading 101–3
    economies of scale 248
    pull systems 88
    push systems 88

paper trading, evolution towards 99
perfect competition 30, 55, 258
planning and control process *see* governance,
        management processes
policies, fiscal 71
pools 102–3
port congestion
    and container industry 37
    Australian 37
    capacity 37
    effect on freight rates 37–8
port delays *see* port congestion
port delays, and dry bulk markets 52
portfolio management 187–214
    and diversity 190, 214
    and risk management 187, 189, 193, 212
    asset selection 193
    car carriers 209
        performance criteria for 194
    commodity sector, success factors 211
    container terminals 209–11
        complexity 210
    exit strategy 189
    gas carriers 208–9
        chartering policies 189

IT as change driver 187
learning curve effect 213
liner and terminal business related 210
logistics business 207–8
niche sector, Gearbulk 212
niche shipping, success factor 212
offshore supply ships 208
strategic process design 213
    cost discipline 212
tramp ship business 207–8
    Morgan Stanley active in 204
portfolio planning 191
    need for liquidity 58–9
    selection problem 191
portfolio strategy 190–2, 194,
        196–204, 232, 249
    A.P. Moller-Maersk 205–11
    and cash flow 191
    and focus on costs 206
    asset choice 192–6
    board, determined by 242
    container liner business 206–7
    CSAV and specialization 206
    diversification 190, 191, 195, 202–3
        time-correlated 195
    exiting 194
    growth patterns, changing 49
    indices for stock market sectors 193
    passive investing 193
    pick the winner 195
    regular revision of 191
    risk, challenge of understanding 200
        profile 250, 254
    Seaspan as long-term model 197
    specialization 207
    stop-loss criteria 194
    success factors for acquisitions 204
    timing and 194
    yield or stock based 199, 200
ports, productivity in US, limited 138
professionalism 13, 252
project initiatives, new firm structure
        along 252
protectionism 71
puts vs. calls 159–60

rates of return, factors dictating 16
rechartering risk 16
research and development, impact for
        shipping 9

risk and revenue management 187, 215–32
  Aker Kvaerner 230
  archetypes, risk different for each 217
  bankruptcy, critical to avoid 218
  benefits 218–22
  capacity and future demand, identifying 219
  capital, competition for 217, 226
  commoditization 224
  currency and interest rates 223
  decision making, key parameters 220
  exposure management key 215
  forecasting scenarios
    and decision maker 220
    and timing purchases 219–22
    Marsoft's approach 220
    need for stress-testing 220
    setting risk levels 221
  forward prices, importance of 231
    stakeholder influences 216
  hedging 218
  innovations 231
  key message 215
  lending, portfolio approach to 225
  new capital 216–17
  Norden, and VaR approach 222
    credit worthiness, perception 224
  performance, dictated by investors 216
  probability estimation 219
  residual values, risk around 228–9
    influencing factors 229
    risk for Seaspan 231
    volatility 228
      rising importance of 80
  risk 217, 218, 219, 226–7
    attitudes to 217
    credit 224
    exposure, income and 224, 227–8
    lower market exposure 223
    management and 223–5, 229–30
    market 224
    minimization, securitization as 229
    profile, and liquidity 89
    requirements for 226
    unintended, elimination 218
  stop-loss management 230
  strategies 217
  trading results, VaR as predictor 222
  Value at Risk (VaR) 222–3
  VaR, limitations 223

risk exposure, understanding 201
  Scandinavian firms 187
risk, diversification 99
risks, trading-related, need to manage 149, 150
Royal Caribbean International 27

safety concerns 9–10
scale benefits 88
scrapping 44
Seaspan Corporation 11, 79, 198
  container shipping lines 113
  containerization 15
  innovation through standardization 181
  lease-inspired niche 13
  long-term charter strategy 93
  newbuilding programme 131
  portfolio model 196–204
  standardization policy 88
  transnational structure 85
Seatrade 27
sector asset management 97–9
Sector Maritime 204
services, top class, near clusters 63
Ship Finance International 102
ship operating companies, largest 100
ship owning, by public companies 102
ship types, segmentation 120
shipbuilders, three biggest 119
shipbuilding 124, 129
  capacity growth 33
  capacity, availability a factor of 118
  financial support for 71–2
  growth, banks drivers of 34
  new prices 124
  productivity 126
  subsidies 71
  see also newbuilding
shipowning 139–40
  adding tonnage 137–8
  and operating, different time horizons 89–91
  business cycles 136
  charter-vessel owners 129
  competitive focus 112–13
  container line, complexity 134
  container ships market 127
  container ships, newbuilding 129–35
  customers 113–14
  customers as infrastructure contractors 114

shipowning (cont.)
cycles, timing in 135–7
emotional elements 89
financial management 141
critical success factor 112
strategies 116
understanding, role of 115
innovation in practice 140
investment behavior, principles 135
large companies, advantageous financial
terms 115
long-term focus 89
orderbook to fleet ratio 131
scale, equivalence to scope 134
scale economies 114–15
scrapping, market in 138
second-hand prices 128
segmentation of ships on order 119 24
sentimentality in 89
ship acquisition, timing in 137
specialization 112
supply and demand 127–9
and financial markets 117
shipping
archetypes 77, 85–111
companies 3
global approach 251
need for analysis 98
crisis, overcapacity as 50
funds, investment in 100
industry, success factors 255
markets, atomistic nature of 55
ocean, stability and growth 8
types of, differing success factors 139
world 1, 75, 79–111
ships, categories 120
ships, demand, macro factors 138–9
ships, new, demand and supply for 118–120
shipyards, growth 124, 127
silo thinking 108, 109, 251
Singapore, growth in maritime
industry 70
single-hull tankers 10, 19, 129
Skaugen I.M. 81
Skipsteknisk 176, 177
specialist firm, types 85–7
specialization 80–4, 86, 91–2
A.P. Moller-Maersk 83
benchmarking as contributor to 87
core activities, aid to defining 83

critical success factors 85
speed reduction 179
SPFAs (Sell Purchase Forward Agreements
for ships) 157
spot market 95
steady steaming 179
steel, innovating 101, 175–83
commercial 175
competitive focus 175–6
customers 176, 177–8
environmental 178–81
Marsoft 177
niches 176–7
online 177
success factors 175
technical 175, 178
see also innovation
steel, operating 100, 170–4
see also operating steel
steel, owning 112–41
see also shipowning and owning steel
steel, using see using steel
stocks and shares 160–1
Stolt-Nielsen 110–11
strategic issues, need for open
discussion 245
strategies, niche 1, 75, 79–111
clear, developing 103
subsidies 71
success, new innovations for 80
succession planning 240
see also family business dimension,
succession
sulfur fuels, low 180

T. Klaveness 151–2
technology, changing 9
Teekay 81
terrorism 9
TEU 11
strategies 113
TK Gas Partners 102
TMT Corporation 150–1
TPM 152
trade, free, barriers to 36
trading instruments, new 157
trading terms 159–63
tramp shipping, Norwegian owners,
focus on 24
transaction costs, and specialization 91–2

Tufton Oceanic 204
turbulence, regional instability reason
    for 8

UBS Blue Sea Index 155–6
uncertainty, need to prepare
    for 59
using steel 142
    bargaining power, shift 146
    branding 146–7
    capital markets, access 142
    customers 144–6, 249
        customer, final 145
    demand-side factors 143
    derivatives 147–8, 168
    DFDS 166–7
    financial capabilities,
        key 142
    Frontline 161
    Golden Ocean 162
    purchase options 163
    routes dictated by
        customers 145

shipbrokers 163–4, 168
    Cargill 165
    transaction oriented 164
    success factors 142, 143, 195
    time charters 161–3
    Western Bulk 162–3
    see also operating

value chain, integrated 82, 104
    decomposition of 82
    economic, stability needed for 8
    enablers 84
    trend to dispersal 84
value creation, volatility in 253–4
van Oord 81
Vietnam, low-cost manufacturing 4

Wallenius Wilhelmsen Logistics 25, 29
World Trade Organization 36
world trade 5
    and world shipping 8

yourship.com 177

For EU product safety concerns, contact us at Calle de José Abascal, 56–1°, 28003 Madrid, Spain or eugpsr@cambridge.org.

www.ingramcontent.com/pod-product-compliance
Ingram Content Group UK Ltd.
Pitfield, Milton Keynes, MK11 3LW, UK
UKHW012155180425
457623UK00007B/41